Irwin L. Joffe
PHOENIX COLLEGE

Achieving Success in College

WADSWORTH PUBLISHING COMPANY
BELMONT, CALIFORNIA
A DIVISION OF WADSWORTH, INC.

English Editor: Kevin Howat
Signing Representative: Ann Cockrum
Managing Designer: Detta Penna
Interior Designer: Rick Chafian
Copy Editor: Dott Morrissey
Cover Designer: Lois Stanfield
Cover photo: Larry Kasperek, Millsaps College, Jackson, Mississippi

© 1982 by Wadsworth, Inc. All rights reserved. No part of this book may be reproduced, stored in a retrieval system, or transcribed, in any form or by any means, electronic, mechanical, photocopying, recording, or otherwise, without the prior written permission of the publisher, Wadsworth Publishing Company, Belmont, California 94002, a division of Wadsworth, Inc.

Printed in the United States of America

4 5 6 7 8 9 10—86 85 84

Library of Congress Cataloging in Publication Data

Joffe, Irwin L.
   Achieving success in college

    Includes index.
    1. Study, Method of—Handbooks, manuals, etc.
2. Note-taking—Handbooks, manuals, etc.
3. Library orientation—Handbooks, manuals, etc.
4. College student orientation—Handbooks, manuals, etc.   I. Title
LB2395.J55   378'.1702812   81-11455
ISBN 0-534-01032-6   AACR2

ISBN 0-534-01032-6

Acknowledgments

Selections in this volume are reprinted from the sources listed below. (Pages on which selections appear are given in parentheses.)

Brooks/Cole Publishing Company: Joseph B. Cook, Marvin A. Hoss, and Robert Vargas, *The Search for Independence*, 1968 (109–110). Gerard Egan, *Face to Face: The Small Group Experience and Interpersonal Growth*, 1973 (89–91). Morris Hein, *Foundations of College Chemistry*, 1967 (185, 186). Richard A. Kalish, *The Psychology of Human Behavior*, Third Edition, 1973 (44–45). Richard A. Kalish, *The Psychology of Human Behavior*, Fourth Edition, 1977 (78–79). Dorothy Rogers, *Adolescence: A Psychological Perspective*, Second Edition, 1978 (44, 184). All used by permission of Brooks/Cole Publishing Company, Monterey, California, a division of Wadsworth, Inc.

Ben Bruce: Ben Bruce and Evelyn Davies, *Beginning Golf*, Revised Edition, 1968 (81–82). Used by permission of the authors.

Irwin L. Joffe: Irwin L. Joffe, *Developing Vocabulary Skills*, 1971 (13–15). Irwin L. Joffe, *Locating Specific Information*, 1971 (120–121, 122, 123, 127). Irwin L. Joffe, *Remembering What Your Read*, 1971 (183). All used by permission of the author.

Robert E. Swindle: Robert E. Swindle, *Fundamentals of Modern Business*, 1977 (71). Used by permission of the author.

United States Government Printing Office: *Area Handbook for the Phillipines*, 1969 (50, 181). *Financial Recordkeeping for Small Stores*, 1966 (57, 83, 94–95, 101). Speech by President Lyndon B. Johnson (183).

Wadsworth Health Sciences Division: May Futrell, Stephen Brovender, Elizabeth McKinnon-Mullett, and H. Terri Brower, *Primary Health Care of the Older Adult*, 1980 (29). Used by permission of Wadsworth Health Sciences Division, Monterey, California.

Wadsworth Publishing Company: Richard A. Ahrens, *Nutrition for Health*, 1970 (84–85, 110–112). Leland D. Baldwin and Erling A. Erickson, *The American Quest*, Volumes I and II, 1973 (46, 49, 77–78, 188–189, 190). Doris W. Barr, *Writing, Listening, Speaking for Business and Professional Students*, 1972 (86–88, 105–107). Vincent Barry, *Looking at Ourselves: An Introduction to Philosophy*, 1977 (49–50). Celia Denues, *Career Perspectives: Your Choice of Work*, 1972 (103–104). Peter Everett and Virginia Dumas Skillman, *Beginning Tennis*, Revised Edition, 1968 (190–191). Dale Hanson, *Health Related Fitness*, 1970 (107–109). Irwin L. Joffe, *Opportunity for Skillful Reading*, Third Edition, 1980 (10–12, 27–28). Howard Kahane, *Logic and Contemporary Rhetoric: The Use of Reason in Everyday Life*, 1971 (92–93, 96–97). Robert E. Kime, *Health: A Consumer's Dilemma*, 1970 (40, 115–116). Judson R. Landis, *Sociology: Concepts and Characteristics*, 1971 (98–99, 112–115). David G. Moursund, *How Computers Do It*, 1969 (70). Roy K. Niemeyer, *Beginning Archery*, Revised Edition, 1967 (101–103). Lloyd Saxton, *The Individual, Marriage and the Family*, Second Edition, 1972 (62–66). Philip. C. Starr, *Economics: Principles in Action*, Second Edition, 1978 (17, 28–29, 59, 60–61). Rudolf F. Verderber, *The Challenge of Effective Speaking*, Fourth Edition, 1979 (41, 185, 187–188). All used by permission of Wadsworth Publishing Company, Belmont, California.

The H. W. Wilson Company: *Readers' Guide to Periodical Literature*. Copyright © 1978, 1979 by The H. W. Wilson Company (120–121, 129–132, 135–138). All used by permission of the publisher.

To Rose and to Scott and Stacie

Preface

This book is divided into two parts. Part 1 is concerned with how information is organized and with how to understand that information. How to outline, how to take notes, how to study a chapter in a textbook, and how to make use of the library are covered. Improving vocabulary skills by becoming sensitive to how words are used is also included. No matter what other skills students possess, they cannot survive in a college setting without being reasonably proficient in these. The sheer quantity of information given to college students can be overwhelming unless they are able to organize and assimilate that input into their own knowledge structure. Part 1 shows the student how to do this.

Part 2 considers some of the practical and psychological aspects of college survival. It is concerned with the ways in which successful students handle the problems that are an integral part of a college student's life.

Each chapter is followed by exercises that are designed to improve poor survival habits and to build new ones with confidence. They should be done carefully and thoughtfully, and the correct answers should be understood thoroughly. By completing the exercises after each skill-teaching chapter, students have an opportunity to test their own skills and develop them further.

This book is flexible. Each chapter is self-contained. Teachers should present the material in any order that they deem appropriate, concentrating on the skill chapters that their students need most. Because students have different skill levels, teachers should encourage them to adapt the book to their own particular needs. In this way, *Achieving Success in College* can be helpful to all students.

Many people helped with this book and I would like to thank them all. My special thanks and appreciation are extended to the reviewers whose helpful comments and suggestions provided insights not otherwise obtainable. They are Denise McGinty, University of Texas at Austin; Margaret Yager, University of Cincinnati; Pat John, Lane Community College; Evelyn Baker Dandy, University of South Carolina; Natalie Rubinton, Kingsborough Community College; Vicki Alvarado, Skyline College; E. Donald Crapps, Clayton Junior College; Ruth Biro, Duquesne University; and William Broderick, Cerritos College.

Contents

Inventory of Survival Habits   xiii
Why Wasn't I Told . . .   xv

PART ONE. ORGANIZING AND UNDERSTANDING INFORMATION

1. Improving Vocabulary   3

    Context Clues   4
    Structural Clues   9
    Practice Exercises   13

2. Learning to Outline   25

    Relating Ideas   26
    Notation   30
    Practice Exercises   35

3. Studying Textbook Chapters   53

    General Study Techniques   53
    The PQ3R Method of Study   55

4. Learning to Take Notes   67

    From Lectures and Class Discussions   68
    From Books Owned by You   75
    From Books Not Owned by You   80
    Practice Exercises   81

5. Using the Library   117

    The Card Catalog   117
    Reference Aids   120
    Other Library Services   124
    Practice Exercises   125

PART TWO. STRATEGIES FOR SUCCESS

6. Becoming a Successful Student   141

    A Balanced PEP Schedule   141
    Characteristics for Success   144
    Personal Problems   145
    Practice Exercises   147

7. Using Time Effectively   151

    Analyzing Your Schedule   152
    Preparing and Using a New Schedule   153
    Practice Exercises   161

8. Working with Professors   165

    How to Choose Professors   166
    What Professors Do for You   167
    What Professors Expect   167
    How to Help Your Professors and Yourself   167
    Practice Exercises   171

9. Remembering What You Learn   173

    Intense Original Impression   175
    Association   175
    Visualization   177
    Concentration   180
    Repetition   181
    Intention   182
    Use of Acronyms   182
    Sequence of Study   182
    Practice Exercises   183

10. Taking Tests 193

    Preparation for Tests   193
    Short-Answer (Objective) Tests   195
    Essay (Subjective) Tests   201
    Practice Exercises   205

Answer Key   **211**

Index   **237**

Inventory of Survival Habits

Decide whether each of the following statements is true or false. Indicate your answer by placing T or F in the space provided to the left of each statement.

_____ 1. It is a good idea to read each textbook chapter three times to be sure that you understand everything in it.

_____ 2. Take only relatively easy courses during your first semester or two. Take the difficult courses later, after you are used to college life.

_____ 3. Always review an exam paper if you have time.

_____ 4. Don't ask questions in class, because it makes you look as if you are unprepared.

_____ 5. You can learn to improve your memory greatly.

_____ 6. When taking an exam, answer the easier questions first.

_____ 7. If you don't like a teacher, it would be better if you dropped the course.

_____ 8. When you answer an exam question, don't volunteer additional information. It won't earn you more points.

_____ 9. When you study a chapter in a textbook, read the summary and the questions at the end, if available, before you read the chapter itself.

_____ 10. The best way to build up a good vocabulary and become sensitive to word meanings is to use the dictionary often.

_____ 11. A successful student seeks counseling or other help when needed.

_____ 12. It's a good idea to arrive late for your first few classes so that your teacher will know you.

_____ 13. If you really want to be a top student, you will have to give up most of your social life.

_____ 14. If you are weak in areas such as mathematics and reading, take courses to clear up this hangup as early as possible in your college career.

_____ 15. How you feel about yourself as a person has a direct effect on your academic success.

The answer to the first statement is false. As you will discover in Chapter 3 (Studying Textbook Chapters), an efficient PREPARE will make rereading unnecessary. Statement 2 is also false. Chapter 6 will point out that while a limited load is suggested for your first semester, you should always schedule a balanced load. Chapter 10 will help you to realize why statement 3 is true. Statement 4 is false for reasons stated in Chapter 8. You really can improve your memory, as statement 5 suggests, and the chapter on memory (Chapter 9) will tell you how. To understand statement 6, you are again referred to Chapter 10. The answer is true. Statement 7 is false. As Chapter 8 points out, you should concentrate on what a teacher says in a lecture, not on how he says it or what his personality is like. Statement 8 is true. Adding information could lose points for you, if the added information is incorrect, and it won't usually improve your exam grade. Statement 9 is true. It mentions some of the things that you do in a PREPARE (see Chapter 3). The answer to 10 is false. This may sound surprising to you, but the chapter on vocabulary improvement (Chapter 1) will tell you why. Statement 11 is true. This is discussed in Chapter 6. Chapter 8 discusses statement 12, which is false. The instructor may get to know you, but in a negative context. In Chapter 7 you will discover that with proper time management you will be able to have a social life, earn good grades, and even have a part-time job. Therefore, statement 13 is not true. Statements 14 and 15 are both discussed in Chapter 6. They are true.

Why Wasn't I Told . . .

- that registration takes only a few minutes if I work out my schedule in advance?
- that there are restrooms in each building—I don't always have to use the one I found the first day on campus?
- that studying for an exam takes less time than secretly writing answers all over my body?
- that my teachers are human and are willing to help me if I ask them to?
- that using someone else's notes doesn't help me when the exam is given?
- that recommended reading is really required reading?
- that the first step in trying to learn is learning to try?
- that I am not a dingbat just because I went to see a counselor?
- that I am not a dingbat just because I took a course to improve my reading?
- that I could have gotten a student loan instead of going to class for the first four weeks without the required textbook?
- that a rap session about intellectual concepts can be just as exciting as a rap session about the opposite sex?
- that the librarian is my friend when I need to do a special report or a term paper?
- that the faculty parking lot is for faculty only?
- that I need to learn to budget time or I won't have time to budget?
- that planning a semester schedule is like going to a restaurant—I get to choose the time and the combination that best suits me?
- that being tutored or visiting the learning center is better than flunking a course?
- that my teachers have already heard all the excuses I can think of as well as those my friends have told me about?
- that in order to learn I have to be curious?
- that being knowledgeable doesn't make me less sexy?
- that college can be fun?

PART ONE

Organizing and Understanding Information

1

Improving Vocabulary

Why is it that in almost every English skills class, whether in high school or college, vocabulary improvement is included? What's so important about developing your vocabulary? After all, you can converse with people and get your message across. You can read a textbook and pretty much understand most of the words used. You don't need to be a trained expert in the use of words to get along in life—or do you? Actually, there are three good reasons, other than being able to read with comprehension, for becoming as sensitized to word meanings as you can. One reason is money. The person with the power of conversation, and especially persuasion (being able to choose just the right word at the right time is a must if you are to be really persuasive), is the person who sells more, gets more raises, rises in the corporate structure. Also, vocabulary ability is a function of intelligence. Even when it's not expressed aloud, complex concept formation is not possible without having the right words. A third important reason for developing your vocabulary ability is self-concept. When you feel really comfortable with words, you tend to like yourself better, because you express your messages more easily and you are confident in both social and business conversations.

How do you improve your vocabulary? Well, you don't do it by memorizing lists of words and their meanings. You don't do it by continually looking up words in a dictionary. The dictionary will not usually tell you the exact meaning of the word you are looking up; it will tell you the various possible meanings of the word. This is not to say that dictionaries are not helpful. They most certainly are. But using a dictionary is not the best way to become sensitive to word meanings. You improve your vocabulary through examining context, structure, and derivation of words. Let's talk about each of these.

CONTEXT CLUES

A word doesn't really have any meaning to you until you use it, and then it gets its meaning from the words around it. This is called using context. For example, what is the meaning of the word *blaze*?

Think about it. Write the meaning on the following line. _____

_____

Is your meaning the same as in the sentence, "The blaze was put out by the firemen," or is it the same as in the sentence, "The scouts were going to blaze a trail in the woods"? Either one is the correct use of the word *blaze*. You can't really tell the author's intended meaning of a word until it is used in context in a phrase or sentence.

Authors often give clues to the particular meaning they have in mind when using a word. If you can become sensitive to these clues, you can discover meanings for words you are not familiar with. There are five major types of clues that you should know about. They are discussed on the following pages.

Restatement

Sometimes an author will help you to understand a word by using another word or group of words that has the same meaning. What does the word *edema* mean in the following sentence? "Symptoms include shortness of breath and edema (swelling) from the accumulation of fluids." Notice that a synonym for the word *edema* is given, in parentheses, directly following it. You don't need a dictionary to tell you that edema means swelling. Now read the sentence, "We mark off on the abscissa, or horizontal line, the units of measurement we are using—meters, inches, seconds, grams, IQ's, or whatever." Here again, the author restates the meaning of the word *abscissa* immediately following it, only this time he uses commas to separate it from the rest of the sentence.

Read each of the following sentences, noting the word in italics. Then, in the space provided, write the meaning of the word as it is used. Do not refer to a dictionary or other reference book. Use the context clue (restatement) to find your answer.

a. An insect's *tropism*, or attraction to light, causes it to swarm around street lights, night after night. _____

b. After hearing the news, he was *jubilant*—joyous, happy, elated. _____

Did you realize that a tropism is an attraction to light, and that jubilant means joyous or happy or elated? The most common ways of restating word meanings are by putting the meaning in parentheses, by separating the meaning by commas, or by using a dash and then giving the meaning.

A variation of the restatement clue is found when an author uses an opposite meaning (usually several phrases rather than one word) to tell you the meaning of the word. What is the meaning of the word *fecund* in the following sentence? "Some soils are barren and sandy and don't produce much, while others are fecund, and can produce bumper crops for the farmer." Here the sentence tells you that fecund soil is soil that is not barren or sandy, thus probably rich and fertile, which is what fecund means in this context. Now read this sentence: "Some college professors are very vociferous, while others hardly talk at all." Do you see that vociferous means talkative?

Read each of the following sentences and write the meaning of the italicized word in the space provided.

a. Joe earned a *meager* income, unlike Sam, who earned close to $100,000 per year. _____

b. Sally's friend is a *misanthrope*, whereas Sally, on the other hand, likes everybody that she meets. _____

Do you see that a meager income refers to a small income and a misanthrope is a person who dislikes other people?

Example

Sometimes authors give examples to help you understand the meaning of a word. What does ornithological mean in the following sentence? "Ornithological creatures such as doves, crows, and robins can be seen in all sections of the country." Even if you didn't know the meaning of the word, the examples that follow make it clear that ornithological creatures are birds. Now look at this sentence: "Some of the most common types of chronographs are wristwatches, stopwatches, wall clocks, and alarm clocks." What is a chronograph? Do you realize after reading the examples that it must be a timepiece?

Read each of the following sentences, noting the word in italics. Then, in the space provided, write the meaning of the word. Allow the examples to give you the meaning. Do not refer to a dictionary or other reference book.

a. *Felines* such as cats, lions, tigers, and panthers are crafty and stealthy, but graceful in their own ways. _____

_____

b. Many *crustaceans*, such as shrimp, crab, or lobster, are considered good food by many people. _____

_____

Felines, of course, are members of the cat family, and crustaceans are shellfish. The examples give you the context clues that you need to learn the meaning of the word.

Definition

Often, especially in factual or textbook-type material, the author will define the word. When this is done, you can usually recognize it immediately. What are the meanings of the words in italics in the following two sentences?

A *bobbin* is a spool to hold thread when using a sewing machine.

Evaporation is the escape of molecules from the liquid state to the gas or vapor state.

These definitions are particularly meaningful if you are taking a sewing class or a chemistry class. Definitions are important and, luckily, very obvious.

Explanation

Sometimes the meaning of a word is explained by the author according to the way he uses it in context. The actual definition may not be there, but the context almost forces the meaning upon you. What does the word *adversity* mean, according to the following sentences?

Her life was full of adversity. Her father died when she was very young; she was badly burned in a fire; her savings were used up when she lost her job.

Can you tell from the context that adversity has to do with hardship and bad luck? Now read the following two sentences, and in the space provided, write the meaning of the italicized word. Try to get the meaning from the explanation given in the context.

    a. He drank an *inordinate* number of cocktails in a very short time and was now at the point where he could hardly stand without support. _____

    b. As a result of the heavy rains, the lowlands were *inundated*. Wherever you looked, the land was covered with water. _____

Explanation is subtle. Can you see, however, that inordinate means excessive and that when an area is inundated it is flooded? Do you see how the context gives the meaning?

Situation

    Situation refers to the way you use context to discover the particular meanings of words that you are familiar with, but which can have several meanings. Look at the following sentence:

    Manuel was *bent* on having his way.

Which of the following dictionary meanings for bent is the correct one according to the way it is used in this sentence?

    a. crooked
    b. determined
    c. a tendency
    d. a type of grass

In different contexts the word bent could have any of the above meanings, but do you see how it can only mean b (determined) as it is used here? Let's continue with the next sentence. From among the choices given, which of the actual dictionary definitions is the correct one for each of the words in italics? Circle the letter to the left of your choice.

    He wouldn't give an *inch*.

The word give means

    a. make a gift of
    b. hand over

c. yield

d. pass along

The word *inch* means

a. measure of length

b. move very slowly

c. close to

d. very small amount

These words are common, everyday words. Yet, you really don't know the meaning even of these words until you see them in context. It's the context (the situation) in which you find the word that allows you to decide the correct meaning. Situation refers to your ability to use your prior knowledge and background to help you find the meaning of words in context.

Read the following sentences. Which of the dictionary meanings for each of the italicized words is the correct one, according to the way in which the word is used? Circle the letter to the left of each correct answer.

The business is expected to *fold* after Christmas.

a. close up

b. blend into a mixture

c. double up on itself

d. intertwine

Henry did things on a large *scale*.

a. series of tones arranged in sequence.

b. outer covering of a fish

c. weighing machine

d. greater or lesser degree or extent

Do you see how the meaning of *fold*, as it is used, is a (to close up) and the meaning of *scale*, as it is used, is d (greater or lesser degree or extent)? Only the context, or situation, can tell you this.

When you use situation, you might also be able to use one or more of the other context clues (restatement, example, definition, and explanation). The idea is to use any clue that can make you more sensitive to the meaning of the word. Another type of clue that, in combination with context, will lead you to meanings for most words is structure, discussed below.

STRUCTURAL CLUES

The structure of a building or a sentence is the way in which it is put together. The structure of a word is the way in which it is put together. The three basic parts of a word in this sense are prefix, root, and suffix. Knowing about these word parts and being familiar with the ones that appear most frequently is a key that can unlock the meanings of hundreds, even thousands, of words. What are prefixes, roots, and suffixes?

Prefixes

A prefix is a syllable or syllables that appear at the beginning of a word and have a special meaning. They are ordinarily attached to a root word. *Dec* is a prefix meaning ten. A *dec*ade is a period of ten years. The *dec*imal system is based on the number 10. The prefix *pre* means before or in front of. When you *pre*cede something, you go before it. A *pre*monition is a warning in advance. Where would you find the *pre*amble to the U. S. Constitution? You would find it at the beginning or in front of it. Use context to help you figure out the meaning of the prefix *micro* as it is used in the following words.

A microscope allows you to see very small objects.

Lilly used an enlarger so that she could read the information that was on microfilm.

A micrometer measures very small distances.

Were you able to realize that *micro* means small? When you are able to use both context and structure to figure out the meanings of words, you have power that will help you whenever you read.

Suffixes

Suffixes, like prefixes, are syllables that have special meaning; however, they appear at the end of a word. The suffix *logy* means the study of. Cosmeto*logy* is the study of cosmetics. Minera*logy* is the study of minerals. Theo*logy* is the study of religion. The suffix *able* or *ible* means able. If something is ed*ible* it is able to be eaten. If it is read*able* it can be read. The suffix *ist* means a person who. A psycholog*ist* is a person who is trained in psychology. A philatel*ist* is a person who collects stamps. What is a chemist? Do you see that it is a person who is trained in chemistry?

Roots

The root of a word, like prefixes and suffixes, has a special meaning and is composed of a syllable or syllables. However, it can appear anywhere in the word—at the beginning, the middle, or the end. *Somn* is a root meaning sleep. When you have in*somn*ia you can't sleep. When you are *somn*olent you are sleepy. If a *somn*ambulist is a person who (ist) walks in his sleep, what do you think the root *ambul* means? Yes, it means to walk. An *ambul*atory patient is one who can walk. A per*ambul*ator is a baby carriage, also known as a walker or a stroller.

Because word parts help you to unlock the meanings of so many words, a list of some of the more common prefixes, roots, and suffixes follows this section. Study them carefully and try to learn as many of them as you can.

PREFIXES AND ROOTS

Root or Prefix	Meaning	Example
ab	away (from)	absent
acer, acr	sour, bitter	acrid, acerbity
ad	to, toward	adhere
ambi	both	ambivalent
ante	before	anteroom
anthropo	man, mankind	anthropoid
anti	against, opposed	antipathy
aqua	water	aquatic
aud	hear	auditory
auto	self	automatic
bene	well, good	beneficial
cede, ceed	go, move	proceed, recede
chron	time	chronological
circum	around	circumference
co, con, com	together, with	cooperate, conspiracy
cogni	know	recognize
counter, contra	against, opposite	counteract, contrary
cred	believe	credential
de	from, away	depart
dent	tooth	dentist
derm	skin	dermatitis
dic, dict	say	dictate
dis	apart, from, away from	distract
duc, duct	lead	aquaduct
ex, exo	out (of)	excise, exodus
fid	faith, faithful	fidelity, confident
gamy	marriage	monogamy
graph	write	graphology
gress	go, move	progress
inter	between	interrupt
man	hand	manicure
mega	big	megaphone

CHAPTER 1 IMPROVING VOCABULARY 11

mis	wrong, wrongly	mistake
miso, misa	hatred	misanthrope
morph	form, shape	amorphous
mort	death	mortality
multi	many	multitude
neb	hazy, cloudy	nebulous
non	not	nonadjustable
path	feeling, suffering	apathy
ped, pod	foot	pedal
pel	push	repel
poly	many	polygamy
port	carry	porter
post	after	postpone
pre	before	preamble
pro	forward	propel
re	back, again	return, redo
retro	backward	retrospect
rupt	break	rupture
scrib	write	transcribe
sect	cut	dissect
spect	see, look	spectator, inspect
sub	under	submarine
super	over, above	superior, supersonic
syn, sym	with, together	synchronize, symmetry
ten	hold	tenacious, tentacle
tend	stretch	extend
tort	twist	distort
trans	across	transport
viv	life	convivial

PREFIXES OF NUMBER

uni	one	uniform
mono	one	monologue
du(o)	two	duet
bi	two	biped
tri	three	triangle
tetra	four	tetrameter
quad	four	quadruplets
penta	five	pentagon
quint	five	quintet
sex	six	sexagenarian
hex	six	hexagon
sept	seven	septet
oct	eight	octopus
nov	nine	novena
dec	ten	decade
cent	hundred	percent
hect	hundred	hectogram
mil	thousand	millimeter

kil	thousand	kilometer
semi	half	semicircle
hemi	half	hemisphere
demi	half	demitasse

SUFFIXES

able, ible	able to	readable
al	pertaining to	musical
ar, er, or	one who	teacher
ful	full of	hopeful
ic	pertaining to	allergic
ish	like, close to	foolish, twentyish
ist	one who	psychologist
less	without	hatless
logy	study of	cosmetology
ous	full of	cancerous

DERIVATION

The study of the derivation of words, or etymology, tells you that words in English come from many sources. Although the greater number of them come from Greek and Roman sources, many of our words come from other languages such as Old Norse, German, or Scandinavian. Knowing the original meaning of a word can make you more sensitive to its various shades of meaning. The root of the word *companion* is *panis*, and it originally referred to bread. A companion, then, was someone with whom you broke bread. Our first month, January is named after Janus, the two-headed god. He could look back at the year just passed and look ahead to the new year at the same time. Can you see any connection between the words *calculate* and *calcium*? *Calculus* means pebble or stone in Latin. The ancient Romans counted with pebbles, hence the word *calculate*. In Latin, a short form of *calculus* is *calcix*, or limestone, and the word *calcium* derives from that.

Your dictionary provides you with the derivation of a word at the beginning of each definition. You can build up an awareness and feeling for words by reading these derivations. Some of the exercises that follow will help you to do this.

EXERCISE 1

In the following exercises, decide upon the meaning of each of the italicized words from its context. Then write your answer in the space provided.

1. An elephant and a hippopotamus formed such a close friendship in the Oakland zoo that when the hippopotamus escaped he was easily *enticed* back into his cage by using the elephant as an attraction.

    enticed _____

2. Their constant, *acrimonious* arguments finally broke up the marriage.

    acrimonious _____

3. He was so *enervated* by the ten-mile walk in the desert that he could hardly stand. It took many hours of rest before he felt strengthened and refreshed.

    enervated _____

4. High blood pressure, or *essential hypertension*, is an unstable or persistent elevation of blood pressure that may lead to increased heart size and to kidney damage.

    essential hypertension _____

5. In a physical examination, the physician looks for clues of existing cardiovascular disease and for symptoms that may precede the development of disease—that is, *precursors* of disease.

    precursors _____

6. Solids that contain water molecules as part of their crystalline structure are known as *hydrates*. Formulas for hydrates are expressed by first writing the usual *anhydrous* (without water) formula for the compound, then adding a dot, followed by the number of water molecules present.

    hydrates _____

    anhydrous _____

7. Acne is a medical problem that has a major effect on the body image. No really effective cure has been found for *acne*, or pimples, even though it is extremely common, particularly during the late teens and early twenties.

    acne _____

8. All axons and dendrites have retaining membranes, and all that serve a transmission function, except those of the smallest diameter, have a white, fatty coating known as the *myelin sheath*.

   myelin sheath _____

9. A six footer on a basketball team impresses nobody; set him down in a village of midgets, and he becomes a *colossus*.

   colossus _____

10. He is a *celebrated* guitarist who is known to kings, presidents, and people in all walks of life.

    celebrated _____

11. Some activities, such as brushing teeth and eating, are *diurnal*. Other activities, such as going to church, are done weekly; still other activities, such as paying rent or paying income tax, are done monthly or annually.

    diurnal _____

12. Don't *equivocate*! It's better to tell the truth.

    equivocate _____

13. He *alleviated* the pain considerably by putting a soothing salve on the wound.

    alleviated _____

14. Although new recruits have *flaccid* muscles, they are in excellent shape after just a few weeks.

    flaccid _____

15. Because she was so *comely*, people were always inviting her to enter beauty contests.

    comely _____

16. His *cognomen* was Jones. His wife's cognomen, before she was married, was Smith.

    cognomen _____

17. Because he disliked the taste so much, he *eschewed* spinach. However, this was the only vegetable he avoided.

    eschewed _____

18. Instead of suddenly going out, the lights in the theater darkened by a gradual *diminution*.

    diminution _____

19. As a result of the accident, the fender of the automobile was *contorted* out of shape. As a matter of fact, the entire auto was twisted and bent. Although the person who hit her tried to blame Sue for the accident, she was finally *exculpated* by the courts.

   contorted _____

   exculpated _____

20. He was the circus *harlequin*. He made people laugh with his funny antics and his gaily colored costume.

   harlequin _____

EXERCISE 2

Determine the probable meanings for each of the following nonexistent words in the exercises that follow. Use context to decide upon the meaning. Write your answers in the space provided.

1. People love to hear their own name. When you meet someone, listen carefully to his or her *bindum* when introduced, and try to remember it.

    bindum _____

2. The young woman, dressed in a bikini, went to the edge of the diving board and *gulded* into the pool.

    gulded _____

3. Politicians need to make speeches during campaign time. They make promises in order to get you to vote for them. I have to think carefully before I cast my *subtuk*.

    subtuk _____

4. How you dress makes an impression on people you meet. When you are being interviewed for a job, you should *insul* more conservatively than if you were going to a party.

    insul _____

5. When you take a test, always read all directions. You should know whether your *remdock* wants you to answer all questions or whether you have a choice of *simburn*. When you do this, you will save time, feel confident, and probably earn a better *tookle*.

    remdock _____

    simburn _____

    tookle _____

6. The federal government should reduce spending in time of inflation and should run a deficit in time of depression by increasing spending without increasing taxes. The federal government thus counteracts the swings in demand by *pernioffing* spending in time of inflation and increasing it in time of *crawlit*.

    pernioffing _____

    crawlit _____

7. If you want to be on the basketball team you must have determination and you must work hard. If you aren't accepted the first time, don't give up. When you are accepted, be prepared to put in many

18   PART ONE   ORGANIZING AND UNDERSTANDING INFORMATION

hours of practice. These two factors then, *gondek* and *borcron*, will make you a successful athlete.

gondek _____

borcron _____

8. The element carbon is very useful in its many forms. Diamonds are used as ornaments and as cutting tools. Charcoal is used in many industries to purify products. Another form of *listur* is lampblack, whose greatest *beldum* is in the manufacture of rubber tires.

listur _____

beldum _____

9. There are three steps in remembering: input, storage, and retrieval. You have input when you are aware that what you want to remember has occurred. The information must then be *korded*, then you need to bring it back at will. If you can learn to do these three steps, you will have a good *rejnill*.

korded _____

rejnill _____

10. Four types of wood used in making bows are yew, osage orange, lemonwood, and hickory. Yew makes a good bow, but it is expensive. Osage orange makes a good hardwood bow. The third type of wood, *boralis*, has a lemon color and is a good beginner's bow. *Sapsog*, though used in bows, has many undesirable features. Probably a *colit* that is made of a material other than wood, such as fiberglass, will be the most popular.

boralis _____

sapsog _____

colit _____

EXERCISE 3

Decide from among the choices given the meaning of each of the following made-up words created from the prefixes, roots, and suffixes listed on pp. 10–12. Refer to the meanings of these word parts if you need to. Circle the letter to the left of your choice.

1. Ambident
   a. yellow teeth
   b. any tooth
   c. both teeth
   d. loose teeth
2. Aquaderm
   a. wet skin
   b. poolside
   c. to live in water
   d. green skin
3. Beneman
   a. kind person
   b. healthy hand
   c. bony hand
   d. male rabbit
4. Demisex
   a. playboy
   b. three
   c. six
   d. devilish
5. Dermrupt
   a. place to sleep
   b. type of crime
   c. sleepless night
   d. broken skin
6. Megapod
   a. large apartment
   b. large pea
   c. big foot
   d. good crop
7. Mortscrib
   a. epitaph
   b. Dead Sea scrolls
   c. death rite
   d. afterthought
8. Polymorph
   a. many shapes
   b. formless
   c. dead bird
   d. twin
9. Ruptgamy
   a. ill spouse
   b. separated married couple
   c. single parent
   d. unfaithful spouse
10. Audmort
    a. place where speeches are made
    b. cemetery
    c. softspoken
    d. deaf

CHAPTER 1   IMPROVING VOCABULARY   21

EXERCISE 4

Notice the words in italics in the passages below. From the choices given, decide the meaning of each of these words according to the way it is used. Circle the letter to the left of your choice. All the choices are dictionary definitions of the word.

1. He will *drive* me to drink.
    a. penetrate
    b. force into a state or act
    c. hit hard or swiftly
    d. control the movement of
2. When will you *dress* the chicken?
    a. put clothes on
    b. decorate
    c. clean and eviscerate
    d. apply medicine and bandages to
3. She received *inside* information.
    a. inner surface
    b. internal organs
    c. secret or private
    d. the part closest to something
4. They reached the *peak* of production.
    a. maximum
    b. top of something
    c. pointed top
    d. droop
5. She *touched* me for some money. I *touched* her hand when I gave it to her. It was a *touching* scene.

    When *touched* is used the first time, it means
    a. put hand on
    b. compared with
    c. fixed
    d. asked for

    When *touched* is used the second time, it means
    a. bordered on
    b. put hand on
    c. cured
    d. caused pain to

    When *touching* is used, it means
    a. tender, emotional
    b. hurting
    c. motivating
    d. asking for

6. The big *wheel* was at the *wheel* of his auto.

   When *wheel* is used for the first time, it means
   a. influential person
   b. circular frame with spokes and a hub
   c. instrument of torture
   d. rotating disks used in gambling

   When *wheel* is used the second time, it means
   a. disk with projecting handles for controlling the rudder of a ship
   b. instrument of torture
   c. influential person
   d. circular frame used to turn vehicles and machinery

7. My *man* will drive you to the airport.
   a. human male
   b. adult male attendant
   c. player on a team
   d. chess piece

8. Take the left *fork* in order to reach her house.
   a. eating utensil
   b. instrument for pitching hay
   c. place where a road is divided into two branches
   d. tuning instrument

9. It was a *fair* day when the *fair*-haired woman went to the *fair*. She thought that the admission price was *fair*.

   a. attractive
   b. unblemished
   c. blond or light in color
   d. clear and sunny
   e. large
   f. average
   g. honest, reasonable
   h. unbiased
   i. a bazaar or exhibition
   j. according to the rules

   Above are ten meanings of *fair*. Write the letter of the correct meaning of *fair*,

   when it is used first _____

   when it is used second _____

   when it is used third _____

   when it is used fourth _____

10. He *ran* through all the money that he made when he *ran* his business after he *ran* away from home. Now he had a cold and a *running* nose.
    a. appeared in print
    b. was a candidate
    c. discharged fluid
    d. managed
    e. moved legs forward rapidly
    f. climbed or crept

g. continued in effect
h. left

i. came to an end
j. used up

Above and left below are ten meanings of the word *ran* or *running*. Write the letter of the correct meaning of *ran* or *running*.

when it is used first ____

when it is used second ____

when it is used third ____

when it is used fourth ____

2

Learning to Outline

Imagine the six-story warehouse of a large furniture manufacturer, with all the new furniture stored according to the room of the house in which it will be used—kitchen furniture on one floor, bedroom furniture on another, family room furniture on another, and so on. The floor that has the family room furniture is set up so that couches are in one section, coffee tables in another, lamps in another. Other floors are also arranged accordingly. Now pretend that a new manager is hired who doesn't care about things being orderly. Instead, he has things stored wherever there might be room and in the order in which they arrive. All the furniture is mixed together. If the manager had a need to deliver 20 couches, he would just have to get them from wherever he could find them—if he could find them. Chances are the business would not last too long. If it did, it would certainly cost a lot in time, energy, and effort to try to locate and move items. A successful and profitable furniture business depends upon an orderly, organized warehouse.

As it is with the furniture warehouse, so it is with organizing and later locating information needed for success in your college classes. If you can organize information well, you will spend less time and effort than you would if you processed information haphazardly. Outlining allows you to do this.

Outlining shows the way in which writers and lecturers organize their ideas and helps you to understand these ideas. Reading or listening to lectures without outlining is like storing furniture in a warehouse without regard to organization—things get misplaced, and it takes longer to find what you are looking for.

RELATING IDEAS

How do you outline? Many students see outlining as a confusing arrangement of roman numerals and capital and small letters (called notation), and they never seem to know which number or letter to place where. Although notation is helpful when outlining, the most important concern is for you to recognize how ideas are related to each other. It helps you to see how thoughts are organized.

Look at the following ideas: *watching TV, mowing the lawn, dusting the furniture, studying for an exam, going to a movie, doing an assigned term paper, preparing a meal, doing homework, going bowling.* How might you rearrange these items into three columns, with each item in a column relating to the others? Write the items on the lines below.

_____   _____   _____

_____   _____   _____

_____   _____   _____

Did you put *watching TV, going to a movie,* and *going bowling* in one column? Were the other two columns *mowing the lawn, dusting the furniture, preparing a meal* and *studying for an exam, doing an assigned term paper, doing homework*? If you listed the items that way, you have constructed an outline. You have put related items together to form an outline. How are the items in the first column related? They might be called recreational activities. Do you see how the other two columns might be titled *activities around the house* and *school activities*? If you were doing a formal outline, it would look something like this:

    I. Recreational activities
       A. Watching TV
       B. Going to a movie
       C. Going bowling
   II. Activities around the house
       A. Mowing the lawn
       B. Dusting the furniture
       C. Preparing a meal
  III. School activities
       A. Studying for an exam
       B. Doing an assigned term paper
       C. Doing homework

You probably thought that this was easy to do. Yet, in order to do it, you had to realize that the first three items are things that you do for recreation, the next three are things done around the house, and the last three are school activities. You had to realize how the ideas related to each other. How do you select the proper items and relate them in an outline? First, you must find the key idea, then you must discover how the author develops the topic. The following suggestions can help you.

Find the most important or key idea. Authors or lecturers always have a topic. They talk about the causes of the revolution, or the properties of a chemical element, or perhaps Freudian theory. Everything that is said is related to this topic. Look at the following words. Which item is the topic (that is, which item includes all the others): *roses, daisies, types of flowers, lilies, tulips?* Did you say *types of flowers?* If so, you have discovered the topic. Now look at the following group of items in which the topic is not included, and you decide upon the topic: *Canada, United States, France, Italy, Japan?* Do you see how *countries* would be the best answer? If so, you have taken another step toward making outlining work for you.

A skillful outliner must think in exact terms. What is the most exact topic that you can think of to cover the following items: *beans, peas, carrots, beets, corn?* Which of the following terms would be the most exact term to cover those items: *foods, vegetables, plants, things that grow?* Each of these topics would describe the list, but *vegetables* is the most exact. *Foods* is too general; it could also include meats and dairy products. *Things that grow* is even more general and could include trees or even animals. *Plants* also includes items other than vegetables. Making sure that you choose exact topics helps you to outline and to analyze and understand the material that is presented to you.

Discover how the author develops the topic. Doing this shows you how the ideas are related. Authors usually develop topics so that you can better understand the points being made. Sometimes they will develop an idea by giving several examples. Sometimes they explain what is meant by certain aspects of the topic. Authors may also use comparison-contrast (such as telling about the theories of different psychologists) or cause-effect (such as discussing the effects of certain medicines). At other times they may develop the topic in chronological order—what happened first, what happened next, and so on. Enumeration may be used—three causes, or four characteristics, or five qualities. At other times the discussion may go from easy to difficult, from specific to general, from general to specific, or even from known to unknown. When you are able to discover these relationships, outlining becomes easy and the most difficult material becomes understandable in less time.

Read the following paragraph. Which of the above methods does the author use to develop the topic?

> There are several things that you can do to improve your reading speed.
>
> 1. *Be flexible.* Adjust your speed for difficulty and purpose.

2. *Be aware of your purpose.* When you are aware of what you are looking for, you are able to sift information and pay most attention to that which is most important at the moment.

3. *Concentrate.* After determining your purpose for reading, concentrate on reading for that purpose. Force concentration by looking away and telling yourself what you have read about. Don't look back when you do this. Try to visualize the *ideas* as you read.

4. *Think as you read.* Relate the ideas to what you already know. Increased rate comes about only as comprehension skills increase.

5. *Practice.* Compete with yourself. Read a specific number of pages of the same type of material each day. (A section in the same novel would be excellent.) Read the material as fast as you can. Then try to beat your own score the next day. Try to read the same amount of material in *less* time.

6. *Have a positive attitude.* When you have confidence in your own ability to increase rate through better comprehension, you will work at it more effectively. As you become more sensitive to and proficient at skills discussed in this book, you will be able to use these skills to increase reading rate.

Before considering what technique the author uses, go back to the first point. What is the topic of this paragraph? You should recognize that it concerns itself with suggestions to improve reading speed. How is this developed? The author uses enumeration. Six suggestions are listed and briefly commented upon. An outline of this paragraph could look something like this:

Suggestions for Improving Reading Rate
  I. Be flexible
 II. Be aware of your purpose
III. Concentrate
     A. Recite from memory
     B. Visualize
 IV. Think as you read
  V. Practice
 VI. Have a positive attitude

Now try this one. Read the following paragraph. Then, in the space provided, write the topic and tell how the author develops the topic.

Not all of the effects of the energy crisis are necessarily bad. Some physicians believe that our buildings and homes are overheated in winter and that we would be healthier if they were cooler. If people drive around less and watch less television, they might get to know each other better. If the airlines fly fewer flights, they may become more efficient (and more profitable). If oil prices rise high enough, entrepreneurs will be motivated to find other sources of power in order to reduce fuel costs. If people become more conscious of ways to conserve energy, they may be readier to form car pools and vote the funds necessary for rapid transit. When more efficient ways of moving people are found, pollution from transportation fuels will be reduced.

Topic _____

How developed _____

(Fill in the above lines before continuing.)

The topic concerns itself with what will probably happen as a result of a continuing energy crisis. How does the author develop the point? Did you notice that he uses cause-effect relationships?

Discover the author's details. When reading for details, however, see them as the author's way of developing major points. In other words, relate the details to an idea that is being made. If you are able to do this, you have related the ideas and you have constructed a mental outline. You will then find it easier to put this outline on paper.

Read the following short selection. Then fill in the lines that follow it. In order to do this successfully, you must discover the topic, the three major points made, and their related details.

> The definition of aging based on chronological age has in recent years undergone some refinement.
> *Middle age* is the time of life when the individual first becomes aware that energy levels are lower and health begins to fail. This period is also the one when children leave home. Middle age often marks a fresh assessment of a marriage, job, or the individual. It is a time when one seriously thinks about the future. These events normally occur during the forties and fifties.
> *Later maturity* should be a period that includes freedom from earlier responsibilities and time to do things one wishes to do when one wishes to do them. However, in this period of the sixties and seventies several predictable crises occur, such as retirement, reduction of income, poor health, and loss of spouse.
> *Old age* finds the individual cognizant of the fact that the end is approaching. Past 80, the likelihood of becoming more frail and disabled increases significantly.

Topic _____

Major point _____
  Detail _____
  Detail _____
  Detail _____
Major point _____
  Detail _____
  Detail _____
Major point _____

(Do the exercise before reading on.)

This exercise may have been more difficult for you to do than the previous one. If so, don't be concerned, because the purpose of this chapter is to help you to develop expertise in outlining. What did you say was the main idea? A correct answer would say something about the stages of later life. The three major ideas were concerned with what are called middle age, later maturity, and old age. Details about middle age included failing health and energy levels, children leaving home (characteristics), and the middle ager's assessments of marriage, job, future, and oneself. Comments about later maturity concerned its relative freedom (characteristics) and the stresses of retirement, lowered income, poor health, and death of spouse.

If you understood all this and filled in the blanks accordingly, congratulate yourself for a job well done. If not, the exercises at the end of this chapter begin with easy-to-understand steps and gradually lead you to more difficult examples.

NOTATION

Notation is the formal method of outlining that is used to mark the relationships of ideas. Remember, the important function of an outline is to recognize how ideas are related so that you can easily understand them. The formal notation is easy to learn, however, and it is universally recognized. It is also a required learning task in many English classes, and so it is presented here. The major points to understand about correct notation in outlining are below:

The importance of the idea determines the type of notation used and its place. Place the most important or major ideas farthest to the left, and assign roman numerals, in order, to these ideas. In other words, the first major idea would be notated I, the second II, and so on, and they should all be placed in their turn near the left margin of the page. The next most important ideas (the major details that help you understand the major ideas) are placed below and to the right of the major ideas. These ideas are notated by using capital letters A, B, C, etc. Minor ideas (details that further develop the major ideas) are placed below and to the right of the major details, and they should be notated with arabic numbers 1, 2, 3, etc.

Generally, outlines are not developed beyond this level of minor ideas. Sometimes, however, especially in complicated material, the author goes into more minute detail. When this is done, these ideas are (in turn) always placed below and to the right of the ideas above. They are notated (in turn):

    a.

       (1)

          (a)

Outline the following words: *kitchen, living room, rooms in a house, bed, stove, bedroom, refrigerator, chest of drawers*. Which term represents the major idea (that is, it includes all the other items)? *Rooms in a house* is the correct term, and it should be placed farthest to the left and notated I. Which items would have capital letters assigned? Your answer should be *kitchen, living room, bedroom*. Where do the remaining terms (*bed, stove, refrigerator, chest of drawers*) belong? *Bed* and *chest of drawers* should be below and to the right of *bedroom*, because they name the type of furniture found in the bedroom. *Stove* and *refrigerator* should be below and to the right of *kitchen*, because they name items that belong in the kitchen. The completed outline should look like this:

  I. Rooms in a house
     A. Kitchen
        1. Stove
        2. Refrigerator
     B. Living room
     C. Bedroom
        1. Bed
        2. Chest of drawers

Outline the following list in the spaces provided: *kitchen, bed, living room, rooms in a school, library, rooms in a house, counseling office, classroom, desks, stove, bedroom, auditorium, refrigerator, chalkboard, chest of drawers*.

    I.

       A.

          1.

          2.

        B.
        C.
            1.
            2.
    II.
        A.
        B.
        C.
            1.
            2.
        D.

Notice that you have two major ideas here. *Rooms in a house* is once again the first one and should have been placed next to I. *Rooms in a school* is the second major idea, and it should have been placed next to II. The major details in I are *kitchen, living room,* and *bedroom* and should have been labeled A, B, C. The minor details are *stove* and *refrigerator* (1, 2) under *kitchen,* and *bed* and *chest of drawers* (1, 2) under *bedroom.* The major details in II are *library, counseling office, classroom,* and *auditorium* and should have been labeled A, B, C, D. There are two minor details under *classroom* (*desks, chalkboard*), and they should have been labeled 1, 2. Your completed outline should look like this:

   I. Rooms in a house
      A. Kitchen
         1. Stove
         2. Refrigerator
      B. Living room
      C. Bedroom
         1. Bed
         2. Chest of drawers
  II. Rooms in a school
      A. Library
      B. Counseling office
      C. Classroom
         1. Desks
         2. Chalkboard
      D. Auditorium

Ideas having equal importance have equal indentation. In other words, all ideas having roman numerals (major ideas) should be placed farthest to the left. All ideas having capital letters (major details) are

CHAPTER 2 LEARNING TO OUTLINE   33

placed at the first level of indentation to the right of the major ideas. All ideas having numbers (minor details) are placed at the second level of indentation to the right of the major details. In this way, you know that any item to the left and above any other item is a more inclusive or more important idea. An item at the same level of indentation is equal in importance or development—whether above or below it. Any item below it and to the right of it is smaller than or a development of the idea.

Read the following items. In the space next to each one mark R if it should be a roman numeral, mark C if it should be a capital letter, and mark A if it should be an arabic number.

_____ sour cream	_____ swiss cheese	_____ sweet cream
_____ cheese	_____ steak	_____ carrots
_____ peas	_____ ham	_____ hamburger
_____ cheddar cheese	_____ beets	_____ eggs
_____ meats	_____ vegetables	_____ milk
_____ dairy products	_____ cream	_____ hot dog

There are three major items presented here that you should have marked R. They are vegetables, meats, and dairy products. You should have marked eleven items C. They are cheese, peas, steak, ham, beets, cream, carrots, hamburger, eggs, milk, and hot dog. You also should have marked four minor details A. They are sour cream, cheddar cheese, swiss cheese, and sweet cream. If you had any difficulty with this exercise, reread this point carefully before going on.

The first word of each item must be capitalized. You can see an example of this if you look at the outline on p. 32.

A period must be placed after each notation symbol. Again, refer to the outline on p. 32.

Don't mix phrases and sentences in the same outline. Outline items are generally expressed as one or the other. It doesn't matter which you use, but the entire outline should be either phrases or sentences.

All levels of outlines should have at least two units. Thus, if you have a roman numeral I, you must have a roman numeral II. If you have a capital A under any roman numeral, you must have a B. The same rule applies to 1 and 2 under a capital letter, a and b under an arabic number, and so on. Most experts at notation feel that if a thought must be divided, it cannot be divided into just one part. You must have at least two parts. If you feel that a thought has only one major idea (a roman numeral) make that idea a title. An example of this can be seen on p. 28.

Several exercises follow that are designed to help you become an expert at outlining. They are presented in gradual, easy-to-difficult steps. Do them carefully and patiently and have confidence in your ability to outline.

EXERCISE 1

Following are lists of words, each of which represents a particular topic. Think of the topic that most exactly describes the list. Then write this topic in the space provided. Sometimes an item may not be familiar to you. You should check it in an encyclopedia or a dictionary. The first one is done for you.

1. *types of fruit*
    grapes
    apples
    pears
    cherries
2. _____
    green
    blue
    red
    yellow
3. _____
    cards
    chess
    checkers
    Scrabble
4. _____
    silk
    rayon
    cotton
    nylon
5. _____
    lipstick
    eye shadow
    nail polish
    mascara
6. _____
    dog
    cat
    turtle
    parakeet
7. _____
    lion
    tiger
    panther
    hyena
8. _____
    London
    Chicago
    Tokyo
    Paris
9. _____
    Los Angeles
    Phoenix
    Boston
    Las Vegas
10. _____
    nose
    mouth
    eyes
    chin

11. _____
    hand
    foot
    face
    chest

12. _____
    heart
    lungs
    stomach
    kidneys

13. _____
    volleyball
    bowling
    wrestling
    golf

14. _____
    football
    baseball
    basketball
    tennis

15. _____
    husbands
    uncles
    sons
    fathers

16. _____
    geology
    biology
    physics
    chemistry

17. _____
    actor
    musician
    comedian
    dancer

18. _____
    nurse
    physician
    dentist
    medical laboratory technician

19. _____
    lawyer
    psychiatrist
    chemist
    teacher

20. _____
    stationery
    scotch tape
    stapler
    typewriter ribbon

CHAPTER 2   LEARNING TO OUTLINE   37

EXERCISE 2

Below are outlines without proper indentation. Decide how the items relate to each other in order to decide the level of indentation that is needed for each one. Then rewrite the outline, properly indented, in the space provided. The first one is done for you.

1. Medical personnel — *Medical personnel*
    Physicians — *Physicians*
    Obstetricians — *Obstetricians*
    Pediatricians — *Pediatricians*
    Dentists — *Dentists*
    Nurses — *Nurses*
    Registered nurses — *Registered nurses*
    Licensed practical nurses — *Licensed practical nurses*
    Legal personnel — *Legal personnel*
    Lawyers — *Lawyers*
    Judges — *Judges*
2. United States presidents
    Washington
    Lincoln
    Roosevelt
    United States rivers
    Mississippi
    Colorado
    United States mountains
    Rockies
    Alleghenies
3. European countries
    Germany
    Sweden
    France
    Type of government

Important cities _____
Paris _____
Marseilles _____
Asian countries _____
4. Federal government _____
Congress _____
House of Representatives _____
Senate _____
Supreme Court _____
State government _____
City government _____
Police department _____
Fire department _____
5. Counseling services _____
Curriculum advisement _____
Scholarships and grants _____
Occupational _____
Job information _____
Job interviews _____
Library services _____
Reference guides _____
Interlibrary loans _____
Exhibits _____
Checkout materials _____
Fiction _____
Nonfiction _____
Recordings _____

EXERCISE 3

Below are lists of items with major and minor ideas mixed together. These items are followed by a partially completed outline. Complete the outline by choosing from the items above it. Be sure to begin each item with a capital letter. The first one is done for you.

1. men's department, bakery items, blouses, dresses, rolls, wedding cakes, bread, clothing store items, cakes, birthday cakes, neckties, shirts, women's department

    Types of Purchases

    I. *Bakery items*
        A. Bread
        B. *Rolls*
        C. *Cakes*
            1. *Wedding Cakes*
            2. Birthday cakes
    II. *Clothing store items*
        A. *Men's department*
            1. Neckties
            2. *Shirts*
        B. *Women's department*
            1. *Blouses*
            2. Dresses

2. treating heart disease, cholesterol, drugs, preventing heart disease, exercise, surgery, diet, cigarettes, weight control.

    I.
        A.
        B. Diet
            1.
            2.
        C.
    II.
        A.
        B. Surgery

3. effective writing, eye contact, tone, grammar, irregular form, effective speaking, enthusiasm, verb form, pitch, punctuation, volume, mechanics, voice, spelling, nouns, subjunctive form

   Communicating Effectively

   I. Effective speaking

      A.

      B.

      C. Voice

         1.

         2.

         3. Tone

   II.

      A. Mechanics

         1.

         2.

      B.

         1.

         2. Verb form

            a.

            b.

Now complete the partially filled in outlines from the paragraph above each one.

4. There are three categories of professional preparation presently recognized that lead to the title R.N. The Baccalaureate Nurse has a bachelor's degree in nursing following four years of preparation in a degree-granting institution. The Diploma Nurse has received three years of training, usually associated with an accredited hospital school of nursing. The Associate Degree Nurse receives two years of professional preparation beyond the high school diploma. Graduates from each of these three categories must take State Board examinations before receiving the R.N. classification. The career possibilities available for individuals prepared in nursing include serving in hospitals, clinics, nursing homes, doctors' offices, public health departments, schools, and industrial plants.

I.

   A.

   B. Diploma nurse

   C.

II.

5.   Because they may be so important to professional speakers and because they can make a classroom speech more exciting, we need to consider three types of mechanical aids: slides, opaque projections, and overhead projections. Slides are mounted transparencies that can be projected individually. In a speech, a few slides could be used much the same as pictures. For instance, for a speech on scenic attractions in London, a speaker might have one or more slides of the Tower of London, the British Museum, Buckingham Palace, and the Houses of Parliament. He or she could show the slides and talk about each of them as long as necessary. Opaque and overhead projections can be used much the same way. An opaque projector is a machine that enables you to project right from a book, a newspaper, or a typed page. It is especially useful for materials that would be too small to show otherwise. An overhead projector is a machine that requires special transparencies. The advantage of an overhead is that the room need not be darkened and you can write, trace, or draw on the transparency while you are talking. Overheads are especially useful for showing how formulas work, for illustrating various computations, or for analyzing outlines, prose, or poetry. Many of the kinds of things teachers use a chalkboard for could be done better with an overhead projector.

Types of Mechanical Aids
I. Slides

   A.

   B.

II.

   A. Definition

   B.

III.

   A.

   B. Use

EXERCISE 4

Once again you will find lists of items with major and minor ideas mixed together. These items are followed by a notated outline. Fill in the outline by choosing from the list of items. The first one is done for you.

1. rip saw, wrenches, hammer, plumber's tools, pipe wrench, saws, monkey wrench, pipe threader, carpenter's tools, crosscut saw, screwdriver, pipe cutter

    I. *Plumber's tools*
       A. *Pipe threader*
       B. *Wrenches*
          1. *Pipe wrench*
          2. *Monkey wrench*
       C. *Pipe cutter*
    II. *Carpenter's tools*
       A. *Saws*
          1. *Rip saws*
          2. *Cross cut saws*
       B. *Hammer*
       C. *Screw driver*

2. automobile insurance, costs of insurance, collision, types of insurance, health insurance, individual costs, term life, fire and theft, group plans, life insurance, bodily injury, limited payment life, homeowner's insurance, endowment life

    I.
       A.
          1.
          2.
          3.
       B.
       C.
       D.

44   PART ONE   ORGANIZING AND UNDERSTANDING INFORMATION

       1.

       2.

       3.

II.

   A.

   B.

Now complete the outlines below from the paragraphs above each one. These outlines have titles.

3.   The study of adolescents may be approached from various frames of reference. One of these, the biological approach, involves defining adolescent behaviors and development in terms of biological criteria. The second, or chronological frame of reference, concerns adolescence as influenced by age. Society uses this frame of reference, for example, in determining the age of adult legal liability. A third approach, the psychological, focuses on personality, values, and individual experiences. Another popular method of characterizing the adolescent, the psychoanalytic, stresses the significance of psychosexual development. Adolescence is perceived as a time when the Oedipal feelings of early childhood are reawakened and produce psychological conflict in teenage boys and girls. From another, or sociocultural, point of view adolescence varies according to time, place, circumstance, and culture or subculture involved.

Frames of Reference for Studying Adolescents

   I.

   II.

   III.

   IV.

   V.

4.   Although all psychologists share a common body of knowledge, the scientific field of psychology, like other fields, is divided into a number of specialties.

    The specialty chosen by most psychologists is clinical psychology. The clinical psychologist is primarily concerned with helping others to cope with their problems. He participates in the face-to-face relationship known as psychotherapy, a form of counseling that involves helping people with personal and emotional adjustment problems. In addition, the clinical psychologist administers and interprets all types of psychological tests. He sometimes does research on tests or on various approaches to psychotherapy. He may have a private practice, or he may work with a government agency, a hospital, or an educational institution.

The social psychologist focuses his attention on the behavior of individuals and groups in a social environment. He studies the formation and change of attitudes and beliefs, the effects of society on behavior, and the actions of people in small groups. He is also likely to be interested in how people communicate with each other, since communication is part of a social relationship.

Quite different from the social psychologist is the physiological psychologist, who studies the physiology, anatomy, and biochemistry of the body as they affect behavior.

The developmental psychologist is primarily concerned with behavior and behavior changes at various stages of development. He tries to discover why some infants learn to walk earlier than others, how adolescent interests change between ages 12 and 18, and why some people seem old at 60 while others are still vigorous at 80.

Industrial psychologists study a variety of topics, including how to design efficient machines, how to evaluate worker morale (and to improve it, if necessary), how to devise training programs for workers, and how to improve marketing and advertising.

Specialities within Psychology

I.

    A.

    B.

    C.

II.

    A.

    B.

III.

IV.

V.

    A.

    B.

    C.

    D.

5. The following were the chief items of legislation in the first session of the Eighty-Ninth Congress.

1. Civil Rights Act of 1965. In states and counties where fewer than 50 percent of the voting-age population were registered or had voted in 1964, the law suspended all literacy, knowledge, and character tests for voters. The Attorney General was authorized to send Federal registrars into such counties to register voters in keeping with the Fifteenth Amendment's guarantee of the right to vote.

2. War on poverty. The antipoverty program initiated in 1964 was continued by (a) greatly expanding the provisions of the Economic Opportunity Act; (b) expanding aid and construction in depressed areas, especially Appalachia; (c) authorizing grants and loans to stimulate business and employment in such areas.

3. Education. For the first time, large-scale aid was given to elementary and secondary education. Parochial schools were aided, but under the supervision of public-school administrators. A feature of the system was the granting of aid to schools according to the number of needy children in a school district rather than according to the wealth of the state. Aid to higher education was continued, and undergraduates were made eligible for scholarships.

4. Medicare and health. A medical care program for those 65 and over was set up under the Social Security system and was financed partly by payroll taxes and optional monthly payments by the enrollees. There was a limit to the amount and duration of aid provided, so that medicare fell far short of meeting the needs of those afflicted by long-term illness. Title 19 of the Medicare Bill gave grants to states which would provide medical benefits to indigents and handicapped of all ages; this was not under Social Security. Other legislation gave aid to medical education and research, combated water and air pollution, and contributed funds to sewage treatment.

5. Immigration. The national origins quota system was repealed; however, quotas were set for each hemisphere. Relatives of Americans, refugees, and immigrants with needed skills were to be admitted freely.

6. Housing and urban renewal. A Department of Housing and Urban Development was established and given Cabinet rank. The first Secretary was Robert C. Weaver; he was also the first Negro to serve in any Cabinet. Housing and urban renewal programs were extended; a rent subsidy plan to aid low-income families was passed, but no money was provided at that time.

Legislation of the Eighty-Ninth Congress

I.

    A.

    B.

II.

    A.

    B.

    C.

III.

    A.

    B.

    C.

IV.

    A.

        1.

        2.

    B.

    C.

V.

    A.

    B.

VI.

    A.

    B.

6.   Junior colleges offer programs designed to meet the needs of three different segments of the population. The transfer program provides the academic courses needed in order to transfer as a junior to a four-year college. There are several advantages to beginning your college career at the junior college level. One is cost. Junior colleges are usually supported by public funds, and tuition is either

free or very inexpensive. Also, attending a college close to your home saves a lot of money on food and lodging. Another good reason for beginning at the junior college is that these schools are usually smaller and more personal than the four-year college or university. Faculty and other students tend to be more interested in you as a person rather than as just another body in a large classroom.

Another group served by the junior college are those seeking the technical or vocational curriculum. This program offers two-year A. A. degree programs in various vocational-technical programs that service the community. Programs to train medical laboratory technicians, electronic technicians, or computer programmers are typical of this category. The technical-vocational curriculum serves the business community, because it provides a source for training the people they require to work in their plants. It also serves the student in the community who can receive proper local training in order to obtain the job he or she seeks.

The third type of program offered is the noncredit adult or continuing education program. Here, a wide range of courses is offered for people who are not seeking a degree, but who seek knowledge or competency in various subjects that interest them. Courses in how to fix your auto, gardening for fun, investments, and ceramics are typical. These courses are popular with retired people, homemakers, and working people seeking leisure activities.

Junior College Programs

I.

    A.

        1.

        2.

    B.

II.

    A.

    B.

III.

    A.

    B.

EXERCISE 5

Produce your own outlines from the short selections below. Write the outline in the space provided.

1. **STAGES OF SETTLEMENT**

   The settlement of new lands followed a rather well-defined pattern. The first stage was that of frontier penetration by fur traders, ordinarily rough characters who had much in common with the Indian way of life—in fact, they were often part Indian. They learned about the country and its possibilities, and they introduced alcohol and the diseases of civilization that made white conquest easier. The second stage, which did not always appear in the North, was the cattleman's frontier. Whenever conditions permitted, the miner, too, moved in, possibly at about the same time as the cattleman, to exploit pockets of "bog-iron," copper, or lead.

   The third stage was that of the agricultural settler. It usually began before the traders or cattlemen passed on, and the first agriculturist was a squatter who mixed his activities. He lived in a rough cabin, girdled trees to kill them and let in light on his corn patch, and then, when neighbors pressed in, sold his "improvements" and moved on to where the hunting or forage was better. The permanent settler, the "equipped farmer," followed close on the heels of the squatter. Last came the mercantile establishments and industries, usually processors of local products; when they were powerful enough to control labor and join the speculators in boosting the price of land, the area had joined the East.

2. THE IMPORTANCE OF CLASSIFICATION

First, classification simplifies our lives. Imagine if every time we came upon a tree we had to name it and then remember that name. Our lives would soon become unmanageable.

Second, classification provides psychological security. Recall the last time you walked into a room full of strangers. You probably felt anxious. That is only natural; after all, you did not know *who* or *what* they were or anything about them. They were unknown, unlabeled, unclassified—and you were uncertain. On the other hand, suppose that just before you entered the room a friend informed you, "Jean Davis is in there." "Jean Davis?" you ask. "Yes, you know, *Doctor* Davis." "Oh, the dentist." "Right." "Oh, great. I've been wanting to meet her to find out how tough it is to get into dental school." Having been classified, Jean Davis would have become a *known* quantity, and you would have entered the room a little more at ease. For the same reason, you sleep better when you can *name* the sound out back that goes bump in the night.

A third desirable feature of classification is that it directs activity. Even if you were really thirsty you would not swig a bottle of Clorox, because you know it is a poison; you have classified it. Or take the case of a dog mooching out of your trash can. At first you just hear the sound. Then you identify it as the neighbor's dog. Armed with this knowledge you can then act: invite him in for a snack or throw a sneaker at him.

Finally, classification permits us to relate classes of things. Suppose a child plays with matches. He strikes one and presto—fire! He might do it again and again. If he survives, he will eventually conclude "Matches cause fire." Think of the classifications in that statement: matches, causation, fire. Notice that he does not conclude "This *particular* match causes fire." Instead, he abstracts—moves from particular instances to classifications—and sees relationships between those classifications. As far as we know, we are the only animal that can do this.

3. MINERALS

The known mineral resources are extensive, though much of the country is relatively unexplored geophysically. Probably the minerals most important to the economy of the country are gold, chromite, iron and copper.

Gold has been important since before the Spanish period and accounts for much of the value of mineral exports. It is found in many widely scattered locations, but mainly in Mountain Province.

Preeminence in importance in the world market, however, rests with chromite, of which the country is the fifth largest producer, furnishing over 11 percent of the world production or over 18 percent of the free-world production. The chief deposits are found in Zambales Province, which has reserves estimated at over 10 million tons of refractory grade ore and over 3 million tons of metallurgical ore.

Extensive iron deposits exist throughout the islands, and the export of iron ores has long been important. Estimated reserves amount to over 1.5 billion tons, of which almost 82 percent is located in Surigao Province and has never been worked. The Surigao field also has a vast amount of nickel, but separation of the nickel and iron ores presents serious difficulties.

Copper is found on many different islands, with known reserves of over 23 million tons of ore averaging 1.4 percent copper. Production of copper is important, as is that of manganese and of mercury.

In the mineral fuels bituminous coal is the most important, being extensively exported as well as being used locally in industry. Known reserves of bituminous coal are more than 70 million tons, and much of the country is still unexplored. Unfortunately, despite extensive exploration, petroleum has not been found in commercial quantities.

3

Studying Textbook Chapters

You can get by without being good at a lot of things, but you really do need to know how to study effectively if you are to be successful in college. It is the key to learning. This chapter will first list several suggestions for improving your study habits and then, most important of all, will discuss with you and provide practice in the PQ3R technique for study. This technique will show you how to study a textbook chapter in less time than it probably takes you now, and will give you good understanding of and an excellent memory for the material covered. What will that do for your grades?

GENERAL STUDY TECHNIQUES

Here are some tips that will help you, no matter what technique you use for study.

1. *Study in the same place all the time.* Do not use this place for any other activity. This will help habit formation and will establish a mental set for study. Do not use this area for playing games or eating, or for anything but studying.

2. *Avoid, or at least minimize, distractions.* Do not study near a window, or have a TV set going, or a clock nearby. Do not have a picture of a friend or member of your family in front of you. It would be a good idea to arrange for someone to take phone messages. If you have a room in which to study, an "off limits" sign on the door during study time is a good idea. Soft, nonvocal music could help you to mask other distractions. However, if it proves to be a distraction in itself, turn it off.

3. *Sit on a comfortable but not an upholstered chair.* The purpose of an overstuffed chair is to overrelax you, and your goal when studying is to be comfortable, but not in a position to fall asleep. Do not study in bed!

4. *Have everything that you need in your study area—paper, pencil, dictionary, notes, textbooks, ruler.* You should not have to leave your study area to get things.

5. *Get right to work.* Don't daydream or wish you were somewhere else before getting started. Concentrate immediately. It might be a good idea to spend the first few moments reviewing your last study session in order to reestablish the momentum you had at that time.

6. *Don't study longer than you can concentrate.* Know your concentration span. Take a short break just before that time. Just standing up and stretching or drinking a glass of water is enough. The break should just be for a moment or two.

7. *Set goals and schedule enough study time to meet them.* Reward yourself for meeting your goals. However, the clock should not be the goal. Resolve to study until a certain amount is finished rather than for a set time period. (For example, study until you finish a certain chapter, or until you feel prepared for the exam.) If you finish as expected, give yourself a little treat—go to that movie or disco spot, or have that pizza you craved.

8. *Be comfortable physically.* Is the temperature right for you? Do you have enough light? Too little light or glare can cause fatigue. Light should come from the side or rear. It should not reflect into your eyes.

9. *Know your biological clock.* Tune it in to your study time. Studies have shown that different people are most effective at different times of the day (or night). Some people do their best work in the morning, and others can't seem to get going until the late afternoon. If you can take classes or do your "hard" studying during your most productive hours, you will be more efficient.

10. *Understand and use to your advantage the results of studies on retroactive interference.* Retroactive interference refers to the idea that you forget things because of information or events that occur between the time that you learned something and the time that you have to remember it. You may be introduced to a person at a party, for example, and remember his or her name perfectly until you are introduced to three or four other people. The names of the people that followed "interfered" with your memory of the first name.

You can take advantage of these studies by doing the following:

a. Study material for a specific class or exam as close to that class or exam time as possible.

b. Unless some of the other factors listed above would interfere, study important material before going to sleep. This would not allow as much time for "interference."

c. Retroactive interference studies have also shown that similar bits of information learned one after another are more easily forgotten than when less similar bits of information are learned one after another. For example, if you had to study chemistry, history, and sociology, it might help you to study chemistry second (that is, between history and sociology, which have more similar content).

11. *Spend part of your study time studying with someone.* To study with someone effectively, you should each study the same material separately. Then, when you meet, ask each other questions or discuss points about which either of you is not clear. This reinforces your studying. The danger here, of course, is that you may turn the session into a social hour (save that as a possible reward for after the study session) or that you will prepare only part of the material and expect your study partner to fill you in.

Sometimes it will be impossible for you to follow all the above suggestions. Even if you do, however, you must have a study technique for success. The PQ3R technique is such a study method. The rest of this chapter is devoted to it.

THE PQ3R METHOD OF STUDY

Many students think that the answer to studying is time. If you spend enough time reading and rereading the material until you know it, and take good notes, you can answer any question about what you have studied. Wrong! You may be successful in absorbing information that way, but it is very costly in terms of time and concentration. It isn't necessary for you to read and reread chapters you are studying. A skilled student prepares the chapter for study and uses techniques that will aid concentration and will allow information to be learned more quickly.

A system for study that allows for this is the PQ3R technique. This technique allows you to study a chapter in less time, understand it better, remember important information longer, and do well on the exam. Using PQ3R is like looking at the picture of a jigsaw puzzle you are working. You have an idea where the individual facts fit in the big ideas presented in the chapter.

The P of PQ3R stands for PREPARE. Just as a painter prepares a room for painting (a tarpaulin is put down, the walls are cleaned, holes are patched, paint is thinned or mixed), an effective student prepares a chapter for study. There are five steps in PREPARE. You should do each step actively. Don't just stare at the items to be read; read and think about them carefully.

1. *Read (actively) the title.* Ask questions. With this title, what will the author probably discuss in the chapter? Does the author have a point of view about the subject? Look at the following title from a textbook chapter.

WILLS AND TRUSTS—HOW TO PROTECT YOUR ESTATE

What kinds of things will the author probably discuss in this chapter? He will probably discuss the nature of wills and trusts, how they differ, their advantages and disadvantages, and how they can be used to pay the smallest amount of estate tax that is allowable under the law. How does the author feel about the value of wills and trusts? He seems to feel positive about them, because the title says that they can be used to protect your estate.

Now look at the following chapter title. In the space provided, write what kinds of things you think the author will talk about in the chapter. Tell whether the author seems to have a point of view.

TAKE CARE OF YOUR DOG—MAN'S BEST FRIEND

What kinds of things will be discussed? _____

_____

_____

_____

How does the author feel about dogs? _____ Favorable _____ Unfavorable

What did you say would be discussed? The title suggests that the author will probably talk about such topics as feeding, bathing, grooming, needed shots, delousing, and other kinds of health care. Now that you know this, studying becomes easier. You know what to expect, and by predicting what is coming, understanding is made easier, and memory for that information is extended. How does the author feel about dogs? Obviously he feels favorable, because he calls them man's best friend.

2. *Read the introduction (if any).* If there are no introductory comments, read the first two or three paragraphs of the chapter. Authors will usually tell you in the opening paragraphs what ideas they are going to develop in the chapter and how they are going to develop them. An author might say, for example:

> In this chapter we will discuss the causes of the war, the significant battles, and the influence of two key generals.

Now you know what the author is going to discuss, and you can prepare your mind for the task ahead. You prepare by searching your mind for any previous information you may have about certain battles or the influence of one of the generals on the outcome of the war. Bringing bits and pieces of prior knowledge to mind before you read the chapter helps your understanding and concentration. Relate the title to the introductory information. In the above example, the title will at least probably tell you which war is being discussed.

Read the following title and brief introductory comments. Think about the information you can glean from it.

RECORDS—FOR THE GOVERNMENT OR FOR YOURSELF?

Why keep records?

If you are a typical small businessman, your answer to this question is probably, "Because the Government (and you mean the Internal Revenue Service) requires me to!" If the question comes in the middle of a busy day, you may add a few heartfelt words about the amount of time you have to spend on records—just for the Government!

Is it "just for the Government," though? It shouldn't be. True, regulations issued in recent years, not only by the Internal Revenue Service, but also by various other governmental agencies—Federal, State, and local—have greatly increased the record keeping requirements of business. But the fact is that this may be a good thing for the small businessman, overburdened though he usually is. Many studies have found a close relation between inadequate records and business failures.

Think about this example before you read on. The title asks who you keep records for and suggests that you, as well as the government, can benefit from record keeping. The introductory statements support this. What kinds of things would you expect to be discussed in the chapter? The author will probably talk about the specific advantages of record keeping, possibly even record keeping equipment (journals, ledgers, etc.).

Do you see how active reading of titles and introductions helps you to predict what is coming?

3. *Read the summary or conclusions, if any, and questions at the end of the chapter.* What kinds of information would you expect authors to summarize or to ask questions about? Would they discuss relatively more important or relatively less important information? Authors would be expected to summarize or to ask about information that they think is important. How often have you read through a textbook chapter, and then closed the book when you reached the page that says "summary"? You feel that you have finished the chapter, because the summary is just a rehash of what you've already read—right? Wrong! Authors place the key information of the chapter in the summary. Smaller details or less important material is left behind; the highlights stand out for you. Reading summaries or questions first, then, will give you a clue on what to pay most attention to when you read the chapter.

Having read and thought about the title, the introductory material, and the summary or questions at the end of the chapter, you should have a good idea of the main points discussed in the chapter and how the author develops these points. Steps 4 and 5 help to refine this information.

4. *Read the subtitles of the chapter.* Ask three questions about each subtitle: (a) How does the subtitle relate to the title? (b) How does the subtitle relate to other subtitles? and (c) What will the subsection probably be about? Suppose that a chapter's title is "Personality-Shaping Factors in Adolescents" and that there are three subtitles, namely, "Influence of Family," "Influence of Peers," and "Influence of the Larger Society." The relationship of each subtitle to the title is, of course, that the author is concerned with the influence of the family, peers, and the larger society on an adolescent's personality development. The subtitles relate to each other in that each one discusses a different personality-shaping factor in adolescents.

Now look at the first subtitle again ("Influence of Family"). What will the author probably discuss here? What are some ways in which your family might shape your personality? You might guess that certain parental beliefs and values are influential here—perhaps religious values, importance of education, importance of job security or money, significance of social status, even sexist attitudes.

What might the author discuss as part of the second subtitle ("Influence of Peers")? There might be a discussion here of an adolescent's need to be like his peers and to maintain a status or image among them. Perhaps some of the seeds of parent-adolescent conflict will be covered—staying out later than permitted, drinking liquor, experimenting with drugs, doing the things that maintain the adolescent's status in his peer group.

The third subtitle should be thought of in the same way. The important thing is that you really stop to think about what may be covered. It doesn't matter whether your guesses are right or wrong. If they are right, you will later realize that you were able to figure out what would be covered (doesn't that make the studying easier?). If they are wrong, as you read you will be telling yourself that this isn't what you thought would be covered, but instead it is making the point that.... Either way, you are forced to concentrate and thus understand more in less time, and probably remember it longer.

5. *Read the first sentence of each paragraph.* Try to relate it to the subtitle. Also, look for clues as to what the rest of the paragraph will say. Sometimes a subtitle will be "characteristics," and the first sentence will say, "There are four *characteristics* of...." You know what will be covered. Try to predict, if you can, what these characteristics might be, but don't read, at this point, to discover them. Doing this for each paragraph in the chapter will give you a tremendous amount of information without spending a lot of time reading and rereading a lot of detail.

Following each of the five steps of PREPARE should tell you, in most textbooks, most of what you want to know. The Q3R steps will fill in the smaller details and help to guarantee that you will remember the information. However, PREPARE forces you to read attentively, with concentration and an attitude of learning. In addition, in a casual survey done by this author, after doing a PREPARE, students were often able to participate in a classroom discussion or take an exam based on the entire chapter and average a B on that exam. How often have you spent hours reading every word of a chapter, taken an exam, and scored less than a B? Try it with your next reading assignment. You will find it to be amazingly helpful.

Now try PREPARE on the following brief section of a book used in college today, *Economics—Principles in Action* by Philip Starr. The title of Chapter 10 is "Unions: The Impact of Organized Labor on the Economy." Think about the title. What might a chapter with that title be about? Certainly you might expect the author to talk about how unions affect wages, prices, and working conditions. There may even be talk about how unions have helped to shape people's lifestyles (having Sundays and evenings free, for example). It doesn't really matter how accurate your assumptions are, but it does matter that you make assumptions. That is what forces active, attentive reading. Now look at the introductory paragraph. Notice the wealth of information that it gives you.

> The aim of this chapter is to help you understand the goals of unions and their impact on the economy. The chapter is divided into six parts: (1) the history and goals of labor unions; (2) the legal status of unions; (3) what is happening to membership in unions; (4) what determines wages; (5) what effects unions have on the levels of wages, prices, and employment; and (6) discrimination and exploitation in labor markets.

Notice how specific the author is about what will be covered in the chapter. He actually lists the six parts that the chapter is divided into. You know what is coming—there are no surprises. Knowing this also helps you to know what is important (items other than the six listed are probably not as important in the author's thinking). Think about each of the items. What will probably be covered in each of them? For example, look at the first item (the history and goals of labor unions). What will probably be discussed in that section? What are some names or dates or events that may be covered? Always bring whatever knowledge you may have about the subject into play. If you are already slightly familiar with labor union history, you might remember AFL or CIO or John L. Lewis. Under the second item (the legal status of unions) you might know something about the Wagner Act of the 1930s or the

Taft-Hartley Act of the 1940s. Think about each part and what may be covered in each one. Assume that there is no summary or no questions at the end of the chapter. The next thing to do then is to read the first sentence of each paragraph in the first part.

THE HISTORY AND GOALS OF LABOR UNIONS

A labor union is an association of workers who join together in an organization for the purpose of negotiating a labor-management contract—as a group rather than as individuals—with employers. Individual workers can easily be fired, but when the employees form a group, the employer is faced with a power that is capable of interrupting his or her business through a strike.

Originally, negotiations leading to a contract emphasized pay and hours of work. While bargaining still covers these, as unions have gained power they have now also become concerned with many details of production—for example, fringe benefits involving medical, dental, and optical care; pension funds (in addition to Social Security); *job descriptions*, which tightly describe exactly who does exactly what and with what tools; *seniority rules*, which state who gets laid off first or promoted first; and the *check-off*, the company's agreement to deduct union dues from the workers' paychecks and to turn the money over to the union.

All these areas for negotiation were usually interpreted by employers as interferences with management, and, until 1935, employers did everything they could to prevent the formation of unions. During the 1920s, employers banded together in associations under what they called the *American Plan*. The purpose of the plan was to crush the unions by getting their members to support the *open shop*—that is, a workplace where an employer could assert the right to hire anyone, whether union member or not. Because none of the employers wanted a union, of course, "open shop" really meant no union. In addition to the open shop, employers often asked newly hired workers to sign *yellow-dog contracts*, whereby the worker agreed not to join a union or engage in union activities. Workers who signed these contracts were called "yellow dogs" by union supporters.

During the 1920s, both sides fought—literally. There was much violence and people were killed. In the West Virginia coal mines, for instance, miners formed an army of 4,000 men, which was crushed by another army of federal troops. In Illinois, two miners were killed during a battle between striking mine workers and strikebreakers brought in by the Southern Illinois Coal Company, and miners retaliated by killing 19 of the strikebreakers. Violence also occurred in many other industries.

The first sentence of the first paragraph defines a labor union. The first sentence of the second paragraph is of special interest. When an author says that "originally" such and such happened, you might guess that things are different now. Think about that. If you read the sentence, "When I first bought my car [originally], gasoline was only $.30 per gallon," what would you expect the next sentence to be? Mightn't you expect the author to say that today, however, gasoline is higher? If negotiations originally emphasized pay and hours of work, and if you assume that unions are more powerful now than they were originally, you might guess that negotiations today emphasize more than just pay and hours of work. If that were so, the major content of the paragraph would have to do with just what else is negotiated. You know what to look for in the paragraph, allowing this active way of reading to make for better understanding and longer memory for the information. Even if you didn't make the first assumption, read the first sentence of the next paragraph (All these areas for negotiations. . . .). Do you see how that sentence reinforces the idea that there were more areas for negotiation than just pay and hours of work? The first sentence of the last paragraph points out that there was fighting during the 1920s. What do you expect the rest of the paragraph to be about? Probably the details of some of this fighting will be given.

Do you see how just reading the first sentence told you the point being made? You can often read first sentences of an entire chapter and know all the points being made. You read the balance of the paragraph for the details and the reinforcement that it provides. If you read it according to the suggestions given for the Q3R of PQ3R, you will be a skilled reader and studier. What is Q3R?

Q stands for QUESTION. Turn the first subtitle into a question. A question sets a goal, a purpose for your reading. When you have a question in mind, you know what answers you are looking for. In the illustration above, you might ask, "What is the history of labor unions, and what are some of their goals?" Questions begin the inquisitive process that learning is all about.

R stands for READ. Now that you have a question in mind, read the subsection to find the answer to the question and for any other important information. If the question isn't being answered, ask yourself why the author is providing this information. Continue to ask questions. Agree or disagree with the author. Try to have a conversation with the author as you read. This is the kind of active reading that you need for success.

R stands for RECITE. Now that you have read the subsection, check yourself. Look away. Tell yourself the answer to the question and any other important information covered in the subsection. The RECITE step forces you to concentrate. It prevents you from reading on without knowing what was previously covered. If you can't do the RECITE step, then redo QRR before going on.

Do QRR for each subtitle and subsection before you do the third R. In other words, turn the first title into a question, and read the first subsection to find the answer to the question and for any other important information. Then do the same for the next subtitle and subsection, then the next, and so on to the end of the chapter. Incidentally, as you do this you will notice how helpful the PREPARE step is. Much of the information covered in QRR can be read quickly, because it was already covered. This will help you remember the information longer (for example, when you are tested), because two important rules of memory are in force. First, you remember longest the things that you see first (have you ever heard the expression "first impressions are lasting"?), and second, you remember longer those things that are repeated. After doing QRR for the entire chapter, you are ready to do the third R.

R stands for REVIEW. Look at each subtitle, and tell yourself what the subsection is about. If you can't do it for any particular subsection, redo QRR for that subsection only. Do you notice the advantage of this step? This forces you to spend more time on what you don't know and less time on what you do know. How often have you reviewed by rereading the entire chapter? When you do this, you give as much attention to what you already know as to what you don't know. When you do the third R of Q3R, you spend most of your time on the sections that you are not sure of.

As a final practice exercise, do PQ3R on the following selection taken from a college textbook. Then answer the questions at the end of the selection. (Read the questions as part of the PREPARE step, of course.) Most important, when you finish, think about how long it took you and how much you learned. Then compare this with your usual way of studying.

THE EFFECTIVE USE OF CREDIT

Properly used, *credit*—"buying now and paying later," for that is what credit is—can make a person's life much richer and fuller. Improperly used, it can bring ruin. In order to take advantage of the good uses of credit (and to avoid its pitfalls), it is essential to know its various forms, to understand how each works, and then to use it—as one would any useful but dangerous tool—with caution and respect.

Three Sound Uses of Credit

There are three sound uses of credit. Two—*open credit* and *profit-making credit*—are obviously sensible and fairly safe if they are properly used. The third—*non-profit-making credit*—is only marginally safe or sensible and requires especially careful consideration. Let us examine these three categories of credit in detail.

Open credit is the term used for credit advanced with no finance charges. The old-fashioned grocer that kept an account of the items a person bought during the month and then settled the bill on payday was extending open credit. Today, open-credit opportunities occur with dairy- and bread-delivery companies, diaper services, the phone company, utilities, newspaper subscriptions, cable television, doctors and dentists, and many other businesses and stores that have the facilities for sending monthly statements to their customers and are willing to provide their services or products in advance of payment.

Department stores, gasoline companies, and multi-purpose bank credit cards also extend open credit if the charge customer or credit-card holder pays the bill in full at the end of the billing cycle (usually 30 to 60 days). However with these formalized charge accounts and with credit cards, if the user fails to pay the full bill within the billing cycle, his account will be financed—that is, charged with interest (usually a minimum of 1½ percent per month on the unpaid balance, which is 18 percent in true annual interest).

It should be clear that a person can use open credit wisely and properly only to the extent that he is certain of being able to settle his account in full at the end of the billing cycle. If he doesn't, the bills will mount rapidly and become more and more difficult to meet; and inevitably, he will be refused further service. If his open-credit account is a formal charge or credit-card account, he will also be charged with high interest rates (as well as service charges), so that the *real* price of his purchase will soar. On the other hand, if open credit is used properly, it is not only a great convenience but a real bargain in that the consumer has the use, almost indefinitely, of the cash he would have spent.

Open credit is also a cost-free way for a person to build up the credit references that become essential when he needs to borrow money for major purchases. People often have the mistaken idea that they will be regarded as a good credit risk if they have always remained solvent and paid cash for everything. The opposite is true. A person is regarded as a good credit risk only if he has borrowed money (or used credit) and demonstrated his ability to repay it. Thus, paying cash for everything can actually create unnecessary hardships for a person when he wants to make a major purchase that requires credit financing (appliances, furniture, a car, a boat, or a house, for example).

Profit-making credit—financed loans or credit purchases that promise a financial return—is a sound use of credit if the consumer will eventually profit more from the use of the borrowed money or credit purchase than he will pay in finance charges. An example of a good use of profit-making credit is borrowing for an education, or for vocational training, thereby acquiring the knowledge or skills that will enable the borrower to earn more. Similarly, good uses of profit-making credit might be borrowing to buy tools that are needed to produce income or to save money (a sewing machine, for example), borrowing to buy or maintain a car that is needed to get to work or school, borrowing to buy work clothes or an office space, or borrowing to move to a new locale and a better job. Businessmen, of course, use profit-making credit in borrowing to build or to buy goods or labor or to make an investment, believing that these steps will bring them more income than the costs of the credit. This use of financed credit is the basis of all commerce.

Non-profit-making credit—the third category for the sound use of credit—is that shadowy region of potential financial difficulty in which a person borrows money or makes a financed-credit purchase to satisfy an immediate and non-profitable need the satisfaction of which he values more than he does the cost of the finance charges. This use of credit requires the greatest exercise of judgment; the borrower must weigh the subjective value of the need satisfaction against the considerable costs of the finance charges and the decrease of subsequent monthly discretionary funds as a result of these charges. This is not only a "buy now and pay later" plan but a "buy now and buy *less* later" plan. If a person makes too many purchases in this way, with each purchase reducing his future spendable income by the amount which he will be paying for credit, he obviously may eventually reduce his standard of living severely and find himself embroiled in months and years of financial stress. It is generally far wiser to follow a deferred-spending, or *saving*, plan.

An example of the sound use of this type of credit, however, might be buying a refrigerator that provides more convenience in storing larger amounts of food, thus allowing the person to shop less often. Similarly, this form of credit might be used wisely in buying a vacuum cleaner that shortens housecleaning time as well as making the time spent more efficient, in buying a piano with which the person can start piano lessons at once instead of deferring them until he is able to save the purchase price, in buying a camera that will provide a great amount of pleasure and capture moments that will never return, or in providing for a vacation or travel opportunity which, once deferred, may not recur in just the same way. There are countless other examples that could be given; for the use of this category of credit is highly subjective. The important point is that the person knows what the costs of the credit are and weighs the relative values carefully; for the routine use of *non-profit-making* financed credit can be a serious drain on even a solvent family's spendable income. For example, the family that carries a continuous average of $1,500 of financed debts (not including a mortgage)—a rather modest amount by today's standards—will pay about $225 a year in finance charges, or $7,000 over its major buying years.

Pitfalls of Credit-installment Buying

The use of *credit-installment contracts* rather than revolving charge accounts or credit cards is often required by stores and dealers when they sell what they call a *"big ticket"* (expensive) *item*, such as furniture, major appliances, carpeting, or a boat or automobile. Credit-installment contracts are a legal agreement between the consumer and the dealer for the financed purchase of a specific item. They provide for a delayed payment for the item on a weekly or a monthly basis for a specified period at the end of which the contract is retired. The payments generally include not only the cost (principal) of the item and the interest charges but also service charges and insurance coverage for the amount. These credit-installment contracts will almost always involve higher interest rates than almost any other source of financing. From the consumer's point of view, therefore, the very worst place to get credit for his purchase is usually the store or dealer who is selling the item. The rule is simple: When buying a "big ticket" item, it is usually advisable to borrow the money elsewhere and then pay cash to the dealer for the purchase.

With an installment-plan purchase, the customer must sign a contract which specifies that the item purchased may be repossessed by the seller if the customer fails to keep up the payments. If repossession occurs, the item may then be resold by the merchant, with the proceeds from the second sale used to cover the expenses of repossession and resale and the remaining indebtedness on the item. If the proceeds from the resale fail to pay everything

66 PART ONE ORGANIZING AND UNDERSTANDING INFORMATION

off, the original customer owes the remainder—even though he no longer has the item. . . .

Answer the following questions according to the information in the selection. Do not refer to the selection for an answer.

1. What is meant by *open credit*? _____

_____

_____

2. What is meant by *profit-making credit*? _____

_____

_____

3. What is meant by *non-profit-making credit*? _____

_____

4. For each of the following credit purchases, write A in the space provided if it is an example of open credit, B if it is an example of profit-making credit, or C if it is an example of non-profit-making credit.

　　_____ home freezer 　　_____ tools for work 　　_____ medical bill

　　_____ newspaper delivery 　　_____ an Easter outfit 　　_____ business loan

　　_____ college expenses 　　_____ Christmas presents 　　_____ a vacation loan

5. Under what circumstances is the use of a credit card considered open credit? _____

_____

_____

6. Name two ways that you can use open credit to your advantage.

_____

_____

4

Learning to Take Notes

Why do you take notes? Stop for a moment—think about it? You have been told for so long that in order to survive in college, you must be a good notetaker. Why? On the lines below, write at least three reasons why you should take notes—how it might help you. Don't write what you think other people would like to hear. Why do *you* think notetaking is important? (If you don't think it can help you, say so—but think about it carefully first.)

What were your reasons? This author and other researchers feel that notetaking is one of the keys to college survival for the reasons listed below. Think about them carefully. If you don't generally agree, then you should skip this chapter, and possibly return to it later if you change your mind.

1. *It keeps you attentive, forcing you to listen and concentrate in class.* You must hear and understand if you are to take a good set of notes in your own words (and that is a must, as you will find out later in this chapter).
2. *It is an aid to memory.* It is possible that you can remember all the important points of the lecture, but you would need a superb mem-

ory to do this in all of your classes. Also, key items in your notes can be used as links to significant details and can start a flow of ideas that might otherwise be left untapped.

3. *Sometimes a lecture may contain information that is the result of the lecturer's reading and understanding that you could not get elsewhere.* Class lectures are often an extension of the information in your textbook, not just a recap of that information. Lectures could be the most important information in terms of both learning and testing, because they more fully explain or analyze the material in the textbook.
4. *It helps in studying for examinations.* You can discover what your instructors think is important, and they make up the exams. Do they, for example, concentrate on big ideas and concepts, or are they concerned about details? Knowing this can help you to predict test questions (see Chapter 3 on studying).
5. *It helps when you want to review.* As will be mentioned later, you should review soon after class and just before the next lecture. Trying to do this from memory for each class is a monumental task, and unnecessary if you take notes.
6. *It improves your self-image.* Taking a good set of notes gives you a feeling of satisfaction and power that comes with a job well done. It helps you to feel good about yourself and about your ability to handle difficult college classes.

Under what circumstances should you take notes? You should take notes in three situations: from lectures and class discussions, from books or other reading material owned by you, and from books or other reading material not owned by you. Each of these circumstances requires its own special techniques, and so they are discussed separately below.

FROM LECTURES AND CLASS DISCUSSIONS

Here are some important points to keep in mind in order to become a skillful notetaker when you attend a lecture or class discussion.

1. Prepare as well as you can in advance of the lecture or class discussion.
2. Take notes in your own words.
3. Be sensitive to clues given by the lecturer that will help you to realize what is important.
4. Take notes in outline form or dash form or a combination of these two.

5. Divide in half the page on which you write your notes. Write your notes on the left side of the page only.
6. If a point is missed, leave a blank space and fill it in later.
7. Be ready to take notes when the lecture begins.
8. Use your personal shorthand to help you keep up.
9. Review your notes as soon as possible after the lecture and again before beginning the next session of that class.
10. Enter certain information at the top of each page of notes.
11. Keep notes in a loose-leaf book.
12. Sit as close to the lecturer as possible.

1. *Prepare as well as you can in advance of the lecture or class discussion.* You might know the topic of the lecture from the instructor's statement about the upcoming lecture or from advance handouts. If you know the topic, do some advance reading before coming to class. Try to predict and even write questions that you think you would want to have answered. Let us say that you know that the topic to be discussed in your next business course class meeting will concern itself with ways that businesses are formally organized. What are some questions that you think will be answered by the end of the lecture? Some might be: "What are the different types of business organizations?", and "What are the advantages or disadvantages of each?" Thinking about these kinds of questions helps you know what notes are important to take, thus making the job of notetaking much easier.

What are some questions that you should keep in mind if you were about to attend a U. S. history class that was going to cover the Civil War? Write three questions below:

_____

_____

_____

Some of the topics that your questions might cover could concern the causes of the war (slavery, cotton), important battles or events, Lincoln's election and his influence and speeches (Emancipation Proclamation, Gettysburg Address), and the aftermath of the war (the Reconstruction Period, the Fourteenth Amendment, carpetbaggers). The more you happen to know about the subject, the more meaningful the questions will be.

2. *Take notes in your own words.* This is especially important. You may have difficulty doing this at first, particularly if you haven't taken notes in this way before. Doing so, however, forces you to understand what is being said. You have to analyze, evaluate, and get key

points if you are to take notes in your own words. Write main points and important details. Use examples only if you think you will need them for full understanding. The only times that you should take notes verbatim (word for word) is when you are given a definition or when you need to remember a quotation or a formula or similar material. You should also copy technical language (jargon) verbatim, because there is no adequate substitute for this precise language.

The practice exercise section of this chapter will provide several opportunities for you to become skillful in taking notes in your own words. Do the exercises carefully. An especially helpful exercise is to take notes from a television newscast. You may find this very difficult to do at first, but keep practicing. Do not take notes from a radio broadcast; the ideas come much too quickly for you to write unless you are a highly skilled expert.

Look at the following paragraph. How would you rephrase the key point or points in your own words? Write your answer on the line that follows.

> A person cannot avoid being aware nowadays that computers play a very important role in the operation of our society. Banking, billing, and bookkeeping procedures, for example, bring us into almost daily contact with the fruits of computer usage. The space program and all missile-associated weaponry are highly dependent upon computers. Computers are used to run factories, handle airline ticket reservations, solve mathematical and engineering problems, perform statistical analyses of data, and aid in record keeping and information retrieval. Indeed, there are few areas of human intellectual endeavor in which computers have not yet been used.

Did you say something about computers being an important part of our lives today? If you didn't, reread the paragraph before going on, and try to understand why that would be the correct response.

3. *Be sensitive to clues given by the lecturer that will help you to realize what is important.* A change in voice or a gesture could be a signal that an important point is being made. Listen for key words or phrases.

Sometimes a lecturer will make a comment such as, "The point is that increased spending in that area will increase the inflation, and increasing the inflation at this time is worse than not spending more in that area." Here the key words, "the point is," tell you that the rest of the statement is especially important and you should be sure to note it. When an author uses the words "in conclusion" or "to summarize," it should be a signal to you. Your attention should be directed to the conclusion or the summary, and your notes should contain that information.

Sometimes a lecturer will say that there are "three causes" or "five methods" or "six characteristics" of something. When that happens, listen for that number of items. Be sure you have all three causes or five methods or six characteristics. If not, ask for them after the lecture.

4. *Take notes in outline form or dash form or a combination of these two.* The chapter on outlining should help you to develop skill in this technique. If you use dash form, you should put a dash in front of each point made rather than the letters and numbers of the outline. The combined form is probably the most useful of all. In using this approach, you should put a dash in front of all points made. In addition, use indentations to separate major and minor points, as you would in an outline.

Read the paragraphs that follow. Then compare the three types of notes below the sample—outline form, dash form, and the combination form.

>   Life insurance is important to businesses. Partners often buy life insurance that is payable to the surviving partner, with an accompanying agreement that the surviving partner will use the money to buy the deceased partner's share of the business from the deceased partner's surviving family. Similarly, corporate managers often buy key man insurance to protect the company against losses that might result from the death of important employees. If a leader in the development of a new and important product should be killed in an accident, for example, the company could lose an important segment of the market because of the delays this person's death would produce.
>   Life insurance protection is also stipulated in many loan contracts. Lenders often require borrowers to buy credit life insurance to guarantee repayment should the borrowers die before repaying the debts.
>   When you decide to buy insurance on your life, the insurance company usually insists that you demonstrate your good health by taking a physical examination. The insurance company pays for the examination and includes the doctor's fee in the premium that you must pay.
>   Insurance companies usually investigate the applicant's lifestyle before issuing a policy. Does the applicant live alone? Where does he work? How does he drive? What kind of person is he? They obtain the answers to such questions from talks with employers, neighbors, and other acquaintances of the applicant.
>   There are four basic types of life insurance: term, straight life, limited payment, and endowment.

Outline Form

Life Insurance

I. Use in business
   A. Partnership protection
   B. Key man insurance
   C. Loan contracts
II. Requirements
   A. Health
   B. Lifestyle
III. Types

Dash Form

—Life Insurance

—Use in business

—Partnership protection

—Key man insurance

—Loan contracts

—Health and lifestyle requirements

—Types

Combined Form

—Life Insurance

—Use in business

  —Partnership protection

  —Key man insurance

  —Loan contracts

—Requirements

  —Health

  —Lifestyle

—Types

Notice in each of the three forms that all needed information is listed. In the combined form, however, you can easily see the relationship of ideas without having to observe the formality of the more structured outline.

5. *Divide the page in half on which you write your notes. Write your notes on the left side of the page only.* The right side of the page should be used for your comments, questions, examples, explanations, or any notes you may want to add from your outside reading. It is very important to use the right side of the page for additional comments, because when you review your notes later, they may not be as clear to

you as they were in class. A phrase or two of explanation to the right of the notes can be very helpful. If nothing else, a word or two will tell you the topic that is covered on the left.

Look at the sample of psychology class notes below. Notice the items on the right side of the page.

—Reasons for females marrying   *Are these reasons as*
  —to establish a family   *valid today as they*
  —for economic gain (or to   *were 20 years ago?*
     stop working)
  —to escape dominating   *This was stressed by*
     parents   *instructor*
  —for more independence   *Probably a test item*

Notice that notes from the teacher's lecture are written on the left side of the page. However, the student taking the notes wondered how valid these reasons are in today's world where women are more independent and self-supporting. The student also had the feeling that the teacher's actions in making this point suggested that a test item would be made out of this information. When this student looks over the notes before test-taking time, this comment will be noticed and given extra attention.

6. *If a point is missed, leave a blank space and fill it in later.* Always be sure to keep up with the speaker. After the lecture, you can ask a fellow student or the lecturer for the missed information. If you try to get it immediately (perhaps by looking over the shoulder of your neighbor), you may miss another point and get even further behind.

7. *Be ready to take notes when the lecture begins.* Have your notebook and writing equipment out and ready. Speakers often begin a lecture with a brief outline of what will be covered (i.e., "Today I will discuss the causes of the revolution and some of the more important battles"). If you are groping for paper and writing material when this is said, you may miss a very helpful overview.

8. *Use your personal shorthand to help you keep up.* Sometimes, even if you are a skilled notetaker, the lecturer speaks too quickly for you to take notes in longhand. Your own shorthand does not have to be a formal one. Use your own set of abbreviations; it doesn't have to be understandable to anyone but you. You might use something like "syk" for psychology or "ecolal" for ecological. Use the same symbols all the time so that you will know them, even if they are not understood by anyone else. Of course, if the subject you are studying uses standard abbreviations, use them. Chemical symbols, for example, should not be changed. Neither should mathematics symbols. N should still be the abbreviation for nitrogen, and water should still be H_2O.

A suggested list of personal symbols for words that are often used in different courses is below. Remember that you should use the same symbols all the time. Also, it is more helpful for you to make up your own symbols. Therefore, only a few, more commonly used words are given.

causes	K
results	Rz
chemical properties	C prps
physical properties	P prps
production (schedule)	pdk (skdl)
business	bsn
mountain	mtn
classification	cls
taxonomy	tx
phylum	phl
because, the reason is	⊙
therefore	△

9. *Review your notes as soon as possible after the lecture and again before beginning the next session of that class.* Research has shown that you will forget most of what you learn within 24 hours unless you review it before that time. Even a brief review will help to place information into long-term memory. To review effectively, you should read each point in your notes and see whether you can explain the point made when the lecture was given. Don't just nod your head, however, and say you understand. Actually recite, preferably aloud, your explanation of the item in your notes. If you can do the first one, go on to the next, and so on. If you can't recite this information, you should try to take more detailed notes, because they would seem to be inadequate as is.

Also, you might write notes that you thought were perfectly clear at the time you wrote them, but which are not so clear when you look at them later. You can explain or elaborate on the right-hand side of the page while the ideas are relatively fresh in your mind. Reviewing again before the next class session refreshes your memory and can help to prepare you for that class.

Three hints about procedures should be mentioned. They are:

10. *Enter certain information at the top of each page of notes.* Enter the date, the course, and the topic that is being discussed, and number the pages. These can act as reference points if you need to ask the teacher for more information, and it helps keep the pages in sequence in case they are moved out of order (see next item).

11. *Keep notes in a loose-leaf book.* Being able to insert additional pages can be very helpful when you want to add explanations or other information and you need more room than is available on the right-

hand side of a page. Also, you may sometimes wish to redo certain notes, and loose-leaf pages allow for easy replacement.

12. *Sit as close to the lecturer as possible.* You can concentrate better, because you are less distracted by what happens in back of you. You can hear better, especially if the instructor speaks in a low voice. You can see the board better.

One question often asked by students is, "Should I tape lectures?" If you wish to tape because you don't think you can keep up with the lecturer and you prefer to listen to the lecture at home, taking notes at your own pace, then taping is not a good idea. Think about this procedure for a moment. For a one-hour lecture, you spend an hour in class and then at least one more hour listening to the tape and taking notes. Each one-hour class becomes at least two hours long. Also, what would you be doing during the actual lecture, if not taking notes? This procedure doesn't allow you to develop the thinking, evaluating, and listening skills needed by good students. You might just as well leave the tape recorder on the desk and do something else during that hour. Of course, if all students taped the lecture, the lecturer might as well just tape his lecture and play that for the students. In that way the lecturer's tape could talk to the students' tapes. Teacher and students could all go out for a pizza and return in an hour to pick up their tapes. (Can you imagine an entire university doing this?)

There is an advantage to taping, however, if you take notes as usual during the class session and use the tape for backup. Then you can listen to the parts that you may have missed or didn't fully understand and fill in your notes accordingly. Doing this can make taping a helpful procedure. (Incidentally, always get the teacher's permission to tape lectures. Some instructors object to this.)

At the end of this chapter are several exercises to give you practice in taking lecture notes. Do them carefully and try to analyze what you have done.

FROM BOOKS OWNED BY YOU

Successful students study from notes made in their books. They know the special advantages that make it especially desirable. You can find what you want in less time—the important information stands out and is easily located. It forces you to concentrate, and this helps you to learn more efficiently. It improves memory, because evaluating and deciding what to take notes on increases concentration. The information is there for faster, more meaningful review.

Note-taking from your book is easier than taking notes from lectures, because you can take the notes at your own pace. Being a good notetaker involves marking in your book. Some students cannot bear to write in their books, because they plan to sell the books after the course or they believe that books shouldn't be marked in. True, you shouldn't mark in a book that doesn't belong to you, but taking notes in your own book makes it more valuable for study and more personal. It then takes on more meaning than just the printed page. You may not be able to sell it for as much later, but not making the most use of the book also diminishes its value to you.

How do you take notes in your own books? You must have an effective approach. A combination of highlighting or underlining and making notes or symbols in the margin is suggested. Have a set of symbols, and use these for all books. It doesn't matter what symbols you use as long as you are consistent and use the same set in each of your books. Some suggestions for using symbols are given below, followed by examples.

1. Main ideas or key thoughts should be noted. You can do this by highlighting the thought, either by underlining it or by putting a double vertical line in the margin. It is suggested that you highlight these because of item 2 below.

2. You should also highlight supporting details. Use different color pens, one for key thoughts and one for significant details.

A word about highlighting is in order here. Items 1 and 2 above are the only things you should highlight. Too often, students highlight their textbooks indiscriminately, so that sometimes most of the page is highlighted. Also, when you highlight two different kinds of thoughts (i.e., main thoughts and supporting details) in the same color, you will need to think your notes through a second time to distinguish between the ideas. Use different colors (for example, yellow for main points, green for details) so that you know at a glance what you are looking at.

3. Indicate items in the book that are emphasized by your teacher in class. Writing *emph* in the margin is a symbol that you might use here. This could be a clue to possible test items.

4. If there is a point that you don't fully understand, even after reading and thinking about it carefully, it should be noted. A question mark in the margin could be used. Be sure to ask your teacher about this point or research it further. When you have the answer, briefly explain it to yourself in the margin or in the space at the bottom of the page.

5. Sometimes you may disagree with a point made by the author. It should be noted. The word *no* in the margin will indicate this. Always add a few words showing the nature of the disagreement.

6. Sometimes a definition of a word or concept is given that you know you must remember. Putting *def* in the margin will show you where it is. It is also a good idea for you to underline the definition in the book.

7. Authors will often mention that there are "three causes" or "six results" or "five characteristics" of something that will now be discussed or elaborated upon. Note where this begins, and then note where each point is discussed. One way to do this is to put 6 *causes* in the margin where it is first mentioned, and then number 1, 2, 3, 4, 5, 6, in turn, in the margin as each cause is discussed.

8. A very significant note to point out is an author's summary or conclusions. A big S or C in the margin covering as many lines as needed is a suggested way to note this.

9. When taking notes in books, it is extremely important that you read several paragraphs first in order to get a feeling for what is being said. Be sure that you fully understand what the key points are, and then go back and take the notes. Read as far as you need in order to get the "gist" of the author's point. In other words, you must understand what is being said before you can take meaningful notes.

10. Make critical comments or evaluations in your own words in the margins or other space on the page. This forces you to think about what you are reading and to understand it. Also, try to summarize important items somewhere on the page.

Below are two examples of notes. The first was taken on a page in a U. S. history textbook; the second, in a psychology book. Each is followed by an explanation or comments about what has been done. Study the illustrations and read the explanations carefully.

TYPES OF COLONIAL GOVERNMENT

The 3 types — *3 types*

All of the Thirteen Colonies were founded by private enterprise, usually without expense to the Crown. Raleigh had learned by hard experience that few individuals had the financial resources to plant colonies. It was therefore natural that, on the conclusion of peace with Spain, colonizers should turn to the joint-stock company, the early form of the modern corporation. It was such a company that founded the first of the colonies, Virginia, and another one later founded Massachusetts Bay. Such companies received charters (articles of incorporation), and the colonies were known as *charter, joint-stock, company,* or *corporate* colonies.

A second type of colony appeared when the king found that his claim to the North American coast provided a cheap way of purchasing political loyalty and rewarding services. Thus *proprietary* grants—of which Maryland, the Carolinas, Pennsylvania, and New York were examples—were made to one or several individuals, who

margin notes: joint-stock company 1; proprietary grant 2; ph.; reasons for jt. stock co.; example; def.

78 PART ONE ORGANIZING AND UNDERSTANDING INFORMATION

[margin note: corporate charter 3 gov't]

not only could sell the land but could exercise governmental powers.

A third type of colony—notably New Plymouth, Connecticut, New Haven, and Rhode Island—emerged when settlers moved onto unassigned or unoccupied lands. Sometimes they purchased Indian land, as Roger Williams did in 1636 in Providence Plantations, or received a land grant without governmental powers, as New Plymouth did in 1621 from the Council for New England. In such cases a government was formed by *compact*—that is, by voluntary association. All but two were eventually absorbed by other colonies; the two exceptions were Connecticut and Rhode Island, which in the 1660s received corporate charters. These two were called *independent corporate* or *charter* colonies, and at the time of the Revolution were the only colonies still governed under corporate charter.

[margin note: 3 types of colonies were formed; each type meeting needs of dif group]

The title, "Types of Colonial Government," suggests that several types will be covered. As you read on, you should notice that three types are discussed, one per paragraph. So that you can realize this without having to reread the material, the words 3 *types* appear in the margin next to the title, and each paragraph is numbered to show the author's organization. Next to each number the particular type of colonial government discussed in the paragraph is noted. The first paragraph discusses why the joint-stock company was needed and gives an example of one, and that is also noted in the margin. The notations next to the second paragraph show that it tells the second type of colonial government, when it was used, and that an example is given. The same kind of information is also noted for the third paragraph. Notice that the entire section is bracketed, and an *emph* reminds you that this information was emphasized by the teacher in class. This is a clue to you to be sure that you understand and remember this section. The brief summary in the white space at the bottom quickly sums up the entire section.

Did you notice that when you are ready to review, the basic information is before you? Also, having written the notes forced you to understand the material and prevented you from daydreaming.

Now examine this brief selection from a psychology book.

THE MEASUREMENT OF INTELLIGENCE

[margin note: 3 types of tests / value / problems]

The most successful and most commonly used individual tests of intelligence, the Stanford-Binet Intelligence Scale and the two Wechsler tests (WAIS and WISC), strongly emphasize the kinds of abilities that predict success in the present school programs. As a result, they have been amazingly valid in predicting school success. However, these tests (and the school systems) have been accused of being highly biased in favor of the verbally capable, already motivated, middle-class child. They assume a moderate amount of interest in exploring the environment, as well as an adequate attention span and a willingness to sit and listen.

[margin note: what are these reasons?]

[Many children do not fit this description. For a variety of social, psychological, and physiological reasons, they are not as verbally fluent, not as well motivated, and not as able to sit still and listen. These children usually get low scores on intelligence tests *and* low grades in school.

[margin note: fair??]

Therefore they are considered stupid, and they are either ignored or placed in special classes with others like themselves.

[margin note: 5 limitations]

The IQ tests have many limitations. <u>First</u>, they assume a good knowledge of English, so that any child brought up in a home in which English is either not spoken or not spoken well has a disadvantage. <u>Second,</u> the child may react negatively to the person giving the test. <u>Third</u>, the child may have a health problem or be emotionally upset by some recent incident (including being required to take the IQ test). <u>Fourth</u>, although psychologists have tried to construct an IQ test that is not influenced by culture or previous learning, they have not succeeded. <u>Fifth</u>, the test only infers intelligence by measuring performance.

[margin note: DEF — Is this def ok?]

The man who created the WAIS and the WISC, David Wechsler, has recently defined intelligence as "the capacity of an individual to understand the world about him and his resources to cope with its challenges." If we accept this definition, then we must term as highly intelligent the child who, in spite of poverty and lack of parental attention, manages to survive to adulthood without serious health or emotional problems. This child may not do well on Wechsler's tests, but he has certainly displayed amazing resourcefulness in coping with challenges that cause others to function well below their potential level of ability.

[margin note: The value? and limits of intel. tests are discussed. Except for predicting school success, the author seems to feel negative about them.]

The notes in the margin next to the first paragraph tell you that this paragraph names three specific intelligence tests, what they emphasize, and that the paragraph suggests that there are problems here. In the second paragraph the student wonders about the statements made. What are the "social, psychological, and physiological reasons"? Also, is being considered stupid under these circumstances a fair appraisal? Noting your questions helps you to think actively about what is being said. It also may be a suggestion to you to bring these questions up in class. The note next to the third paragraph tells you that five limitations of IQ tests are pointed out. The notes next to the fourth paragraph indicate that a definition is given, and again the student wonders about the adequacy of the definition—another point for class discussion. The brief summary indicates how the student interprets what is being said.

At the end of this chapter are several exercises in which to practice this skill on your own. Do them carefully. Then try to take notes in your own textbook.

FROM BOOKS NOT OWNED BY YOU

Very often you need to take notes from books that do not belong to you—notes from library research, for example. You must use your notebook to record the notes. (Another advantage of using a loose-leaf notebook is that these pages can more easily be placed in the appropriate place among your notes.) Some suggestions for doing this are:

1. Take the notes in outline form. Remember that the author had an outline when he wrote the book that you are taking notes from—try to use that outline. However, take notes only on the information that you need for your purposes.
2. There are some things that you may want to copy verbatim—quotations, definitions, formulas, certain statistical information.
3. Be sure that you put the source of the material that you are taking notes from on the top of each page. In that way, you know where to look if you have to refer to that source.

Good note-taking is a very difficult task, but it is well worth the effort, because skillful note-taking is one of the keys used by successful students. The following exercises will give you an opportunity to develop this skill. Do them carefully. Do them all, even though you may feel competent after doing just a few. After completing each exercise, it might be helpful to you if you exchanged your notes with a classmate and analyzed each other's note-taking procedures.

EXERCISE 1

Pretend that each of the following exercises is a lecture. If you can, find someone to read the material to you—a fellow student (you can take turns reading the material to each other), a relative, or a friend. If you can't find anyone, take notes from the material as if it had been read. Analyze your notes after you finish each one by comparing it with the printed exercise.

1.   Plan your play. Playing any round of golf calls for intelligent thinking and planning to achieve the best results. A player who uses good judgment will score better than one who shoots with reckless abandon and with little concern for strategy.

1. *Avoid tension.* Many times when a golfer is playing before a group, tension can cause a poor shot. Always take practice swings to ensure a good stroke. Blot out the spectators from your mind. Hit the ball as though it were a practice shot. Frequently, overstudying a putt causes tension and thus stroking off line. If tension is felt at the address, walk away from the ball and relax.

2. *Take the offensive.* Hit all shots so they will force your opponents to try to do as well or better. Don't be concerned if an opponent hits a longer drive than you do. You have the opportunity to hit the green in position for a par or birdie, while the burden of getting as close as your ball rests with your opponent. Play the course, and induce your opponent to play your game.

3. *Allow for mistakes.* A match is no place to experiment with your game. If you are slicing, play to the left side so that the ball will come to rest in the middle of the fairway. If you are pulling your pitch shots consistently, aim for the right side of the green. If the error is a minor one, make the correction, but don't experiment; you may lose the match.

4. *Don't gamble.* When the opponent has the advantage, too many players attempt shots of which they are incapable. For example, an opponent may be on the green in two strokes, 20 feet from the flagstick, while you may be in the bunker in the same number of strokes, with the flagstick quite near the edge of the bunker. If you try to play the ball close to the pin rather than merely to the green, you may find the next shot still in the sand. Trying to hit the flagstick every time is too risky and may add extra strokes. All long approach shots should be played to the center of the green; short pitch or chip shots may be aimed at the flagstick without as much chance for error.

When in the deep rough, don't try for distance, but play for position on the next shot. Be more concerned with getting a decent shot from the rough than with attempting to hit the green.

5. *Concentrate.* Play each shot as it comes. Attempting to figure too far ahead may cause a poor shot. Think each stroke through, visualize the ball in flight, think positively. If you are convinced you can't hit a shot, or sure it will slice or hook, in all probability it will. Decide how the shot should be played, then play it that way. If on your backswing you feel you have too much club, trying to compensate with an easy swing will probably result in a poor and inaccurate shot. A poor shot should be forgotten and not allowed to influence the next stroke. Be careful in selection of club.

6. *Play in turn.* When near or on the green, many players think they are being courteous by hitting their ball as soon as they come to it, instead of waiting for the person who is away. The player having the right to hit first should be allowed to do so. Hitting out of turn may cause a poor shot, and thus encourage the opponent, or place him in a position to play safe on his shot.

7. *Lag or "lay up" on putts.* The objective of a putt is to get the ball into the cup. There are times, however, when it is wise to play just close enough to assure sinking the next shot. An example of this strategy may be found in the following situation: the opponent is 30 feet from the flagstick in three strokes, and you are 45 feet from the flagstick in two strokes. You need only two putts for a tie, if he sinks his next shot. You may be sure of a tie and a possible win if you don't three-putt. In this situation, it would be better to lag to within a foot or so from the cup, rather than to try to sink the putt, only to roll the ball several feet beyond the three-putt.

Playing Golf

1. Avoid tension
    practice
    ignore spectators
    try to be relaxed
2. Take the offensive
    play best game
    play to compensate for errors
        slicing, pulling
3. Play conservatively
    go for green rather than flagstick
    lag on putts*

4. Concentrate
    take one shot at a time
5. Wait your turn

*This was placed in this position rather than at the end, because it really belongs here. Very often, lecturers will skip around, and you usually have to rearrange the notes later. If a point obviously belongs in a category already noted (as this point might have been), you should immediately make the adjustment. This shows that you are taking notes actively—thinking about what is said. This should make you feel good about yourself and your notetaking ability.

2.   The financial records of a business begin with bits and pieces of paper—sales checks, credit memos, cash-register tapes, written receipts, check stubs, petty-cash slips, bank statements, and so on. These papers are important. They are the bricks from which you will build your organized, permanent records. Some sort of written record, however informal, should always be made *at the time a transaction takes place*.

The Journal

The information from these various papers is first brought together in one or more *journals*—sometimes called "books of original entry." A journal is simply a record of the daily transactions of the business. Each journal entry shows (1) the date of transaction, (2) a brief description of it, (3) the amount of money involved, and (4) the assets, liabilities, capital, or type of income or expense affected by the transaction.

The Ledger

To make the information recorded in the journal more usable, each item is later transferred, or *posted*, to a ledger account. An *account* is a record of the increases and decreases in one type of asset, liability, capital, income, or expense. A book or file in which a number of accounts are kept together is called a *ledger*.

Sometimes the income and expense items are posted to a profit-and-loss statement and only the net profit or loss posted to a ledger account. This method is used in the record keeping system described in this booklet.

A business uses as many accounts as it needs for keeping track of its operations. A small firm with a few pieces of equipment, for instance, may have only one account for all its equipment. A larger business will probably need an account for each type of equipment or even, in some cases, for a single piece of equipment. A business with only one owner will need only one capital account; a partnership will need a capital account for each partner.

3. VITAMIN A

Vitamin A may be synthesized in the body from **carotenes** or from cryptoxanthin (yellow corn pigment). To supply a given amount of vitamin A to the organism, about twice the given amount of these **provitamin A** substances are required in the diet. Deficiency symptoms include stunted growth, night blindness, and diseased conditions of the skin and membranes. **Xerophthalmia** is a deficiency disease which affects the membranes of the eye and causes permanent blindness in 20,000 children every year. Vitamin A appears to be involved in the formation of mucopolysaccharide, a substance which is needed for the health of the epithelial cells which make up the lining membranes of the body. Vitamin A is also a structural component of **rhodopsin**, the "visual purple" of the eye. Rhodopsin is required for vision in dim light and it is involved in the adaptation of the eye to light and dark. When vitamin A is deficient, an insufficient amount of rhodopsin is formed and a person has difficulty in adjusting his vision when he moves from a brightly illuminated room to a dim room. Sufficient vitamin A is needed to maintain the unity of the **adrenal** cortex, which produces hormones involved in body salt balance and in the utilization of protein for energy purposes. A vitamin A deficiency results in a chemical **adrenalectomy**.

Vitamin A is stored in animal bodies, primarily in the liver, with the other fat-soluble vitamins. Because of the storage, repeated high intakes of vitamin A can cause the vitamin to accumulate to **toxic** levels. Such toxicity is called a hypervitaminosis syndrome; there have been instances of hypervitaminosis A and hypervitaminosis D among children who were given injudicious amounts of vitamin supplements. The overdosages occur because of the availability of vitamin concentrates in our society and because of the common belief that if a little is good, more is better.

For adults, the recommended daily allowance of vitamin A is 5,000 **international units** (I. U.). The richest sources of vitamin A (or provitamin A precursors) are liver, butterfat, egg yolk, and green and yellow vegetables. The provitamin content of vegetable foods is variable, because it is dependent upon the way these foods are prepared and served. The use of mineral oil in certain "low-cal" salad dressings interferes with the absorption of all the fat-soluble vitamins. Mineral oil is almost totally unabsorbable, yet the fat-soluble vitamins and provitamins dissolve in the mineral oil and therefore tend to pass unabsorbed through the intestinal tract. Fortunately, the U.S. Food and Drug Administration banned such salad dressings from our markets. But chronic ingestion of mineral oil as a laxative can have a similar effect. About 25% of U.S. families use foods which furnish less than the amount of vitamin A recommended by the N.R.C.

4.
During the period of his job research, the career applicant should prepare a resume or summary of his background and experience. This resume contains facts relevant to the position for which he is applying. Many applicants also prepare a job card, a short form of the resume that they can carry in their billfolds or purses, to use when they fill out application forms at places of employment.

Dean Clifton Matz, head of the career curriculum at Parkland College, tells this true story: A major manufacturing firm instructs its personnel interviewers to watch the large room where people fill out applications for work. When the interviewer sees an applicant using a job card or resume to answer questions on his form, the interviewer is to take the applicant past the small cubicles where regular interviewing is done and into the private interviewing offices. The firm's management has instituted this policy because it believes that a person who comes to an interview prepared to fill out an application is probably better trained than the average worker and may be eligible for the company's supervisory or junior executive programs. Not all firms have such immediate policies, but many do judge applicants by the way in which they prepare application forms.

Job Card

The job card is not submitted to the employer. The career person keeps it to use in filling out the application form, as well as other forms requesting information which he may need to fill out after he gets the job.

The job card contains information about his experience that the career person might not be able to remember on the spur of the moment. This may include:

1. Social Security number.
2. Graduation dates from grade school, high school, and college. (If the person was not graduated, he should use the dates he attended school. He should make this distinction when he fills out the form so he cannot be accused of misrepresentation.)
3. Beginning and ending dates of all former jobs with gross monthly salaries.
4. Full names, titles, and present work addresses of former supervisors.
5. Dates of armed service and of discharge.
6. Full names, occupational titles, occupational addresses and telephone numbers of persons who have previously agreed to serve as references.
7. Awards or honors and dates received.
8. His own telephone number if it is a new one and he might not be able to remember it.

References

While preparing the job card and resume, the job seeker must select his references. References are those persons who will vouch for the applicant's character and working ability. Relatives and close friends should not be used as references in most cases because they might give biased recommendations.

The career person should always inform a prospective reference that he would like to use his name. This is not only courteous but prudent, because sometimes a person one thinks would be glad to act as a reference would rather not.

Most employers do not like to give open letters of reference to employees when they leave jobs. If they do so, they run the risk of recommending people for jobs they may be unable to perform, and of being held responsible by other employers. If an open letter of reference has been obtained, however, it may be presented to the interviewer, and the reference may be listed on the job card, resume, and application for work without the reference's specific permission.

The resume is an expansion of the job card. Typed resumes are preferable, but they may be handwritten neatly in ink on unlined paper. The employer should always receive an original copy. Applicants who are investigating a number of companies sometimes have their resumes printed by offset process. Whether to have this done is a delicate question: although there is no rule regarding multiple reproduction, employers tend to prefer original, typed copies.

The resume provides information not only about the writer's background, but also about his communicative skills as demonstrated by the layout, neatness, and writing technique.

Most applicants enclose their resumes in their letters requesting interviews. This enables the employer to decide if he is sufficiently interested in the applicant to grant the interview. If the resume is sent to the employer before the interview, it is still wise for the applicant to take a copy of the resume to the appointment. The employer may have misplaced his copy or sent it to another office of the company and thus may not have it on hand. This kind of forethought on the part of the applicant also tends to impress the employer favorably.

5. DIFFERENT KINDS OF LANGUAGE

Language That Brings about Human Contact

This kind of language permits a person to translate his real self into words and by doing so to make deeper contact with his fellow man. It is language filled with the person who is speaking. Negatively, it implies a refusal to use speech merely to fill interactional space and time or as a smoke screen behind which to hide.

The ability to speak in such a way as to make human contact must be clearly differentiated from the ability to speak fluently or elegantly, for both fluency and elegance are at times used to camouflage rather than reveal one's identity. If the encounter-group member is to develop new ways of being present to the other members of the group, then he must discover "new" ways of speaking.

Commercial Speech

"Commercial speech" refers to the language of the marketplace, the use of language in the commercial transactions of men. Such language is lean, utilitarian, pragmatic; it deals with objects rather than persons for it is a medium of exchange rather than of interpersonal contact. Much of such language today is left to computers. It would be of no interest to us here were it not for the fact that there are people who use commercial speech as their principal mode of speech in interpersonal transactions. They see people as objects to be manipulated, rather than persons to be contacted, and this is reflected in the quality of their speech.

Cliché Talk

"Cliché talk" refers to anemic language, talk for the sake of talk, conversation without depth, language that neither makes contact with the other nor reveals the identity of the speaker (except negatively, in the sense that he is revealed as one who does not want to make contact or does not want to be known). Cliché talk fosters ritualistic, rather than fully human, contact ("Do you think that it is really going to rain?"—"The way they're playing, they'll be in first place by the first of September!"). Cliché talk fills interactional space and time without adding meaning, for it is superficial and comes without reflection. Perhaps it is the person who is overcommitted to maintenance functions, a person who is either unaware (because he lacks the requisite social intelligence) or afraid of possibilities for further interpersonal growth, whose speech will be predominantly cliché talk.

Cliché talk is just words, while language-that-contacts is speech filled with the speaker. Some people speak endlessly about themselves and say nothing (if they were really disclosing themselves, others would not find it boring). They say nothing about themselves because they have no real feeling for themselves—they are deficient in the emotional dimension of life—and could hardly be expected to relate what they don't experience.

Speech as a Weapon

Sometimes language is actually used to destroy interpersonal contact rather than foster it. There are a number of forms of speech that are really violations, rather than uses, of language. For instance, in the heat of anger, language can become a weapon. When married people stand shouting at each other, their language has more in common with the sledgehammer than with a process of communication.

Translating Nonverbal Messages

When two or more people are talking, there are usually at least two levels of communication: (1) what is conveyed by the verbal interchange (the content mentioned above) and (2) a variety of other messages that are transmitted in a number of different ways—for example, the qualities of the verbal exchange itself such as speed, tone, inflection, intensity, and emotional color, and nonverbal cues such as eye contact, bodily stance, facial expressions, and gestures. These messages are "metacommunicative processes," the purpose of which is to interpret or classify the content of the verbal message or to send a parallel message more or less unrelated to verbal content. These metacommunications can even negate or deny the explicit meaning of the verbal message (for instance, it is a rather common occurrence to hear "no" on an explicit verbal level and at the same time to experience "yes" on a metacommunicative level, the latter being the real message).

6. APPEAL TO AUTHORITY

No one knows everything. So we often have to consult experts before making decisions. But there are good and bad ways to do this; improper appeals to experts constitute the fallacy of appeal to authority.

The problem is to distinguish proper from improper appeals to authority, a problem about which the relevant authorities (logicians and writers on rhetoric) have had relatively little to say. There are, however, a few rules of thumb which are of some practical use:

1. An authority in one field is not necessarily worth listening to in another. The opinions of famous athletes who endorse Gillette blades in TV commercials are a case in point; there is no reason to suppose that athletes know any more about razor blades than anyone else. Similarly, to cite an example from politics, a man who is expert in making and selling automobiles (whether his name is Charles Wilson or Robert McNamara) is not thereby qualified to oversee the defense of the nation.

2. It is generally fallacious to accept the *opinion* of an authority (as opposed to his arguments) on topics about which experts disagree. The same is true of opinions in fields about which relatively little is known.

Judges and juries often violate this principle, and thus commit the fallacy of *appeal to authority*, when they decide about a defendant's sanity or competence *solely* on the basis of one psychiatric *opinion*. Judges, of all people, ought to know how easy it is to obtain contrary expert testimony on most psychological matters.

3. When experts disagree, the layman must become his own expert, turning to acknowledged experts for *evidence*, *reasons*, and *arguments*, but not for conclusions or opinions. This is especially true with respect to political matters because of the tremendous controversy they arouse. But it applies elsewhere too. The judge who merely accepts a psychologist's opinion ought instead to ask for the *reasons* which led the psychologist to his opinion. Similarly American presidents need to go into the complex details which lie behind the opinions of their economic advisors, rather than confining themselves, as President Eisenhower is said to have done, to whatever could be typed onto one side of one page.

4. Finally, anyone who feels that he must appeal to an expert in a way which violates any of the above rules should at least consult the past record of that authority. Experts who have been right in the past are more likely to be reliable than those who have been wrong.

It is surprising how often even this rule of last resort is violated. Think of the many senators and congressmen who accepted expert military opinion that the war in Vietnam would end in 1969 or 1970, even after having heard military experts testify incorrectly so often over the years about the end of the longest war in American history. Or recall President Nixon's economics advisors, who remained in favor with the president even though their predictions for 1970 on inflation and unemployment proved to be way off the mark. If you have to rely on expert opinion, at least choose experts with a good track record.

The danger of the fallacy of *appeal to authority* results largely from the tendency to trust in the authority of all pronouncements by high officials and other famous people. Senator Joseph R. McCarthy's charges in the early 1950s that Communists infested the Department of State ("I have here in my hand the names of . . .") were taken seriously, and caused so much trouble for our country, precisely because he was a *United States Senator*.

7. When you are sure that the balance in your checkbook is mathematically correct, you are ready to reconcile your record with the bank's. You will need the preceding month's reconciliation, the checkbook stubs, and the canceled checks and bank statement received from the bank. Then take these steps:

1. Arrange all the canceled checks in numerical order.
2. Compare deposits listed on the bank statement with deposits entered in your checkbook. List in the first section of the reconciliation any deposits recorded in your checkbook during the month but not appearing on the bank statement. (If deposits are made daily, only one or two deposits at the end of the month should have to be put on this list.)
3. There will probably be some canceled checks from the previous month. Check these off the list of outstanding checks shown on the preceding month's reconciliation. List in the first section of the current reconciliation the checks still outstanding.
4. Check off on the corresponding check stubs all canceled checks drawn during the month being reconciled. Add the checks recorded on the remaining stubs to the list of outstanding checks on the reconciliation. (Disregard any checks that you may have written after the end of the month.)
5. If any errors in amounts are discovered in the preceding steps, list them in the second section of the reconciliation statement as adjustments to be added or deducted.
6. Examine the bank statement for service charges or other adjustments to your account and enter them in the second section of the reconciliation.
7. Carry out the additions and subtractions shown on the bank reconciliation. The adjusted balance per bank statement should equal the adjusted balance per your checkbook.

Errors Made by the Bank

Occasionally, you may find that the bank has made a mistake in your account. The following types of errors can occur:

Deposit or check of another person posted to your account.

Your deposit or check posted to another person's account.

Deposit or check posted in the wrong amount.

Preceding month's balance incorrectly brought forward on your bank statement.

Addition or subtraction incorrectly carried out on the bank statement.

Any such errors should be reported to the bank at once. They must also be shown as adjustment items in the first section of your bank reconciliation. When the next month's bank statement is received, make sure that any bank errors from the previous month have been corrected in the statement.

8. HISTORY TEXTBOOKS

The need for students to know the history of their own nation is, of course, one reason for the great emphasis on American history in our public schools. But in view of the actual content of the history texts used, it can hardly be the only reason.

Given the portrayal of American history in typical public school textbooks, it seems reasonable to conclude that history is taught to public school children as much to *indoctrinate* them as to teach them the truth about the history of their own land:

1. History as a subject matter is inherently value-tinged, first in the very selection of "facts" to be presented, and second in discussing the quality of political and social systems. History also is inherently *controversial*, unless all controversial topics are ignored, in which case we have pablum. Yet these texts have an "objective" and "evenhanded" tone, which is used to create the impression that it is an *objective fact* we as a nation hold and *live up to* the highest ideals, and in general are the greatest nation on earth.

2. This impression is enhanced by omission of as much as possible that is sordid in our past (the fallacy of *suppressed evidence*), and by playing up all that is good (the fallacy of *distortion*). In general, the skeletons in our national closet that cannot be ignored are discussed only at the point in history when they have somehow been corrected or atoned for, or else, on a note of optimism, as being in process of solution.

3. Minority groups, in particular those we have treated the worst, are made as close to "invisible" as possible. The

exceptions to this are "token" figures, such as Indian guides, Susan B. Anthony, Booker T. Washington, and George Washington Carver.

These sorry facts would be out of place in a book on reasoning, argument, and political rhetoric were it not for the subtle (often not so subtle) bias most of us bring to many political arguments in later life, a bias produced in part by the history and civics textbook brainwashing we all suffer through as youngsters. We are ill-prepared to face the problems of today because we were never taught the evils of the past which in large part produced them.

In addition, history texts ill prepare students to face today's challenges because they perpetuate falsehoods about the relative importance of events and (in particular) people. They portray the great men in our history as (roughly in descending order of importance) U.S. presidents, other politicians, explorers and adventurers, military men, inventors, businessmen, settlers (pioneers), religious leaders and, last, artists, scientists, and "intellectuals." In the elementary school text to be discussed, we are told about every president, twenty-two other politicians, twenty explorers, fifteen military men (excluding those who later became politicians), sixteen inventors, three businessmen, ten settlers, and thirteen religious leaders. We are told about two social workers (white), five men granted land in what is now the U.S., one adventurer, one "bad man," and two Wild West types. But we read the names of only one labor leader, two artists, four Indians (three friendly to white men), three scientists (none of them theoretical scientists, or of the first rank), two (token) Negroes, and no philosophers whatsoever.

9. When an instructor walks into class the first day of the semester, he knows without thinking what the students will expect of him and what he will expect of them. These things are known even though they have not seen each other before. The students know that the instructor will stand in front of class behind a lectern, that he will have a coat and tie on, that he will probably call roll, assign reading, and dismiss them early the first day. The instructor knows that, unless he is teaching a required class, students will be shopping around. They will be trying to decide whether to take this class, and their decision will be based on course content, the viewpoint and personality of the instructor, the amount and type of work required, or on how the instructor grades.

We know these things about each other partly because of the system of norms discussed previously. The concepts of status and role are closely related to norms, and they play a major part in the situation described above. By *status* we mean a position in society or in a group. There are innumerable positions that one may occupy—teacher, student, police officer, president, football player, father, wife, convict. Furthermore, each of us may occupy several positions at once—teacher, handball player, father, husband, and so on. By *role* we mean the behavior of one who occupies a particular status. As Bierstedt puts it, a role is what an individual *does* in the status he occupies; statuses are occupied, roles are played.

A set of norms surrounds each status and role. These norms, called *role requirements*, describe the behavior expected of persons holding a particular position in society. Recalling our earlier example, the behavior of the student who refused to stand up was disturbing because it was unpredictable. He was occupying the status or position of student, but the role he played—his behavior—was contrary to the expected behavior of a person in that status. His behavior was outside the limits set by the norms or role requirements.

Within the boundaries set by the role requirements, there is often extensive variation in how a role is played. On a football team, status would refer to the positions, role to the behavior of the incumbent of the position. One status would be quarterback. Role requirements of quarterbacks are generally that they call the plays, direct the team, and try to move the ball down the field. But now look at the actual performance of several quarterbacks. One passes frequently, another seldom passes but runs with the ball often, and a third does neither but usually blocks. Compare four or five of your instructors in their role behavior. Although all occupy the status of college professor, no doubt their behavior varies markedly. One paces the floor, another stays behind the podium while lecturing. One demands class discussion, the next dislikes having his lectures interrupted. One has beautifully organized and prepared lectures, and another has a disorganized, stream-of-consciousness presentation that he put together on the way to class. Or, compare the role behavior of the last three presidents of the United States. Again we see marked difference in role performance within a given status. These differences in role behavior obviously occur because people holding the same status define the role differently. They also have different skills, interests, abilities, and personalities. Therefore, although each status carries with it certain role requirements, there is still variation and flexibility in actual role behavior.

Achieved and Ascribed Status

How do we happen to occupy the statuses that we do? Some, probably most, statuses are earned or achieved in some way, and hence these are called *achieved* statuses. Astronaut, policeman, college professor, and truck driver represent achieved statuses. Some statuses are automatically conferred on us with no effort or choice on our part. These are *ascribed* statuses. One's sex, race, and nationality are ascribed (although occasionally some changes can be made). Sometimes it is difficult to tell whether a status is ascribed or achieved. Take the fellow who is "forced" to go to college because of the wishes of his parents—is his status of student ascribed or achieved? Or how about statuses that a child "inherits" from his parents, such as political and religious affiliations—are they ascribed or achieved?

CHAPTER 4 LEARNING TO TAKE NOTES   101

EXERCISE 2

Now pretend that each of the following exercises is in a book that belongs to you. Take notes that you can use for future reference. The first one is done for you.

1.   ADVANTAGES OF KEEPING GOOD RECORDS

Advantages

1. for organization

2. to be competitive / competitive needs

A simple, well-organized system of records, regularly kept up, can actually be a timesaver by <u>bringing order out of disorder</u>. Furthermore, <u>competition</u> is very strong in today's business arena. A small businessman needs to know almost on a day-to-day basis where his business stands profitwise, which lines of merchandise or services are the most or the least profitable, what his working-capital needs are, and many other details. He can get this information with reasonable certainty only if he has a good record keeping system—one that gives him all the information he needs *and no more*.

emph. in class (Test items?)

3. Safeguard assets / how assets are safeguarded

Good records can also help to <u>safeguard your assets.</u> Accurate records of cash transactions will disclose any shortages, so that steps can be taken to find and correct the source of trouble. Accounts-receivable records disclose any shortages in the customers' balances and also help to control bad-debt losses. Inventory shortages are somewhat harder to detect, but here, again, a good system of records makes it possible to keep the shrinkage at a minimum.

4. prep of financial reports

Still another important use of well-organized financial records is in the <u>preparation of financial reports</u> showing the progress and current condition of your business. Such reports can be invaluable if you need a bank loan, or if the business must be evaluated for a sale or merger.

2.   How archery was discovered can only be conjectured. Possibly a man idly experimenting with a tree branch that had a piece of vine, gut, or rawhide attached to it discovered that it could cast a light stick of wood farther than he could throw a heavier spear. As the idea developed, better pieces of wood were found for bows, and feathers or leaves were added to the sticks to guide them better in flight. The idea of adding sharp stones to the ends of the arrows was probably the next stage of development. Once the bow was perfected, it became man's most important weapon. We can imagine his feeling of relief when he no longer had to flee the beasts or to fight in close combat with clubs or spears or when he could take game at greater distances than previously.

The bow is thought to have been known to all Eastern Hemisphere tribes except the aboriginal Australians. The Israelites, Babylonians, Mongolians, Assyrians, Chinese, and Japanese all favored the bow and arrow. The Egyptians used bows and arrows in overthrowing the Persians and then successfully waged war on many other countries. The success of the bow and arrow as a weapon of war spread rapidly, and many nations gave up their chief weapons—slings and javelins—for this more efficient device.

The Greeks and Turks are credited with originating composite bows made of wood, horn, and sinew and shaped like a "C" when unstrung. These composite bows were extremely efficient. Interestingly, many of our modern bows tend to resemble them. An ancient Turkish bow is said to have shot an arrow more than 800 yards. This record flight was unsurpassed until Danny LaMore won the National Flight Championship at Lancaster, Pennsylvania, on August 17, 1959, with a free-style flight (bow held by the feet and pulled with both hands) of 937.17 yards and a regular flight (hand-held) of 850.67 yards. At the same meet Norma Beaver set a women's national record of 578.7 yards.

The bow was the chief weapon of warfare for centuries—until the battle of the Spanish Armada in 1588. For that battle, the English had experimentally equipped ten thousand troops with firearms, with outstanding success. The bow soon became a secondary weapon, and after the last big battle was fought with bows and arrows by the Chinese at Taku in 1860, it became obsolete as a weapon of war. However, some tribes in Africa and South America still use bows and arrows in warfare (as is evidenced by small, slow-flying planes that become "pincushions" over certain jungle areas) and also depend on them as their chief means of taking game and fish.

After the decline of the bow as a weapon, archery was forgotten until countries such as England saw its merit as a sport. King Henry VIII was an enthusiastic archer and an ardent bettor who staged large matches and invited wide participation. With the help of this kingly interest, archery became very popular in England, and proficiency in the use of the longbow was common.

Archery was known to the Indians of America when the Pilgrims arrived. The Indians soon gave up their bows and arrows for the more efficient firearms, and so history repeated itself. Archery began as an American sport in 1828 when a group of archers formed the United Bowmen of Philadelphia—which still exists. In 1879, the National Archery Association was founded and yearly national tournaments were begun, the first being held in Chicago.

For more than 100 years, target-archery competition prevailed in America. In 1934, when the NAA held its tournament in Los Angeles, a group of archers interested mainly in bow hunting began agitating for a new kind of game that was suited for off-hand shooting, which was more usable for hunting. Six years later, in 1940, the National Field Archery Association was organized. For ten years competition was restricted to bare-bow shooting, or the use of a single-pin sight. Today, the values of the two main styles of shooting are recognized and tournaments are conducted in two divisions, free style and instinctive.

The future of the sport looks bright. Archery tackle sales are among the highest of all sporting goods and still rising. People of all ages are taking up the sport. There were 1.7 million bow twangers in 1946, according to the National Recreation Association; in 1960 they numbered more than 4.7 million—up 176 percent and the trend is still upward. The greatest increase can be seen in the large numbers of newly licensed bow hunters each year. From 1950 to 1966, the number of licensed archery deer hunters in Michigan alone jumped from a few thousand to over forty thousand. Practically every state has special bow seasons which commonly precede the regular deer seasons and usually last much longer. In Michigan, for example, the bow season is five weeks long, while the regular deer season is only fifteen days. Because archery has many merits, it is probable that people of all ages will continue to enjoy it in the years ahead.

Since its inception, the Outdoor Education Project of the American Association for Health, Physical Education, and Recreation has done much to promote archery, primarily in schools and colleges. The numerous workshops conducted throughout the country have enabled thousands to receive training under expert instructors. This effort is expected to continue.

3. **Aptitude Tests**

Entrance examinations taken for acceptance into college are a kind of intelligence test, usually divided into several areas. In order to be accepted in many universities you must achieve stated minimum scores on individual tests or an accepted combination of scores. Girls generally make higher scores on verbal tests and lower scores on mathematical or quantitative tests.

A standard entrance test for many colleges and universities is the *Scholastic Aptitude Test* (SAT), which is a three-hour objective test designed to measure your verbal and mathematical skills. It is offered by the College Entrance Board, a nonprofit membership organization that provides tests and other educational services for schools and colleges. The College Board also offers achievement tests in various subjects which you may take the same day as the SAT if the college you plan to attend requires it.

Another test that many colleges use for their entrance examination is the *American College Test* (ACT) which gives scores in four areas (English, mathematics, social science, and natural science) followed by a composite score. Some colleges, particularly public junior colleges, do not require a minimum score in order to be accepted, but use the scores to supplement high school grades for placement in various courses.

Another entrance test, the *School and College Aptitude Test* (SCAT), is divided into two areas (verbal and quantitative) with a total which is not an average of the two.

The purpose of all these aptitude tests is to determine the ability of a person to succeed in academic work, and in this sense, the tests reveal the intellectual ability of the person taking the test. However, since the questions are related to particular bodies of knowledge, the tests also measure achievement. An individual who has had little or no familiarity with the information being tested will not do well and still may be intelligent.

Intelligence Tests

An intelligence test refers to the intelligence quotient (IQ) or "ability" of the person taking the test. When comparing aptitude tests and IQ tests, it is important to realize that the aptitude test gives scores in different kinds of mental ability, that is, English and mathematics; an IQ test reports mental perception with only one score. That score can then be compared with the average scores made by thousands of others.

The *Otis Quick Scoring Mental Ability Test* and the *Henmon-Nelson Tests of Mental Ability* give the test taker a rough estimate of his IQ. A more nearly valid test of an individual's IQ can be obtained when a test is administered individually by a skilled tester.

One problem with all aptitude and intelligence tests is that the individuals taking them must have come from homes with similar cultural and linguistic backgrounds. If they have not, the scores are not valid. Schools and test centers have gradually become aware that there are other ways to measure intelligence than through a measure of verbal skills, because intelligence may be defined as the capacity to profit by experience or as the ability to solve problems.

4.   Everyone likes a good listener, but not everyone likes to listen. Often we have our own ideas, and we would prefer that others listen to us. However, approximately one-third of career communication is now oral, and new devices such as televised telephones and conference telephone systems will make listening even more important.

Employers often complain that their employees, especially their new employees, make mistakes because they do not listen carefully enough. There is some truth in their complaint, but listening is not the employees' responsibility alone. It is just as important for employers and managers to be good listeners. In fact, listening may be used to define power: the president of an organization is the most powerful person in it because he has more sources for listening than anyone else.

Anyone who wants to learn to listen more effectively should first realize that he can never completely understand what another person says. Understanding is always imperfect because the backgrounds of the speaker and listener are never identical, and therefore no word means exactly the same thing to both. As a result, the listener always over- or under-reacts to the message. However, if he learns about the factors that influence listening, a person can understand the message more completely and recall its details more exactly.

Factors that influence listening include the clarity of the message, the importance of the message to both speaker and listener, the listener's preparation for receiving the message, and the physical conditions under which listening takes place. Many things, then, can go wrong in the listening experience. A good listener must eliminate as many of the possibilities for error as he can—before, during, and after listening.

Blocking

Inaccurate listening usually occurs because the listener has composed a message of his own that competes in his brain with the speaker's message. The result of this competition may be total blocking: the listener simply does not hear the speaker. Or it may be partial blocking: the listener hears only a portion of the speaker's message. In this case he may confuse the details of this portion with the details of his own message.

The basic reasons for blocking are to be found in the very nature of listening. Listening requires that the listener accept the speaker's goals, at least temporarily, in order to comprehend them. Listening also usually requires the listener to accept the speaker's techniques for reaching these goals. Therefore, even if the listener disagrees with the goals and with the speaker's techniques for reaching them, he must overcome his opinions enough to be able to recall the information he has been given.

Creative listening goes beyond simple good listening. The creative listener uses material he hears to form new thoughts and ideas of his own, during or after the listening experience. There is always some danger in listening creatively because one's own thoughts may interfere with the speaker's message. However, creative listening should be the goal of the career person who wishes to train himself not only to understand oral information, but also to use it to stimulate and expand his own thought.

Boredom

One of the greatest threats to effective listening is boredom. Boredom usually occurs because the listener already knows the material, or because he believes it irrelevant to his own goals.

Even the most boring listening experience can be made interesting if the listener tries to listen critically. Critical listening involves determining if the speaker is presenting the details in a logical order, if other listeners are properly involved in what he is saying, and if they appear to understand the message. Critical listening should always be undertaken for positive goals, not for the negative goal of enhancing the critical listener's prestige. A good critical listener can be very helpful to a speaker. He can ask questions that will help other listeners to learn, and he can tell the speaker where his message needs clarifying or expanding.

Information outside his own field need not bore the career listener. He should realize that careers are highly interrelated, and it is precisely where career fields meet that executive management is needed. Therefore, listening to information outside one's field is a form of management training. The career person who wishes to advance to the management level should listen eagerly to information both inside and outside his immediate area of responsibility.

Anxiety

Everyone is slightly afraid of even the kindest superiors. Everyone wants to be considered intelligent and promotable. But everyone sometimes fears that he is not outstanding, and this fear can make it hard for the listener to understand what his superior is saying.

A certain amount of anxiety about one's career abilities and listening skills is normal, and some tension is believed necessary for learning to occur. However, excessive anxiety prevents one from receiving the message. The anxious listener must therefore decrease his nervousness. He can do this by concerning himself with the physical and organizational techniques of listening.

Getting oneself in a proper physical position to listen greatly increases one's ability to take in facts. People who sit near the door at the rear of a large auditorium soon become tired from straining to hear; they expend effort needlessly. A good listener tries to get away from distractions such as swinging doors, windows open on street sounds, and even certain people who he knows may become restless and fidgety during the listening period.

The listener himself is often his own greatest distractor. He may tap his foot, drum a pencil, twist his hair, bite his fingernails, and thereby create small, distracting pains that prevent him from paying full attention to the speaker.

By maintaining eye contact with the speaker, a listener not only prevents himself from becoming distracted, but he increases the number of cues that he receives from the speaker. If he is listening to a mechanical source such as a tape recorder, he should look at the recorder rather than at another person. If printed material is being used with the mechanical source, the listener should look at the printed material when the source instructs him to look at it. If the source does not tell the listener where to look, and the listener grows bored looking at the source, he should look at a neutral area such as a wall or desk surface; he should not look at pictures on a wall or out a window at passing cars because these stimuli may distract him.

5. SOMATOTYPING

People are built differently. Some are slight with long levers and small muscles; others have short levers and large muscles. Some are streamlined; others are truncated. The basic build of most people is between these extremes. Biological heredity is responsible for basic body structure. The size of bony segments, bone length, number of muscle fibers, and even intestinal length are relatively fixed from conception.

A number of attempts have been made to classify the human body. Sheldon offers a reasonable scheme. His system is called somatotyping and recognizes three main categories: endomorphy, mesomorphy, and ectomorphy.

The endomorph is characterized by a large soft bulging body—the so-called "pear-shaped" build. Identifying traits include short neck, large round head, wide feminoid hips, short arms, broad stubby hands, hammy legs, and small feet. Body mass is concentrated toward the center of the body in fatty breasts, protruding abdomen, and heavy buttocks. Generally, endomorphs have fragile tendons and ligaments and intestines of great length—some 12 to 15 feet longer than the average. They usually reach sexual maturity late. Their response to fitness training is slow, but they are capable of vast improvement. Running is hard for endomorphs because they are troubled by foot problems. Endurance work is also difficult because they have great body bulk, but strength work is more promising because of their lever advantages.

The ectomorph is characterized by linearness and slight build. Identifying traits include poked neck (thin with slight musculature; short torso; shallow chest depth; long arms, legs, and feet; thin wrists; and knees and elbows that appear to be knotted. Ectomorphs have light musculature; and, generally, their ligaments and tendons are flimsy. They carry little body fat and their intestines are about 12 to 15 feet shorter than the average. Their response to training is slow, and they are easily injured. Strength development poses a problem because they have slight muscling and long levers, but endurance development offers greater promise.

The mesomorph is characterized by a body mass that is away from body center: he has extremely well-developed and well-defined muscles. Identifying traits include long torso, short heavy neck, short powerful levers, narrow waist and hips, wide shoulders, deep chest, and flat abdomen. Their ligaments and tendons are strong, and their skeletal muscles are capable of great strength and endurance. Intestinal length is average—about 32 feet. They respond quickly to training and are capable of incredible physical feats.

Every individual has some characteristics of each of these three components; *extreme cases are rare*. Each component is rated on a scale from one to seven, seven being the largest amount and one being the least. The endomorphy rating is given first, followed by mesomorphy and ectomorphy, in that order. Three numbers in sequence give the rating. For example, a 4 5 2 is an endomorphic mesomorph—mesomorphy is most prominent and endomorphy is next in prominence. A 3 5 3 is a mesomorph and a 2 5 6 is a mesomorphic ectomorph. The average male falls in the "average" category for each component, while most women are higher than "average" in endomorphy because of biological sex differences. Females tend to have wider hips and more subcutaneous fat stored in the hip and thigh areas.

Somatotyping permits an understanding of individual differences. It focuses on the individual and on the characteristics of his physique, illustrating that basic structural differences may be the result of biological inheritance. Most people would probably choose to be mesomorphs, but an individual's will cannot determine his body structure.

The health needs of each category are unique. For example, the endomorph should know that his group is prone to degenerative and hypokinetic disease. He should be aware that he may always have a serious problem with weight control and that his motor potential is less than average. However, he should also realize that, within the limitations of this inheritance, he can contribute maximally to his health, although his life may be prematurely terminated if he does not pay close attention to his health needs. Health problems in the endomorph are common and often severe.

The body-type classifications described here are subjectively determined and are variable. By constant exercise and extreme dieting, the mesomorphic endomorph may appear more mesomorphic and less endomorphic than an endomorphic mesomorph who eats too much and does not exercise. The concern is to recognize *gross* individual differences and to personalize fitness goals accordingly rather than to assume that every person has the same physical potential and that his present physique is solely the result of his choosing. The somatotype is only one of many factors to consider in forming a realistic self-image. It is not very useful alone, but when combined with other measurements, it increases understanding of individual fitness.

6. LEARNING TO LISTEN

Part of learning in college comes through listening to a lecturer. Sitting and listening is rather passive and not always conducive to learning. To give yourself the best opportunity to learn in the classroom, you must become as actively involved as possible. The first step in becoming a good listener is very simple. Sit up straight in your chair! This first step sets the stage for your *active* listening.

A second step for making classroom listening an active process is to develop the habit of using questions to analyze what the speaker is saying. Ask yourself questions that will help capture the essential meaning in the lecturer's flow of words: "Why is he saying that?" "What does he mean by that?" "What is the main point of what he is saying?"

A third step that will help you develop into an active listener is to take notes on what the lecturer is saying. The act of writing will make you physically as well as mentally active as you try to determine the important ideas and facts that should be captured in your notes.

A fourth step involved in becoming an active listener is to familiarize yourself with the lecturer's topic before the lecture through assigned reading. If you have prior knowledge of the lecturer's subject, you can develop a keener interest in what he is saying and the time you spend in class will be more valuable for you. By contrast, if the subject is "foreign," then what the lecturer is saying will mean little and the hour will be lost.

Remember the four steps of active listening: (1) be physically alert; (2) ask yourself questions; (3) take notes; (4) develop familiarity with the topic to be discussed.

7. It is unfortunate that a significant number of physicians have found it lucrative to abandon general practice in order to "treat" the obese. In some areas of the United States this abandonment has helped to create a "doctor shortage." It is perhaps tragic that most obesity "treatments" dispensed by these men are unsuccessful, although they are dispensed at great cost to the patient. One of the areas notoriously neglected in the education of physicians is the area of nutrition, and most fad diets or ill-considered nutritional regimes published in popular magazines carry the endorsement of a physician. Fortunately, some physicians are very knowledgeable in the area of nutrition in spite of their limited initial preparation.

Following is a discussion of some of the chief misapprehensions about weight reduction which have made huge profits for the unscrupulous or the ill-informed.

Perspiration

Steam cabinets, plastic steam-bath suits, and portable sauna baths are just a few of the many devices used to cause the body to perspire. When the body perspires, moisture and its corresponding weight is lost. But as soon as one drinks water, all the lost weight is restored and the body's fatty deposits remain untouched.

Salt

One well-known beauty expert has urged women to omit some of the salt they use in meals, because this salt is used by the body for fluid retention. A number of self-proclaimed obesity experts have therefore recommended dietary salt restriction for weight reduction. The salt and water balance of the body is a basic and critical matter of health and is controlled by the cortex of the adrenal glands. Except in cases of severe edema, salt restriction is not a wise practice from the standpoint of health. As in forced perspiration, the dehydrating of the body can cause weight losses of short duration but it does not reduce the fatty deposits which cause obesity.

Appetite Killers

One method of reducing the fat stored by the body is the decrease of the amount of food consumed. Many people soon find that the limiting of food intake is often difficult; they become receptive to any "crutch" which will help support their will-power in their attempts to eat less. One of the earliest "crutches" did not rely on drugs, but did fit very well with the concept of body dehydration for weight reduction. The consumption of water or of any beverage with meals was strictly forbidden. It is still rather common today for students to enter college with the deeply ingrained misconception that "Water with meals makes fat."

In recent years an entire family of anorexigenic drugs has been developed. Anorexigenics have proven to be temporary and useful "crutches" in the early treatment of the individuals for whom weight loss is difficult. Too great a reliance on the anorexigenic, however, causes the treatment of obesity to fail. The use of anorexigenics in a patient who has a deeply rooted neurosis, the outward manifestation of which is compulsive or emotional overeating, is dangerous. Such patients need treatment aimed primarily at the correction or alleviation of their real illness, the neurosis. Neurotics need crutches. They are the least likely to be properly motivated to reduce and are the most likely to depend excessively on medication; there is a great chance that they will become habitual users of the drug. Excellent appetite suppression is obtainable with drugs, but anorexigenics, although useful in the treatment of obesity, are never the *only* treatment.

The drugs preferred and most commonly used because of their anorexigenic potency and lack of side effects are phenmetrazine, dextroamphetamine, phendimetrozine, methamphetamine, diethylpropion, chlorphentermine, benzphetamine, and phentermine. Of these, phenmetrazine and dextroamphetamine are the most popular. They are stimulants of the benzadrine and dexedrine category and in some patients they can cause coronary attacks or cerebral hemorrhages. These drugs can only be obtained legally through a physician's prescription and are of greatest therapeutic value in patients whose obesity stems from compulsive overeating due to a depressed mental state.

Other appetite killers are called "bulkers" and are supposed to function by expanding in the stomach and causing the stomach to feel full. Research by Jolliffe showed that these "bulkers" were no more effective than a placebo, which also helped patients to lose weight. The primary value of these "bulkers" seems to be as a psychological aid for those who have insufficient will power to reduce the amount of their food consumption. "Bulkers" are dangerous for people with ulcers, colitis, or ileitis.

One of the more popular commercial preparations for appetite suppression is a milk-sugar candy which supposedly contains a few vitamins and minerals and which is supposed to reduce the appetite if it is taken shortly before a meal. The theory behind this preparation is similar to the theory of parents who exhort children not to eat sweets before meals. The vitamins and minerals have no therapeutic value; one could expect the same effect from any candy which was eaten in the same way. A half-slice of bread taken shortly before a meal would be just as effective. The effect of such before-meal snacks toward the reduction of appetite is minor.

The Machines

In general, "reducing" machines specialize in arm and leg exercises or in surface agitation to increase blood flow to certain areas of the body. Although a half hour of special arm and leg exercises may be very tiring, one could lose far more weight by spending that half hour in a leisurely walk. Most studies agree that physical activity involving the large muscle system of the legs expends the most energy. Stair climbing requires the expenditure of more calories than is required by almost any other activity. Accordingly, an increasing number of physicians recommend running and walking as an aid to weight control. Regular running also helps to strengthen and maintain the health of the cardiovascular and respiratory systems. Atherosclerosis is more apt to occur in vascular systems where blood flow is slow and is seldom accelerated by vigorous exercise. A daily walk of about an hour's duration interspersed with weekly running to the point of exhaustion has been recommended by Mayer as a practical aid to the maintenance of better weight and health.

8. CROWD

An outline of the major collective behavior concepts would start with the crowd. A *crowd* is a temporary collection of people in close physical contact reacting together to a common stimulus. For example, the passengers on the flight from New York to San Francisco whose pilot suddenly decides he would like to go to the North Pole might be transformed from an aggregation into a crowd (or even a mob). Crowds have certain characteristics in common. *Milling* usually occurs as a crowd is being formed. In one sense *milling* refers to the excited, restless physical movement of the individuals involved. In a more important sense *milling* refers to a process of communication that leads to a definition of the situation and possible collective action. Not long ago, a Berkeley classroom suddenly started shaking with the first tremors of an earthquake. Almost at once the people began turning, shifting, looking at each other, at the ceiling, and at the instructor. They were seeking some explanation for the highly unusual experience and, whether spoken aloud or not, the questions on their faces were clear: "What is it?" "Did you feel it?" "What should we do?" Buzzing became louder talking, and some shouted, "Earthquake!!!" The students began to get up and move toward the doors. Many continued to watch the ceiling. . . . Milling may involve the long buildup of a lynch mob, or the sudden reaction in a dark and crowded theater when someone shouts, "Fire!!!" Milling helps ensure the development of a common mood for crowd members.

A person when he is part of a crowd tends to be *suggestible*. He is less critical, and he will readily do things that he would not ordinarily do alone. This is in part because, as a member of a crowd, he is *anonymous*. There is a prevailing feeling that it is the crowd that is responsible, not the individual. Once one becomes a member of an acting crowd, it is extremely difficult to step back, get perspective, and objectively evaluate what one is doing. Crowd members have a narrowed focus, a kind of tunnel vision. The physical presence of a crowd is a powerful force—a person almost has to separate himself from the crowd physically before he can critically examine his own behavior. There is also a *sense of urgency* about crowds. Crowds are oriented toward a specific focus or task: "We've got to do *this*, and we've got to do it *now!*" Some form of leadership usually appears in the crowd but, as the mood of the crowd changes, the leadership may shift quickly from one individual or group to another.

There are many different types of crowds. Some are passive—those watching a building burn or those at the scene of an accident. Some are active—a race riot or a lynch mob. Some crowds have a number of loosely defined goals. Other crowds are focused on a specific goal.

Turner and Killian distinguish between crowds that direct their action toward some external object—harassing a speaker until he leaves the platform or lynching a criminal—and expressive crowds, that direct their focus on the crowd itself—cheering at a football game or speaking in tongues at a church service.

Audience, Mob, Riot

Audiences and mobs are specific types of crowds. An *audience* at a concert, football game, lecture, religious service, or burning building may usually be likened to a passive crowd. Emotional contagion is possible in such situations, and individuals are responsive in a group in ways that they would not be as individuals. Audiences at performances of rock and roll stars and in Pentecostal church services may become very expressive in a variety of possibly unpredictable ways. Comedians expect audiences to laugh at their jokes. But most comedians have "bits" that they do when audiences are unpredictable and don't laugh (Johnny Carson gets audience sympathy by jokingly mentioning his "war injuries"). Much of audience behavior is predictable, or at least predictably unpredictable. The football fan knows he is going to cheer at the game, the comedian's "rejection bits" are well prepared, and rock concerts are adequately staffed with police to protect the musicians and nurses to minister to the fans that pass out. At the same time, audiences demonstrate collective behavior characteristics in that their behavior is frequently spontaneous, and members are suggestible and anonymous.

A *mob* is a focused, acting crowd. It is emotionally aroused, intent on taking aggressive action. A lynch mob would be an example of such a crowd. A water-fight between several fraternities in Berkeley on a warm spring day in 1956 spontaneously turned into a panty raid. Thousands of eager young males marched with determination through the campus community methodically stealing panties from numerous sorority houses. Afterwards, many of the participants expressed amazement that they had been involved in such behavior.

A *riot* describes the situation in which mob behavior has become increasingly widespread and destructive. Riots may involve a number of mobs acting independently. Throughout our history, the United States has had riots over the issue of race: New York, 1863; Chicago, 1919; Detroit, 1943. In the 1960s, urban riots occurred with increasing frequency. The issues were social class and poverty as well as race. The Watts riot in Los Angeles in the summer of 1965 lasted six days. Nearly 4,000 people were arrested, and property damage was estimated at over $40 million. Thirty-four people were killed and over 1,000 people injured. Most of the killed and injured were Negroes. More than forty people died, and property damage was estimated at $50 million in the Detroit riot in the summer of 1967. The relatively minor incident which set off the week-long confrontation was the police closing of a "blind pig," an after-hours tavern. A crowd collected as the police carted off the tavern's patrons, a stone was thrown, a shoe store was set on fire, and the riot was on. Campus disturbances occurred in the late 1960s at San Francisco State, Berkeley, Harvard, Columbia, Cornell, and at a number of other schools. It is likely, however, that to call these occasions riots, as the press often did, is an exaggeration of what actually happened. Riots have taken place at prisons and sporting events. A highly unusual situation occurred in 1969 when a disagreement at a soccer match led to a riot which in turn led to a short war between the two countries Honduras and El Salvador.

Summary

In this chapter we examined a form of activity that is outside the organized, ordinary, and predictable—collective behavior. Collective behavior refers to spontaneous, unstructured, and somewhat unpredictable actions by groups of people. A number of concepts and terms central to the study of collective behavior were discussed. We examined types of collectivities: crowds, audiences, and mobs.

9.   A number of other professions are specially prepared to work with physicians or independently to assist in adjunct areas:

Optometry

The optometrist is an individual who has received special preparation to measure visual acuity and to prescribe corrective lenses for visual defects. The optometrist examines eyes without the use of drugs, and he does not treat diseases of the eye. Most optometrists have been prepared to recognize pathological conditions of the eye and to refer these conditions to an ophthalmologist. Optometry is a well-recognized profession and preparation leads to a bachelor's degree or, for advanced study, the degree O. D., Doctor of Optometry.

Opticianry

An optician is a skilled technician specially prepared in compounding, filling and adapting prescriptions written by an ophthalmologist or optometrist.

Nursing

Nurses are prepared to staff a variety of positions. The primary preparation leading to the title R.N. (registered nurse) is instruction in caring for the sick. Minimum preparation beyond high school is not specified in a number of states, but individual curriculum requirements dictate the length of the programs in these states, with a two-year minimum required for licensing in 31 states.

There are three categories of professional preparation presently recognized that lead to the title R.N. The Baccalaureate Nurse has a bachelor's degree in nursing following four years of preparation in a degree-granting institution. The Diploma Nurse has received three years of training, usually associated with an accredited hospital school of nursing. The Associate Degree Nurse receives two years of professional preparation beyond the high school diploma. Graduates from each of these three categories must take State Board examinations before receiving the R.N. classification. The career possibilities available for individuals prepared in nursing include serving in hospitals, clinics, nursing homes, doctors' offices, public health departments, schools, and industrial plants. The demand for Registered Nurses far exceeds the supply.

Hospital demands have necessitated creation of the practical nurse. The licensed practical nurse (L.P.N.) must meet certain requirements in 48 states and in the District of Columbia. Texas and California license a vocational nurse (L.V.N.). Usual preparation of the L.P.N. or L.V.N. is one year of study beyond the high school diploma.

Medical Technology

Medical technologists provide services under the supervision of physicians. Laboratory technologists are primarily prepared to work under the direction of a pathologist in making tests on blood, urine, and tissues. The findings from these tests are used by the physician in making a diagnosis. Because of the scientific demands of their work, laboratory technologists must have at least three years of college work in the basic sciences plus a year of supervised laboratory experience.

Laboratory technicians are prepared to carry out types of work similar to those undertaken by technologists but not requiring as high a degree of specialized preparation. X-ray technicians are prepared to operate X-ray machines by taking pictures and developing the plates for reading by a radiologist.

5

Using the Library

The library is probably the most important building on a college campus. It's a major source of knowledge, a place to supplement what is learned in the classroom and a place to acquire information to bring back to the classroom. It's a way of making difficult-to-read textbooks easier to comprehend, difficult concepts easier to understand. Yet it's a place of mystery, even fear to many students. Why?

The aim of this chapter is to introduce you to your library—to show you what it can do for you and how to use it for learning and even for fun. If you are familiar with the library, you may find some of the information in this chapter very elementary. Do stay with it, however, and you will probably find much of the contents of importance to you. What are some of the things you need to know about to use the library effectively?

THE CARD CATALOG

The card catalog is really the lifeblood of the library. It contains an orderly listing of all the books there. Each book is listed on a 3 x 5 card which contains all the information that you need to find what you are looking for. The card catalog is usually divided into three separate catalogs: author cards, title cards, and subject cards. All cards in the card catalog are listed alphabetically: author cards are listed alphabetically by author, title cards alphabetically according to the title of the book, and subject cards alphabetically by subject. When looking for an item in these catalogs there are two things you should be aware of. The words *a*, *an*, and *the* are not used for alphabetizing when they are the first word. If, for example, you were looking for a book entitled *The Single Parent*, it would be listed under S for single rather than under T for the. Also, abbreviations are spelled out. Thus, *Dr.* would be listed alphabetically as doctor.

Let us say that you needed to locate the book entitled *The Memory Book* by Harry Lorayne and Jerry Lucas. Here is what the three cards (author card, title card, and subject card) would look like, followed by an explanation of each.

```
                    LORAYNE HARRY

     BF         The Memory Book by Harry Lorayne
     385        and Jerry Lucas.  Stein and Day (1974)
     L755

                1.  Mnemonics
```

```
                    MNEMONICS

     BF         Lorayne Harry
     385        The Memory Book by Harry Lorayne
     L755       and Jerry Lucas.  Stein and Day (1974)

                1.  Mnemonics
```

```
                    THE MEMORY BOOK

     BF         The Memory Book by Harry Lorayne
     385        and Jerry Lucas.  Stein and Day (1974)
     L755

                1.  Mnemonics
```

Notice that all the cards have the same group of letters and numbers at the left side. This is known as the call number, and its purpose is to tell you where the book can be found in the library. There are two standard systems for classifying books and assigning call numbers to them. One is the Dewey Decimal System, and the other is the Library of Congress System. Unless you are planning to be a librarian, it isn't really important for you to know details about these two systems except that you use them to locate the books. Books are located either in the areas of the library that you have access to (open stacks), or in areas that only library personnel have access to (closed stacks). If books are on open shelves in the public area, you should tour the library to become familiar with where different books are kept. In a large library you should refer to a map showing where books with different call numbers are located. Libraries ordinarily have such guides available to you.

Notice that the author card has the author's name at the top of the card, the title card has the book's title on top, and the subject card has the subject on top. Notice also that the body of each card tells the name of the book, the author(s), the publisher (Stein and Day), and the copyright date (1974). The item under that on each card can be important to you. It tells under what subject, or subjects, this title is listed. If you are interested in finding other books on the subject, this listing is a hint as to where to look. If the listing "mnemonics" were not there, you might look under "memory" and, not finding it, think that the library did not have that book.

There is another important type of listing that you might find in the card catalog. That is the "see" or "see also" listing. An example of this type of comment is shown below.

Garden Architecture
see
Architecture, Domestic
Landscape Gardening

Notice that if you want information about the topic "Garden Architecture," you can check "Architecture, Domestic," or "Landscape Gardening." "See" or "see also" listings, in other words, direct you to other books about the same subject.

There is an additional way to use the card catalog. Let us say that you have purchased a textbook for a course in statistics and that you have difficulty understanding the explanations for some of the principles as they are written in your textbook. Go to the subject cards in the card catalog of the library, and under "statistics" (or any other subject titles the card refers you to) find the call numbers of books on statistics. Most statistics textbooks will have call numbers that will show them to be shelved in the same section of the library. You can then go there and, hopefully, find another book which will explain in simple language the principle that you are trying to understand.

REFERENCE AIDS

Magazine articles, encyclopedias, biographies, and certain other reference materials are usually not listed in the card catalog. Following is some helpful information about these very important sources of information.

The Readers' Guide to Periodical Literature

We are in the midst of an information explosion. Information is being accumulated faster than ever before in the history of civilization; our knowledge is doubling every few years. As a result, books are often inadequate for obtaining information, because by the time a manuscript is published, the information it contains may be obsolete. More and more you will find that you must rely on magazines, newspapers, and other periodicals for up-to-date information.

Suppose your instructor asked you to prepare a report on a current controversial issue. Books will probably not be of much help to you, because besides not being current, they will tend to use many pages to promote one point of view. Three or four magazine articles, on the other hand, can provide you with good insights into both sides of the issue. But how do you know which magazines to look at? Certainly, you can't search through hundreds of them to find articles on a particular subject. The *Reader's Guide to Periodical Literature* will help you. It indexes articles in more than 150 magazines by both subject and author, and stories, in addition, are indexed by title. There are also subheadings which guide you to articles about a particular aspect of a subject. Because there are so many magazines indexed and because so many different kinds of information are provided, the *Readers' Guide* uses many abbreviations. You should look at the key to abbreviations which is always provided. (There is one on pp. 129–132 of this book.) It will be less confusing for you if you study it carefully before looking at any of the listings. Of course you may refer back to it at any time. A short exercise to help you become familiar with and skilled at reading these abbreviations can be found on p. 127.

Some of the different kinds of listings and their abbreviations are described below.

Author Listings One way in which magazine articles and stories are listed is by author. Look at the following listing taken from volume 38 of the *Readers' Guide.*

>ARONSON, Harvey
> In praise of monogamy. por Newsweek 91:14-15
>   Mr 27 '78

The author's name (Aronson, Harvey) is given, last name first, in heavy type, on a line by itself. This is followed by the name of the article (In praise of monogamy), which in turn is followed by the abbreviation *por* which, if you refer to the list of abbreviations on p. 129, tells you that a portrait is included with the article, followed by the name of the magazine in which it appears (in this case, *Newsweek*). Following this are the numbers and letters 91:14–15 Mr 27 '78. The first number, 91, is the volume number in which the article appears. The numbers after the colon, 14–15, tell you the page numbers of the article. The rest of the listing, Mr 27 '78, tells the month, day, and year of issue (March 27, 1978). In other words, if you found a copy of *Newsweek* magazine, volume 91, dated March 27, 1978, there would be an article on pp. 14–15 entitled "In Praise of Monogamy" by Harvey Aronson.

Look at the following author listing.

>WATSON, James Dewey
> DNA folly continues. New Repub 180:12+ Ja
>   13 '79

What is the name of the article? (DNA folly continues.) Who wrote it? (James Dewey Watson.) What magazine did it appear in and on what date? (*The New Republic*, January 13, 1979.) On what pages does it appear? (p. 12, continued on later pages of same issue.) You may have to refer to the page of abbreviations to understand some of the symbols.

Subject Listings The *Readers' Guide to Periodical Literature* also lists articles by subject. (Incidentally, all listings, whether they are author, subject, or story title, are in one alphabetical listing. They are not in separate author or subject or story title listings.) Look at the following listing.

>LOCAL finance
> Backlash to the tax revolt. il Bus W p69-70
>   Jl 31 '78

Notice that the subject appears on a line by itself with the first word in capital letters in boldface type (**LOCAL** finance). This is followed by the name of the article (Backlash to the tax revolt.) This is usually followed by the name of the authors. In this case, the article is written by a staff writer of *Business Week*, and so no particular author is acknowledged. The article is illustrated (il), and appears on pp. 69–70 of the July 31, 1978, issue.

Look at the following subject listing.

> WEALTH
> Chariots of the insurance salesmen; get rich quick mail order trade. R. Rosenbaum. il N Y 11:26-31 Jl 3 '78

What is the subject of the article? Who wrote it? In what magazine did it appear? When?

"See" References Sometimes when you check the author's name or the subject heading, you are referred somewhere else. This is a "see" reference, because it asks you to "see" another title. These "see" references are of many kinds. An example of one kind is "schoolbooks. See Textbooks." In this case the information you want will be under another title (Textbooks). In another kind of "see" reference, information is provided, followed by a referral to another heading for additional information. This is called a "see also" reference. An example of this is found on p. 138 under "Waxes." Notice that three "see also" references are given. A third type of "see" reference is a story title listing. Story titles are listed, followed by a "see" reference to the author.

Subtitles Sometimes you may only be interested in a particular phase or category of a broad subject. The *Readers' Guide* will often provide subheadings so that you can refer directly to the particular category of the subject that you are interested in. Look at the listing under "United States," p. 137. Notice the subtitles in the middle of the column (rather than at the left side) in darker type. It is important that you understand about these subtitles or you will be confused by titles that appear to be out of the alphabetical order of the listings.

There is one additional point to understand about the *Readers' Guide to Periodical Literature*. It is published twice a month, on the 10th and on the 25th, except during July and August, when it appears only on the 10th of the month. Its publishing year runs from March through February. Each issue published on the 25th of the month contains listings for a two-week period. Each issue published on the 10th of the month combines the listings of the previous issue with its own listings. This means that it is not necessary to refer to the issue of the 25th of the month once the following issue is published, because it will be included in that issue. For example, the issue of March 25th includes listings for two weeks only. However, the next issue, that of April 10th, will include the listings of the March 25th edition. In addition, the issues of May 10, August 10, November 10, and February 10 include all the listings of the previous three months. At the end of the year, a combined annual volume is published, and this contains listings for the entire year. All of this means that you will usually not have to refer to more than a few issues of *Readers' Guide* in order to get all the information you need.

Other Reference Aids

Encyclopedias Your library probably has an entire area devoted to encyclopedias of various kinds. An encyclopedia may be defined as a book or set of books which contains information on all branches of knowledge or which specializes in and contains detailed information about one particular branch of knowledge. You are probably familiar with the first kind of encyclopedia mentioned (usually called a general encyclopedia). Even as a youngster you may have used a general encyclopedia to find out about a particular person, or place, or event. If you have never used one it is important that you realize that information is listed in alphabetical order and that there are guide words at the top of each page, just as in a dictionary. Often the listings under one letter will make up as much as a complete book, or at least half a book. A complete encyclopedia set is often composed of 20 or more books. Some encyclopedias have indexes which often make up a complete book by themselves.

There are four important general encyclopedias that you should know about. Which one you use depends on the subject and on how sophisticated you want the information to be. The easiest to understand, the one that assumes that you know almost nothing about the subject, is *The World Book*. Because of its simple level of sophistication you may not even find it in a college library, but if you do, it is valuable as an introduction to the subject you are investigating. *Collier's Encyclopedia* is an "in-between" set, in between the level of difficulty of *The World Book* and the two encyclopedias most often found in college libraries. These are *The American Encyclopedia* and *The Encyclopedia Brittanica*. These two cover items at a vocabulary level and depth geared to better than high school educated adults.

For more detailed references, such as you may need for college courses, there are many specialized encyclopedias. These are sets of reference books which contain detailed information about a particular field or about people in a particular field. There are specialized encyclopedias of wild flowers, of American antiques, of advertising, of music, of American history, and of many other special subjects. There are also specialized biographical encyclopedias. These give information about people who have become distinguished in various fields. A brief, annotated list of some encyclopedias often used by college students follows.

Who's Who. There are various types such as *Who's Who in America*, *Who's Who of American Women*, and so on.

Current Biography. This reference gives information about prominent people in many fields. It is issued monthly, with every 12 issues bound into an annual volume.

Contemporary Authors. Here you will find short biographical sketches about living authors.

Book Review Digest. This reference will give you summaries of books that have been published and reviewed. You may find this helpful if you want to know something about a book before you read it.

The New York Times Index. This refers you to items that have appeared as newspaper articles.

Masterplots. If you need information about book plots, mostly those of classics, you may find it here. A summary of the plot, a description of the characters, and other information are contained in these informative articles.

Psychological Abstracts. This very important reference for psychology students presents abstracts of research and articles in various psychological journals and allied publications. The use of these abstracts is a must if you are doing a research project in psychology.

The Nursing Index. This reference is a guide to articles in nursing and allied health journals. It is an important source of information for nursing students doing research.

There are, of course, many other source books too numerous to mention. You should make a tour of the reference section of your library. Browse through the shelves and even leaf through some of the materials in order to have a better feeling for what is there.

Librarians There is one major reference source which has not been stressed enough—your librarian. Librarians have advanced degrees in library science, and they are experts on what is in the library. Your librarian will help you feel comfortable in the library. If you are not sure of how to find what you are looking for, ask your librarian. Librarians will suggest card catalog titles in order to find what you are seeking. They will show you how to use reference sources you are not sure of. Librarians often offer library orientation tours or information pamphlets to help you use the library; if they are available, make use of them. If the library doesn't have what you want, your librarian can arrange for an interlibrary loan or suggest other ways that you can get the information you need. The important thing is to realize that librarians are eager to be of help to you if they can. Don't hesitate to ask for help when you need it.

OTHER LIBRARY SERVICES

Many college libraries also have other services available, such as typewriter use, copy machines, interlibrary loans, or paintings or records for loan. Often, pamphlets are available that describe these services. If you are not sure, ask the librarian.

The exercises following these pages will help make you an expert in the use of the *Readers' Guide to Periodical Literature.* Do them carefully.

EXERCISE 1

Check the card catalog of your library for the information needed as indicated below. Then write your answer in the space provided.

1. Book title: *Future Shock*

    Author's name _____

    Call number _____

2. Book title _____

    Author's name: Henry Steele Commager

    Call number _____

3. Book title: *I'm OK—You're OK*

    Author's name _____

    Call number _____

4. Book title _____

    Author's name: Sigmund Freud

    Call number _____

5. Book title: *A History of Modern Music*

    Author's name _____

    Call number _____

6. Book title _____

    Author's name: John Dewey

    Call number _____

If you were looking for information about each of the following items, tell under what subject heading you would find books having that information. Write your answer in the space provided. Also, list one book title mentioned there and its call number.

7. Subject: Hurricanes

    Subject heading _____

    Book title _____

    Call number _____

8. Subject: President Lyndon Johnson

    Subject heading _____

    Book title _____

    Call number _____

9. Subject: Finding a job

   Subject heading _____

   Book title _____

   Call number _____

10. Subject: How to fix an automobile

    Subject heading _____

    Book title _____

    Call number _____

EXERCISE 2

On the pages following these questions you will find the key to abbreviations used in the Readers' Guide *and a list of abbreviations for the periodicals indexed (pp. 129–132). Study them carefully and then answer the following questions.*

1. In the spaces provided, list the abbreviations used for the different months of the year.

    January _____ April _____ July _____ October _____

    February _____ May _____ August _____ November _____

    March _____ June _____ September _____ December _____

2. Which abbreviation tells you that more than one person wrote the article or story? _____

3. Which abbreviations tell you that there may be a picture with the article or story? _____

4. List all the abbreviations that tell how often a periodical is issued.

    _____

    _____

5. When did *Retirement Living* change its name? _____

6. When did *New Times* discontinue publication? _____

7. Name three periodicals that are available in special types of editions for physically handicapped readers. _____

    _____

8. Which magazine, available during the summer of 1978, might be of interest to a senior citizen? _____

9. Name three magazines that give health information. _____

    _____

10. Name two magazines that are concerned with religious topics.

    _____

    _____

ABBREVIATIONS

*	following name entry, a printer's device	Jr	Junior
		jt auth	joint author
+	continued on later pages of same issue	Ltd	Limited
Abp	Archbishop		
abr	abridged	m	monthly
Ag	August	Mr	March
Ap	April	My	May
arch	architect		
Assn	Association	N	November
Aut	Autumn	no	number
Ave	Avenue		
		O	October
Bart	Baronet		
bibl	bibliography	por	portrait
bibl f	bibliographical footnotes	pseud	pseudonym
		pt	part
bi-m	bimonthly	pub	published, publisher, publishing
bi-w	biweekly		
bldg	building		
Bp	Bishop		
		q	quarterly
Co	Company		
comp	compiled, compiler	rev	revised
cond	condensed		
cont	continued	S	September
Corp	Corporation	sec	section
		semi-m	semimonthly
D	December	Soc	Society
Dept	Department	Spr	Spring
		Sq	Square
		Sr	Senior
ed	edited, edition, editor	St	Street
		Summ	Summer
		supp	supplement
F	February	supt	superintendent
Hon	Honorable		
		tr	translated, translation, translator
il	illustrated, illustration, illustrator		
Inc	Incorporated	v	volume
introd	introduction, introductory		
		w	weekly
		Wint	Winter
Ja	January		
Je	June	yr	year
Jl	July		

ABBREVIATIONS OF PERIODICALS INDEXED

Aging—Aging
Am Artist—American Artist
Am Educ—American Education
Am Heritage—American Heritage
Am Hist Illus—American History Illustrated
Am Schol—American Scholar
America—America
Americana—Americana
Américas—Américas
Antiques—Antiques
Antiques J—Antiques Journal
Archit Rec—Architectural Record
Art in Am—Art in America
Art News—Art News
Astronomy—Astronomy
Atlantic—Atlantic
Atlas—Atlas World Press Review
Audubon—Audubon
Aviation W—Aviation Week & Space Technology

Bet Hom & Gard—Better Homes and Gardens
BioScience—BioScience
Black Enterprise—Black Enterprise
Blair & Ketchums—Blair & Ketchum's Country Journal
Bull Atom Sci—Bulletin of the Atomic Scientists
Bus W—Business Week

Car & Dr—Car and Driver
Center Mag—Center Magazine
Change—Change
Changing T—Changing Times
Chemistry—Chemistry
Child Today—Children Today
Chr Cent—Christian Century
Chr Today—Christianity Today
Commentary—Commentary
Commonweal—Commonweal
Cong Digest—Congressional Digest
Conservationist—Conservationist (Albany)
Consumer Rep—Consumer Reports
Consumers Res Mag—Consumers' Research Magazine
Craft Horiz—Craft Horizons
Crawdaddy—Crawdaddy
    Continued as Feature. Ja '79

Creat Crafts—Creative Crafts
Cur Health—Current Health 2
Cur Hist—Current History
Current—Current (Washington, D.C.)
Cycle—Cycle

Dance Mag—Dance Magazine
Dept State Bull—Department of State Bulletin
Design (US)—Design (United States)
Down Beat—Down Beat

Earth Sci—Earth Science
Ebony—Ebony
Educ Digest—Education Digest
Encore—Encore American & Worldwide News
Environment—Environment
Esquire—Esquire
Essence—Essence

FDA Consumer—FDA Consumer
Fam Handy—Family Handyman
Fam Health—Family Health incorporating Today's Health
Feature—Feature
    Formerly Crawdaddy
Field & S—Field & Stream
50 Plus—50 Plus
    Formerly Retirement Living
Film Comment—Film Comment
First World—First World
Flower & Gard—Flower and Garden (Northern edition)
Flying—Flying
Focus—Focus
For Aff—Foreign Affairs
For Pol—Foreign Policy
Forbes—Forbes
Fortune—Fortune
Futurist—Futurist

Glamour—Glamour
Good H—Good Housekeeping
Gourmet—Gourmet

Harp Baz—Harper's Bazaar
Harpers—Harper's
Hi Fi—High Fidelity and Musical America

Hist Today—History Today
Hobbies—Hobbies
Holiday. See Trav/Holiday
Horizon—Horizon
House & Gard—House & Garden incorporating Living for Young Homemakers
Hum Behav—Human Behavior
Humanist—Humanist

Int Wildlife—International Wildlife
Intellect—Intellect
  Continued as USA Today. Jl '78

Ladies Home J—Ladies' Home Journal
Liv Wildn—Living Wilderness

M Labor R—Monthly Labor Review
McCalls—McCall's
Macleans—Maclean's
Mademoiselle—Mademoiselle
Mankind—Mankind
Mech Illus—Mechanix Illustrated
Money—Money
Mother Earth News—Mother Earth News
Motor B & S—Motor Boating & Sailing
Motor T—Motor Trend
Ms—Ms.

N Y—New York
N Y R of Bk—New York Review of Books
N Y Times Bk R—New York Times Book Review
N Y Times Mag—New York Times Magazine
Nat Geog—National Geographic Magazine
Nat Geog World—National Geographic World
Nat Parks & Con Mag—National Parks & Conservation Magazine
Nat R—National Review (48p issue only, pub. in alternate weeks)
Nat Wildlife—National Wildlife
Nation—Nation
Nations Bus—Nation's Business
Natur Hist—Natural History
Negro Hist Bull—Negro History Bulletin
New Leader—New Leader
New Repub—New Republic

New Times—New Times (New York)
  Publication discontinued with January 8, 1979 issue
New Yorker—New Yorker
Newsweek—Newsweek

Oceans—Oceans
Opera News—Opera News
Org Gard—Organic Gardening
Org Gard & Farm—Organic Gardening and Farming
  Continued as Organic Gardening. Jl '78
Outdoor Life—Outdoor Life

Parents Mag—Parents' Magazine
People—People Weekly
Peter Phot Mag—Petersen's Photographic Magazine
Phi Delta Kappan—Phi Delta Kappan
Phys Today—Physics Today
Pol Today—Politics Today
  Formerly Skeptic
Pop Electr—Popular Electronics
Pop Mech—Popular Mechanics
Pop Phot—Popular Photography
Pop Sci—Popular Science
Progressive—Progressive
Psychol Today—Psychology Today
Pub W—Publishers Weekly

Radio-Electr—Radio-Electronics
Read Digest—Reader's Digest
Redbook—Redbook incorporating American Home
Ret Liv—Retirement Living
  Continued as 50 Plus. S '78
Road & Track—Road & Track
Roll Stone—Rolling Stone

Sat Eve Post—Saturday Evening Post
Sat R—Saturday Review
Sci Am—Scientific American
Sci Digest—Science Digest
Sci News—Science News
Science—Science
Science and Public Affairs. See Bulletin of the Atomic Scientists
Sea Front—Sea Frontiers
Seventeen—Seventeen
Sierra—Sierra

Skeptic—Skeptic
 Continued as Politics Today. Mr '78
Skiing—Skiing
Sky & Tel—Sky and Telescope
Smithsonian—Smithsonian
Society—Society
South Liv—Southern Living
Space World—Space World
Sport—Sport
Sports Illus—Sports Illustrated
Sr Schol—Senior Scholastic including World Week (Scholastic Teacher's edition)
Stereo R—Stereo Review
Suc Farm—Successful Farming (Midwest edition)
Sunset—Sunset (Central edition)

Tech R—Technology Review
Teen—Teen
Theatre Crafts—Theatre Crafts
Time—Time
Todays Educ—Today's Education
Trav/Holiday—Travel incorporating Holiday

UN Chron—UN Chronicle
UNESCO Courier—UNESCO Courier
U.S. Cath—U.S. Catholic
U.S. News—U.S. News & World Report
USA Today—USA Today
 Fomerly Intellect

Vital Speeches—Vital Speeches of the Day
Vogue—Vogue

Wash M—Washington Monthly
Weatherwise—Weatherwise
WomenSports—WomenSports
 Discontinued publication February '78
Work Wom—Working Women
Workbench—Workbench
World Health—World Health
World Tennis—World Tennis
World Week See Senior Scholastic
Writer—Writer

*Available for blind and other physically handicapped readers on talking books, in braille, or on magnetic tape. For information address Division for the Blind and Physically Handicapped, Library of Congress, Washington, D.C. 20542

ARMBRISTER, Trevor, and Clark, Katharine
What's your real tax bite? Read Digest 112:35-8 Ap '78
ARMCHAIRS. See Chairs
ARMCO Steel Corporation
Overseeing Armco's shift away from steel. L. Maloney. il pors U.S. News 84:66-7 F 27 '78
ARMED Forces
See also
Commandos
National service
Appropriations and expenditures
Bigger bang; report by R. L. Sivard. New Repub 178:2 My 27 '78
Expenditures and transfers; report of World military expenditures and arms transfers 1967-1976. Sci Am 239:85 O '78
World arsenals in 1977; report of the Stockholm International Peace Research Institute. F. Barnaby. il Bull Atom Sci 34:10-13+ My '78
World's skewed priorities; social costs and the arms race. R. L. Sivard. Nation 226:730-2 Je 17 '78
ARMED Forces Radiobiology Research Institute. See United States—Armed Forces Radiobiology Research Institute
ARMED Services Committee. See United States—Congress—House—Armed Services, Committee on; United States—Congress—Senate—Armed Services, Committee on
ARMENIAN cookery. See Cookery, Armenian
ARMENIANS
Proud Armenians. R. P. Jordan. il map Nat Geog 153:846-73 Je '78
ARMI Beretta (firm) See Firearms industry—Italy
ARMOIRES
Reactivating an antique armoire. il Bet Hom & Gard 56:40 Mr '78
ARMOR, David J.
Forced busing and white flight. il por Time 112:78 S 25 '78 •
ARMORED automobiles. See Automobiles, Armored
ARMS, Tom
CIA Octopus engulfs terrorists. Encore 7:12 Jl 10 '78
ARMS, Artificial. See Limbs, Artificial
ARMS, Coats of. See Heraldry
ARMS control. See Disarmament
ARMS Control and Disarmament Agency. See United States—Arms Control and Disarmament Agency
ARMS control legislation. See Firearms—Laws and regulations
ARMS trade. See Airplane industry—Export-import trade; Munitions—Export-import trade
ARMSTRONG, Bess
On their own; TV's newest odd couple; interview. ed by M. S. Miller. pors Ladies Home J 95:143-4 Mr '78
ARMSTRONG, Bob
Texas legacy. por Forbes 121:78 F 6 '78 •
ARMSTRONG, Denny
Confessions of a car salesman. J. S. Coyle. il por Money 7:98-9+ Ap 78 •
ARMSTRONG, Edwin Howard
Injustice of the patent system—one scientist's story. H. L. Poss. Phys Today 31:9+ Ja '78 •
ARMSTRONG, Frank A.
Enough Moxie? il por Forbes 122:138 O 2 '78 •
ARMSTRONG, Garner Ted
Big shift to Big Sandy. J. M. Hopkins. Chr Today 22:45-6 My 5 '78 •
Fall from the family. J. M. Hopkins. Chr Today 22:39-41 S 22 '78 •
Spirit. V. Junger. il pors People 10:83-4+ N 20 '78 •
Strong-arming Garner Ted. il pors Time 111:54 Je 19 '78 •
Wonderful world of Garner Ted Armstrong. S. Edwards. il pors Humanist 38:8-13 Ja '78 •
ARMSTRONG, Herbert W.
Apocalypse now? K. L. Woodward and others. por Newsweek 93:61 Ja 15 '79 •
Fall from the family. J. M. Hopkins. Chr Today 22:39-41 S 22 '78 •
Power struggle in Pasadena. J. M. Hopkins. Chr Today 22:41-2 Je 2 '78 •
Strong-arming Garner Ted. il pors Time 111: 54 Je 19 '78 •
ARMSTRONG, O. K.
All-consuming crime. il Sat Eve Post 250:22+ Mr '78
Scandal in our public schools. il Sat Eve Post 250:40-2+ My '78
ARMSTRONG, Richard
Tangled web. Commonweal 105:334-6 My 26 '78
ARMSTRONG-JONES, Antony Charles Robert, 1st Earl of Snowdon. See Snowdon, A. C. R. A.-J.
ARMSTRONG Cork Company
Far from the madding crowd... il por Forbes 122:43 O 2 '78
ARMY Air Force. See United States—Air Force, Army
ARMY Engineers. See United States—Army—Corps of Engineers

ARMY food. See United States—Army—Commissariat
ARMY life. See Military life
ARMY rations. See United States—Army—Commissariat
ARMYTAGE, Stephen Green-. See Green-Armytage, S.
ARMYWORM moths. See Moths
ARMYWORMS
Toxicity of a furanocoumarin to armyworms: a case of biosynthetic escape from insect herbivores. M. Berenbaum. bibl il Science 201:532-4 Ag 11 '78
ARNAZ, Desi, 1953-
On the move. M. Smilgis. il pors People 9:113-14+ Je 19 '78 •
ARNAZ, Lucie
Stage. M. Smilgis. il pors People 11:68-70 Ja 22 '79 •
ARNESON, Howard D.
(ed) Economic diary. Bus W p23-4 My 22; 13-14 Jl 3 '78
ARNETT, Keith
Flame texturing wood. il Theatre Crafts 12: 86 Mr '78
ARNGRIM, Alison
Alison Arngrim; not-so-nasty Nellie. pors Teen 22:54 Ag '78 •
ARNOLD, Abraham J.
Sometimes words fail, and the word that's failed us most is multiculturalism. Macleans 91:8 Jl 24 '78
ARNOLD, Charleen
Who's who & what's what in fibers. E. Sommer. il por Creat Crafts 6:14-15 Ag '78 •
ARNOLD, Eve
Shooting the '50s. D. Davis. il por Newsweek 92:106-7 S 25 '78 •
ARNOLD, Glenn F.
Christian collegium after a decade of change. il por Chr Today 23:22-6 N 3 '78
Consumerism and Christian higher education. Chr Today 23:12 N 3 '78
ARNOLD, Richard M.
Sincerely motivated. il por Forbes 122:157 O 16 '78 •
ARNOLD, Walter
Trade winds. Sat R 5:37 Jl 8; 58 Ag; 50 S 16; 62 N 11; 55 D '78; 6:66 Ja 20 '79
ARNOLD'S Turtle (restaurant) See New York (city)—Hotels, restaurants, etc.
ARNONE, William J.
Mobilizing the elderly in neighborhood anti-crime programs. il Aging 281:23-5 Mr '78
ARNOT, Michelle
Massage: how to give a really good one. il Esquire 90:81-3+ O 24 '78 •
ARNSON, Cynthia, and Klare, M. T.
Pipeline to Pinochet. Nation 226:502-5 Ap 29 '78
ARNSTEIN, George E.
Two cheers for accreditation. bibl Phi Delta Kappan 60:357-61 Ja '79
ARODAKY, Badr Eddin
Madrasahs. il UNESCO Courier 30:35-6 D '77
AROMATIC hydrocarbons. See Hydrocarbons
ARON, Raymond
Can 50 million Frenchmen be wrong? interview. ed by R. E. Tyrrell, Jr. il Sat Eve Post 250: 26+ O '78
U.S. is enormously powerful if it decides to be; interview. il por U.S. News 85:66-7 N 27 '78
ARONOFF, Stanley
Gamesmanship. T. Mathews and T. Fuller. il pors Newsweek 92:54 N 20 '78 •
ARONS, Arnold
Toward a more reasonable physics: the inquiry approach. B. Mitzman. il por Change 10:52-5 Ja '78 •
ARONS, Marjorie. See Barron, J. jt auth
ARONS, Stephen
Is educating your own child a crime? il pors Sat R 5:16-20 N 25 '78
ARONSON, Harvey
In praise of monogamy. por Newsweek 91:14-15 Mr 27 '78
AROUND the world flights. See Aviation—World flights
AROUND the world tours. See Voyages around the world
AROUND the world voyages. See Voyages around the world
ARP, Halton M.
NGC-1199. il Astronomy 6:15 S '78
ARPEL, Adrien
In her own words; interview. ed by H. Shapiro. il pors People 10:58-60+ Jl 3 '78
about
Behind the best sellers. C. Lawson. por N Y Times Bk R 83:42 Jl 9 '78 •
ARRANGEMENT (music) See Musical arrangement
ARRANGEMENT of flowers. See Flowers, Arrangement of
ARRANGEMENT of fruits, vegetables, etc. See Fruits, vegetables, etc. in decoration

LOBSTER fisheries. See Shellfish fisheries
LOBSTERS
  Behavior and the crustacean molt cycle; changes in aggression of Homarus americanus. G. R. Tamm and J. S. Cobb. bibl il Science 200:79-81 Ap 7 '78
  Bursting neural networks; a reexamination. D. F. Russell and D. K. Hartline. bibl il Science 200:453-6 Ap 28 '78
  Experimental transformation of muscle fiber properties in lobster. F. Lang and others. bibl il Science 201:1037-9 S 15 '78
  See also
  Cookery—Shellfish
LOCAL control of schools. See School management and organization
LOCAL finance
  Backlash to the tax revolt. il Bus W p69-70 Jl 31 '78
  Reform of taxation; with questions and answers. F. Layfield. il Center Mag 11:60-9 Ja '78
  See also
  Municipal finance
LOCAL government. See Municipal government
LOCAL service airlines. See Airlines—Local service
LOCAL taxation
  Rebellion or no, local taxes keep rising. il U.S. News 85:102 O 23 '78
  State & local tax bills; a report from 62 cities. il Changing T 32:25-9 N '78
  Taxpayers in revolt. il Nations Bus 66:19-22 Jl '78
  Why drives to limit taxes are spreading. J. J. Kilpatrick. Nations Bus 66:11-12 Jl '78
LOCAL transit
  Future of transit in the U.S; some projections. J. Coomer and R. Herbert. Futurist 12:171 Je '78
  Going to work in the 1980s. R. Adams. il Mech Illus 74:32+ Mr '78
  Mass transit and appropriate technology. L. Bell. il Futurist 12:169-70+ Je '78
  See also
  Bus lines
  Buses
  London—Transit systems
  New York (city)—Subways
  New York (city)—Transit systems
  Port Authority of New York and New Jersey
  Portland, Ore.—Transit systems
  Prague—Subways
  Street railroads
  Subways
      Federal aid
  Shifting gears in urban transportation. H. Leavitt. il New Leader 61:12-13 Mr 13 '78
  Story of transitory madness; question of federally funded transit system for Greenwich, Conn. D. Oliver. Nat R 30:1416-17 N 10 '78
LOCALIZATION of brain functions. See Brain—Localization of functions
LOCATION in business and industry
  Adieu, Montreal; Sun Life shifts to Toronto. Time 112:62 My 8 '78
  Bedroom to board room; Fairfield County, Conn. il map Time 112:54-5 Ag 28 '78
  Cities where business is best. il U.S. News 84: 68-71 My 15; 85:60-3 O 30 '78
  Connecticut's happy colony of corporate refugees. S. Solomon. Fortune 97:286+ My 8 '78
  Curious flight of American Airlines; move from New York to Dallas-Fort Worth airport. T. Morse. il por N Y 11:51-4 D 11 '78
  Dallas' lure for American; move headquarters to Dallas-Fort Worth Airport. il por Bus W p 144+ N 20 '78
  Delaware works hard to stay a corporate home sweet home. L. Smith. il Fortune 97:132-4 F 13 '78
  Economic fallout from Proposition 13. il map Bus W p 101-2+ N 13 '78
  Georgia-Pacific looks southward to home, move from Oregon to Atlanta. Bus W p32-3 D 4 '78
  Job meccas for the '80's. J. S. Coyle. il Money 7:40-7 My '78
  Nasty case of Sun-burn. D. Thomas. il Macleans 91:20-2 Ja 23 '78
  New migration shift; where Americans are moving now. G. Helman. il Nations Bus 66:42-6 F '78
  O pioneers; Harper and Pinnacle stake out the West. P. Holt. il Pub W 214:38-41 D 11 '78
  One-stop permits to woo new industry; environmental permits. il Bus W p55-6 S 11 '78
  Pan Am sours on New York. il Bus W p92+ Mr 13 '78
  Quebec warms to business. il Bus W p50 Jl 24 '78
  Sun Life leads off in fleeing from Quebec. Bus W p28 Ja 23 '78
  Why the future no longer looks so golden in California. J. Quirt. il Fortune 97:130-2+ Mr 27 '78
  Wrong-way Carter and the Dixie slum kings. M. Kramer. N Y 11:35-8 F 20 '78

You can come home again; businesses that left and returned to New York City. T. Clifford. N Y 11:116 Je 5 '78
  You can go home again; move to the South by forest products companies. K. K. Wiegner. il Forbes 122:81-2 D 11 '78
  See also
  Airports—Location
  Atomic power plants—Location
  Automobile factories—Location
  National Development Council
  Petroleum refineries—Location
  Shopping centers—Location
  Supermarkets—Location
LOCATIONS, Motion picture. See Motion pictures—Setting and scenery
LOCH NESS monster
  Elusive Nessie. J. N. Baker and D. Shapiro. il Newsweek 92:26+ D 4 '78
  Search at Loch Ness; excerpt. D. L. Meredith. il Sci Digest 83:66-74 F '78
LOCHER, David
  Catching the wind; poem. America 139:45 Jl 29 '78
  Rooftops; poem. America 139:471 D 23 '78
LOCK, James & Company, Ltd. See London—Stores
LOCKARD, Geraldine
  Mainstreaming: one child's experience. Phi Delta Kappan 59:527-8 Ap '78
LOCKARD, Jon Onye
  Ideology for black artists. il First World 2:42-4 Spr '78
LOCKE, Raymond Friday
  George Catlin and the Mandans. il por Mankind 6:8-13+ Ag '78
LOCKE, Richard
  Can these bones live? N Y Times Bk R 83:3+ Ja 29 '78
  Joseph Conrad: problem child. Atlantic 243:86-9 F '79
  Man of the year. il N Y Times Bk R 83:3+ F 26 '78
  Spring fevers. N Y Times Bk R 83:3+ Ap 23 '78
  Three young writers. il N Y Times Bk R 83:3+ My 21 '78
LOCKE, Sondra
  Off the screen. L. Armstrong. il pors People 9:56-8+ F 13 '78 *
LOCKE, Calif.
  U.S. journal; Locke, Calif. C. Trillin. New Yorker 54:107-8+ F 20 '78
LOCKERBIE, D. Bruce
  Pilgrimage to joy. Chr Cent 95:983-5 O 18 '78
LOCKHART, Carl Ford
  Name game. il por Forbes 122:218 N 13 '78 *
LOCKHART, William L. See Stokes, J. C. jt auth
LOCKHEED Corporation
  Aluminum study funds sought. C. Covault. Aviation W 109:14-15 Jl 31 '78
  Annals of crime. R. Shaplen. New Yorker 53: 48-50+ Ja 23; 74-91 Ja 30 '78
  L-1011 TriStar heads toward profitable production program. J. M. Lenorovitz. il Aviation W 108:23-4 Ap 10 '78
  Lockheed boosting L-1011 production. W. H. Gregory. Aviation W 109:34 N 27 '78
  Lockheed chairman predicts earnings will rise by 1980. Aviation W 108:22-3 My 15 '78
  Lockheed negotiating L-1011 sale to El Al. Aviation W 108:40 Je 19 '78
  Lockheed 1977 earnings increase over 1976. Aviation W 108:24 F 27 '78
  PSA, Lockheed sue in L-1011 dispute. J. M. Lenorovitz. Aviation W 110:30 Ja 8 '79
  U.S. policies hamper exports of C-130. K. Johnsen. Aviation W 109:57-8 N 13 '78
LOCKLIN, Gerald
  Divorcée; poem. Am Schol 47:231 Spr '78
LOCKRIDGE, Richard
  Murder for two. J. Filstrup. il New Repub 179: 35-8 Jl 22 '78 *
LOCKS and keys
  Auxiliary door locks. il Consumers Res Mag 61: 19-23 Mr '78
  Bicycle locks. il Consumers Res Mag 61:27-30+ My '78
  High security padlocks and hasps. il Consumers Res Mag 61:32-6 Ag '78
  Homeowner's guide to the super locks. R. Graf and G. Whalen. il Fam Handy 28:40-1+ My '78
  How to install a deadbolt. D. Green. il Pop Sci 213:166+ O '78
  Kryptonite K-4 lock; motorcycle use. D. Phillipson. il Cycle 29:120+ Jl '78
  Locks. il Workbench 34:50-2+ My '78
  Magnetic locks; pickproof but hardly foolproof. il Consumer Rep 43:64-5 F '78
  7-bolt door lock offers high security. il Workbench 34:44 Jl '78
  16 products that make it tougher for burglars. J. Provey. il Pop Mech 151:90-1+ Ag '78
LOCKWOOD, Allison
  Times of Samuel Curwen. il por Am Hist Illus 13:22-32 Ap '78
LOCKWOOD, George Wesley, and others
  New absolute calibration of Vega. il Sky & Tel 56:286-9 O '78

UNITED STATES—Arms Control and Disarmament Agency—*Continued*
U.S. and Soviet strategic capability through the mid-1980's; report. il Dept State Bull 78 24-8 O '78
Verification assurance criticized; report of Arms Control and Disarmament Agency. Aviation W 108:59 My 8 '78

Army
Better USAF/Army coordination sought. Aviation W 108:197+ F 6 '78
See also
Association of the United States Army
United States—Air Force. Army

Appropriations and expenditures
Army accelerates helicopter purchases. S. W. Harlamor. Aviation W 108:26-7 Ja 30 '78
Army budgets for nerve gas again. il Bus W p16 N 20 '78

Aviation
See also
United States—Air Force. Army

Cavalry
Union lancers in the Civil War. C. Worman. il Hobbies 83:146 N '78

Commissariat
Army still plugging for FDA approval of irradiated meat. C. Holden. Science 202:500 N 3 '78
C-rations—new look, new taste. K. Murphy. il Pop Sci 213:148 N '78

Corps of Engineers
Field & Stream annual Dumb-Dumb Award; alleged mismanagement of Missouri's rivers. G. Reiger. il Field & S 83:24+ Ja '79
In trouble; D. A. Wisdom. S. Hinson. il pors People 9:55-6 Ja 23 '78
Rising flood of dam repairs. il Bus W p21 Ja 30 '78
Search for dangerous dams—a program to head off disaster. G. Shaw. il Smithsonian 9:36-45 bibl(p 124) Ap '78
Town that took on the Corps of Engineers; North Bonneville, Wash. S. D. McBride. Read Digest 112:191-2+ F '78
Trickery on the Tenn-Tom. J. N. Miller. map Read Digest 113:138-43 S '78
U.S. civil works construction shows decrease in required labor. B. J. Bingham. bibl il M Labor R 101:24-30 O '78
Winter of discontent heats up; plan to enlarge St Lawrence River for winter shipping. R. H. Boyle. il map Sports Illus 49:69-70+ N 20 '78
See also
United States—Waterways Experiment Station

Education
See also
United States Military Academy, West Point

Equipment and supplies
See also
Tanks, Military

Forces in Europe
Cobra bolsters U.S. stance in Europe. D. A. Brown. il Aviation W 107:40-1+ N 14 '77
Europe's GI drug scene. K. Labich and others. il Newsweek 92:44 Jl 3 '78

Forces in Germany, West
Dollar's drop: GI's learn about it the hard way. R. A. Haeger and J. N. Wallace. il U.S. News 84:44-5 Mr 13 '78
GI's on the dole. S. Strasser and T. M. Nater. il Newsweek 91:52 Mr 20 '78
Time to bring the boys home. Sat Eve Post 250:25 O '78

Forces in Korea, South
Carter's Korean catch-22. T. Szulc. il N Y 11:10+ My 1 '78
Old soldier who won't fade away; interview, ed by F. W. Martin. J. K. Singlaub. il pors People 10:24-7 Jl 10 '78

History
Accomplished villain; Gen. J. Wilkinson. J. M. Taylor. il pors Am Hist Illus 13:4-9+ Ja '79

Medical and sanitary affairs
Military medicine; L. T. Davis case. D. A. Williams and M. Hager. por Newsweek 92:70 N 13 '78

Officers
Thinking like a captain; how to make general. N. Lemann. il Wash M 10:20-8 My '78
See also
Generals

Parachute troops
Jump into Sicily; excerpt from On to Berlin. J. M. Gavin. il pors map Am Heritage 29:46-61 Ap '78

Pay, allowances, etc.
Dollar's drop: GI's learn about it the hard way. R. A. Haeger and J. N. Wallace. il U.S. News 84:44-5 Mr 13 '78
GI's on the dole; effects of dollar's decline in West Germany. S. Strasser and T. M. Nater. il Newsweek 91:52 Mr 20 '78

Recreation
See also
United Service Organizations

Religious life
See also
Chaplains, Military

Research
See Military research

Special Forces
Black Berets to the rescue; Ranger battalions. G. Norman. il Esquire 89:43-6 Ap 11 '78

Training
See Military training

Training camps
See Military training camps

Women
See Servicewomen

Art
See Art—United States

Atomic Energy Commission
How Israel got the bomb; question of missing uranium from Nuclear Materials and Equipment Corp. D. J. Fialka. Wash M 10:50-8 Ja '79
Oppenheimer case: a study in the abuse of law; 1950's investigation by Atomic Energy Commission. H. P. Green; reply. J. G. Beckerly. Bull Atom Sci 34:3+ Ja '78
Seaborg: U.S. must remain in A-energy game; interview, ed by D. S. Smith. G. T. Seaborg. por Sci Digest 83:20-1 Ja '78
West Valley; remnant of the AEC; N.Y. facility of Nuclear Fuel Services. G. I. Rochlin and others. il Bull Atom Sci 34:17-23 Ja '78
See also
United States—Nuclear Regulatory Commission

Bibliography
Home scene. J. P. Parkes. America 139:337-8 N 11 '78

Bonneville Power Administration
Bottom of the pork barrel. B. Mitzman. Progressive 42:32-3 S '78
New barrier to more Northwest power. map Bus W p75 Mr 6 '78

Boundaries
Berlin wall on the Rio Grande? map U.S. News 85:11 D 4 '78
Challenge of the U.S.-Mexico border. J. Prieto. il Chr Cent 95:1258-62 D 27 '78
4,000 miles of friendship. A. Keller. il maps Am Hist Illus 13:4-9+ N '78
Justice's wall; fence to be erected on U.S.-Mexican border. Time 112:47 O 30 '78
Mexican wall. America 139:326 N 11 '78
Second thoughts; US-Mexican border fence. C. McWilliams. Nation 227:632 D 9 '78

Cabinet
Cabinet eavesdropping; message of the leaked minutes; symposium. Nation 227:289+ S 30 '78
Carter's cabinet: how it rates. il U.S. News 85:20-5 O 16 '78
Carter's harried businessmen. il Bus W p80+ My 29 '78
Curbing cabinet government. il Time 111:22 My 15 '78
Giving Commerce the ax? E. Lewis. Bus W p 157-8 D 11 '78
Research questions from the Cabinet. Chemistry 51:34 Je '78
Scoreboard on Carter's Cabinet. il Bus W p54+ My 1 '78
Tightening the ship. D. M. Alpern and others. Newsweek 91:29-30+ Ap 21 '78
Tough talk from the boss. P. Goldman and others. il pors Newsweek 91:20-2 My 1 '78
Unlocking Cabinet conversations. il Time 112:36 O 9 '78

Capitol
All is not quiet on the West Front. J. P. Carlihian. il Archit Rec 163:101-6 Mr '78

Castles
See Castles

Cavalry
See United States—Army—Cavalry

READERS' GUIDE TO PERIODICAL LITERATURE March 1978–February 1979

WATKINS, T. H.
American characters. il Am Heritage 29:92-3 D '77
Astley David Montague Cooper and the matter of Mrs Stanford's jewels. il por Am Heritage 30:70-1 D '78
Chief Satanta, I presume? il por Am Heritage 29:66-71 O '78
Heritage preserved. il Am Heritage 29:32-3 Ap; 62-3 Je; 48-9 Ag; 36-7 O; 30:48-9 D '78
On the air, forever. il Am Heritage 29:62-3 Je '78
Out of the shadow of ruin. il Am Heritage 29:32-3 Ap '78
Purloined past. il Am Heritage 29:48-9 Ag '78
WATKINS, William Jon
(ed) See Brown, T. Jr. Tracker
WATSON, Aldren, A.
Tools for the country handyman. bibl il Blair & Ketchums 6:50-66 Ja '79
WATSON, Bernard C.
Excellence: what it is and how it can be achieved: address. bibl por Phi Delta Kappan 60:207S-210S N '78
Responsibility is ours. il Encore 7:13 My 22 '78
WATSON, James Dewey
DNA folly continues. New Repub 180:12+ Ja 13 '79
In his own words; interview, ed by C. P. Andersen. il pors People 9:93-4+ Ap 17 '78

about
Annals of science. H. F. Judson. il New Yorker 54:46-8+ N 27; 89-90+ D 4; 122+ D 11 '78 •
WATSON, James H.
Real-life company born in a B-school class. il por Bus W p90+ Ap 10 '78 •
WATSON, Jeannette
To the wall isn't a sentence but a compliment at the popular new Books & Co. H. Shapiro. il pors People 11:24-5 Ja 15 '79 •
WATSON, Peter
Military alliance with behavioral science. Psychol Today 11:109+ Ap '78 •
Psychologists go to war. il Time 112:68 Jl 10 '78
WATSON, R. E. and Perlman, M. L.
Seeing with a new light: synchrotron radiation. bibl il Science 199:1295-1302 Mr 24 '78
WATSON, Stanley J. and others
Adrenocorticotropin in rat brain; immunocytochemical localization in cells and axons. bibl il Science 200:1180-2 Je 9 '78
Effects of naloxone on schizophrenia: reduction in hallucinations in a subpopulation of subjects. bibl il Science 201:73-6 Jl 7 '78
WATSON, Thomas John, 1914-
Palawan in the peaceful sea. il Motor B & S 141:65-7+ Ap '78
Preparing for paradise. il por Motor B & S 141:86-9+ Mr '78
World I have seen. il por Sat Eve Post 250:66-9 S '78
WATSON, Tom
Come, Watson, the game's afoot. D. Jenkins. il Sports Illus 48:20-1 Ja 16 '78 •
King Nicklaus and the great pretender. D. Anderson. il pors Sport 66:36-8+ F '78 •
WATT, David
Global response? Atlas 25:36-7 Ja '78
WATT, Douglas
Popular records (cont) New Yorker 54:126-8+ Mr 13; 90-3 My 29; 146+ S 18; 153-4+ O 16 '78
WATT, Tom
History appears to be ready to repeat itself—and that's just fine. R. MacGregor. il por Macleans 91:47-8 Ja 9 '78 •
WATTLE fences. See Fences
WATTLETON, Faye
To have or have not...children: interview, ed by J. C. Warsaw. il por Work Wom 3:48-51 Je '78

about
Family planning's top advocate. S. D. Lewis. il pors Ebony 33:85-6+ S '78 •
To the top. N. Collins. il pors People 9:111+ My 22 '78 •
WATTS, André
Bio. J. R. Gaines. il pors People 9:48-50+ Je 26 '78 •
Musician of the month: André Watts. H. E. Phillips. por Hi Fi 28:MA4-5 D '78 •
WATTS, D. Randolph, and Olson, D. B.
Gulf Stream ring coalescence with the Gulf Stream off Cape Hatteras. bibl il maps Science 202:971-2 D 1 '78
WATTS, Franklin Mowry
Obituary
Pub W 213:20 Je 5 '78
WATTS, Geoff. and Muller, Mike
Global health care challenge. il Atlas 25:23-6 O '78
WATTS, Heather
Where will your next paycheck come from? E. Elliot. il pors Work Wom 3:28-31+ D '78 •
WATTS, Lester
Few dead men. S. Chapman. New Repub 179:9-10 D 16 '78 •

WAUER, Roland H.
Head start for an endangered turtle. il map Nat Parks & Con Mag 52:16-20 N '78
WAUGH, Evelyn
Man who liked Dickens; story; condensation of Handful of dust. Read Digest 112:197 Je '78

about
White mischief of Evelyn Waugh. G. Wolff. por New Times 10:58+ Ja 23 '78 •
WAVE guides
Guided-wave optics. A. Yariv. il Sci Am 240: 64-72 bibl(p 164) Ja '79
WAVE power
Flexible rafts harness wave power. D. Scott. il Pop Sci 213:94-5 S '78
Waking up to wave power. il Time 112:92 O 16 '78
WAVEGUIDES. See Wave guides
WAVERLY, Mary Wade
Amazing and irrepressible Charles Darwin. il por Sat Eve Post 250:46-8+ My '78
Inside line. il Sat Eve Post 250:66-8 My '78
WAVERLY Consort. See Instrumental ensembles
WAVES
Experiments with controlled Langmuir circulations. A. J. Faller. bibl il Science 201: 618-20 Ag 18 '78
Nightmare waves are all too real to deepwater sailors. P. Britton. il Smithsonian 8:60-7 F '78
Weather course: waves and currents. Motor B & S 141:56-8+ My '78
Weather course: wind waves and swells. il Motor B & S 141:94-6 Ap '78
See also
Gravity waves
Shock waves
Sound waves
Tidal waves
Ultrasonic waves
Wave power
WAVES. Brain. See Brain waves
WAVING of arms. See Gesture
WAX, Judith
You bright up my life; poems. Newsweek 92:21 D 11 '78
WAX dolls. See Dolls
WAX moths. See Moths
WAXES
See also
Automobile waxes
Floor finishes, waxes, etc.
Paraffins
The WAY International (movement)
Uproar in Emporia: community and college relations. A. A. Denton. Chr Cent 95:588-90 My 31 '78
WAYBURN, Edgar
Alaska's future: a matter of momentum. por Sierra 63:5 My '78
President's greatest environmental opportunity; Alaska 1978. Sierra 63:7 O '78
Priority—update on Alaska. il Sierra 63:2 Jl '78
WAYBURN, Peggy
Alaska: where the sun stays up all summer. il Sierra 63:43-5 My '78
Redwoods: jobs and environment. il Environment 20:34-9 Ap '78
WAYLAN, Cecile
Here is a detachable pot hanger in macramé style. il Flower & Gard 22:65 D '78
WAYNE, John
Celebrity visit with: John Wayne. il por Good H 186:140-3+ My '78 •
Full ahead, Mr Wayne. M. Goodman. il por Motor B & S 142:58-61+ N '78 •
Great Fox Powell, John Wayne, magic-dirt medicine show. T. Alexander. il por Fortune 97:64-6+ Mr 27 '78 •
John Wayne: what makes him an American institution. M. Zolotow. il pors 50 Plus 18:12-17 O '78 •
WAYS, Max
Virtues, dangers, and limits of negotiation. il Fortune 99:86-90 Ja 15 '79
WAYS and Means Committee. See United States—Congress—House—Ways and Means. Committee on
WAYSIDE Chapel for All People. See Houston, Tex.—Chapels
WAZEE Saturday Market. See Denver—Markets
WEAGRAFF, Patrick J.
Scandal in the use of voc ed funds. R. A. Rumstead. Phi Delta Kappan 59:477-8 Mr '78 •
WEALES, Gerald
Stage (cont) Commonweal 105:81-2, 178-9, 244-5, 498-9, 594 F 3, Mr 17, Ap 14, Ag 4, S 15 '78
Television. Nation 227:189-90 S 2 '78
WEALTH
Chariots of the insurance salesmen; get rich quick, mail order trade. R. Rosenbaum. il N Y 11:26-31 Jl 3 '78
Distribution wars: effect of tax cut proposals. R. Lekachman. New Repub 179:15-18 Jl 29 '78
Free! Free! Free! The priceless world of tomorrow. B. P. Beckwith. il por Futurist 12:307-12 O '78
Gluttoned on riches or the beauty of restraint. K. E. Boulding. Tech R 81:6+ D '78
Haves and the have-nots: views of R. W. Tucker. il Futurist 12:399-400 D '78

EXERCISE 3

On pp. 133–136 you will find four pages taken from volume 38 of the Readers' Guide to Periodical Literature. *Refer to these pages in answering the following questions.*

1. In which magazine will you find an article about Armenians?_____

2. Under which listing besides "lobsters" would you find an article about lobsters?_____
3. In which issue of which magazine is a bibliography included with an article about waves?_____
4. What is the title of the most recent article listed that was written by Richard Locke?_____
5. What is the name of the article that H. Leavitt wrote about helping local transit?_____
6. Under what heading would you have to look to find out about art in the United States?_____
7. In which volume of a *State Department Bulletin* is there a report on arms control?_____
8. What is the name of the article that K. Murphy wrote about Army food?_____
9. Who wrote an article with Marjorie Arons?_____
10. Where would you find an article written in September 1978 about Faye Wattleton?_____
    Who wrote the article?_____
11. What is the name of the article in volume 51 of *Chemistry* that discusses the Cabinet of the United States?_____
12. In which volume of which magazine might you learn how to install a dead-bolt lock?_____
13. Which town took on the Army engineers?_____
14. In which volume of which magazine might you find the name of the best city to locate a business in?_____
15. In which magazine would you find out about the GI drug scene in Europe?_____

138   PART ONE   ORGANIZING AND UNDERSTANDING INFORMATION

16. Who wrote an article about John Wayne that appeared, with a portrait, in *Fortune* magazine? _____
17. An article was written about the Loch Ness monster in *Newsweek* magazine. Who wrote it? _____
18. Information about two different listings can be found under "Voyages around the world." What are the two listings? _____
_____
19. Under which listing might you find information about United States military chaplains? _____
20. In which magazine can you find most of the articles listed about the Lockheed Corporation? _____

PART TWO

Strategies for Success

6

Becoming a Successful Student

A BALANCED PEP SCHEDULE

So you've finally made it to college. You've been accepted, and you have received registration materials, and you've been assigned a time to sign up for your classes. Now, how do you decide which courses you should take? Oh, you know the courses you need or want to take during your first year or two. But how should you schedule your courses?

If you have read the chapters preceding this one, you know about the importance of balance and skill in order to be a successful student. If you spend almost all your time working on school assignments you really will not feel successful, because you need some time for a social life, for recreation, and possibly for a job. Only if your college life is well balanced can you really enjoy it and feel a sense of accomplishment and self-worth. What do you need to know in order to plan your course schedule each semester?

First, as a successful student you should try to balance your course load with other facets of your life. Unfortunately, too many students feel that there is a rule that insists that unless you take 15 course hours per semester you are an inadequate student. Nonsense! You should proceed at a rate which meets your needs and which balances your life. The key word is *balance*. If you need or desire to work 20 or more hours per week, you are probably doing an injustice to yourself if you take a full load. If your subjects include one or more laboratory courses, you will probably want to balance them with other courses that are not as demanding. If you have a family and have personal and social obligations, a full load is just too much. Better to do well with fewer courses, and feel good about yourself and your academic accomplishments, rather than to feel frustrated and possibly withdraw from a class or two. Incidentally, you have no right to expect your instructor to lower his standards because you have mitigating circumstances. It is your responsibility to adjust your selection of classes to your unique situation.

Even when you can take a full load, there are some things to consider in order to maintain balance. There are three general classifications of courses, called PEP. You can balance your course load if you take a mixture of PEP each semester. What is PEP and what should you know about it?

The first P stands for PLUG AWAY courses. These are courses that require continuous day-by-day study and preparation for class and laboratory work. These courses usually involve lots of practice and many tests. Any of the laboratory science courses, such as chemistry or biology, come under this grouping. Skills courses, such as mathematics, English, or reading, also appear here, as do courses such as foreign languages or accounting. They are demanding and require that you do the following if you are to be successful.

1. Try not to miss any classes for any reason. These classes are usually taught in sequence, so you can't understand the second lesson if you didn't understand the first lesson, and you can't understand the third lesson if you didn't understand the second, and so on.

2. Because of the above situation, it is important that you keep up with each lesson. You can't let yourself fall behind. This, of course, means that daily study and review are absolutely necessary. In other courses you sometimes have more time to prepare lessons, but not in PLUG AWAY courses.

3. If you don't understand a point made in your classes or in your reading, see your instructor immediately. If you wait, you will fall behind. If too much time elapses, you will fall hopelessly behind and may have to withdraw from the class—an unnecessary and costly step.

E stands for ENJOYMENT. Take a fun-type course which you know you will enjoy, or perhaps a course which will help you relax. This category includes courses in art appreciation, drawing, ceramics, music appreciation, speech, or physical education, perhaps golfing, swimming, volleyball, or modern dance. These courses normally have few exams, although they may have long-range goals such as the creation of a ceramic object or drawing or the development of a physical skill. Don't take these courses too lightly, however. There are some dangers that you need to watch out for.

1. Self-discipline is needed. In these courses you are often left on your own with a long-range project. Sometimes you need to practice to develop a skill. Although the particular scheduling of time is left up to you, you must be sure to schedule that time on a regular basis. You should not allow it to wait until the end of the semester, or you will become harried and stressed and all of the fun is gone. You must discipline yourself (no one will be looking over your shoulder to scold you if you don't) and set up a regular schedule in order to succeed.
2. Don't look upon this course as a "snap" or as something unimportant. To do so puts you into the position of taking it for granted, which is a position that can lead to failure.

The third type of course (the second P) is the POWER course. These courses do not usually require a lot of daily work, but they do require a lot of outside reading which, more often than not, can be done on a weekly basis. Also, there are often long-range projects to be done. Although there are fewer tests, this very fact means that these tests take on added importance, because you have fewer opportunities to show what you know. A poor grade in one of these tests is difficult to overcome. English literature, history, sociology, psychology, and anthropology are examples of POWER courses. In order to be successful in this type of course, you should note the following suggestions.

1. Once again, you must have self-discipline. You should not leave the weekly reading until the night before it is required. Plan your work for the semester in relatively equal, but manageable, steps.
2. It is important that you take good notes (see Chapter 4) and that you study them regularly so that you don't fall behind. Because there are so few tests (usually no more than two or three plus the final exam), they will cover work done over a long period of time. Only by taking and then keeping up with your notes can you study effectively for these tests.

You should try to balance your course load each semester by taking one or two courses from each of these categories. An ideal situation is to take one, or two at the most, PLUG AWAY courses in one semester. If you need to take more than two, you might want to consider taking a smaller course load that semester so that you can do justice to these courses.

There are two other items that you should consider. If this is your first semester at a particular school, you should take a limited load, perhaps no more than ten credits. This will give you time to become adjusted to a new situation without having to spend the time and energy involved in carrying a full load. A second and very important point—take "preparatory" courses first. If you know that you need help in mathematics or in reading, or perhaps even in typing, be sure to sign up for these courses during your first semester, if possible. Get these hangups out of the way once and for all so that you can zero in on the course work in full possession of the skills needed for success.

CHARACTERISTICS FOR SUCCESS

What are some other characteristics of successful students? As a successful student, you should:

1. *Think positively.* You need to have good self-image so you can turn what seems like defeat into a positive learning situation. If you expect that you can do better, and you try to do better, then overall you will do better. Babe Ruth was known as the home-run king. He was also the strike-out king. However, if he thought of himself as the strike-out king, it could have defeated him and he would not have been the home-run king. You might want to read a book that discusses the importance of thinking positively. Read *Psychocybernetics*, by Dr. Maxwell Maltz (Simon and Schuster, 1960).

2. *Be interested in your courses.* Even if you think a course is the most boring one in the world, force yourself to be interested. Take a minor point and read as much as possible about it in order to become an expert in just that little bit of information. Talk about it, live and breathe that minor point for a few days. That kind of interest can beget interest in the entire course.

3. *Seek help when you need it, before it's too late.* If you have special problems, don't be afraid to seek help. See your teacher, your counselor, your advisor, anyone that you think may be able to help you. It is important that you be aware of where you can go for help. As a student, find out what kind of help is available, and where, before you need it. Some schools have special courses in reading and mathematics and other basic skills. Some have tutoring centers where you can get help in understanding the material for a particular course. Special counselors are usually available to help you with personal problems. Most campuses can help with money—student loans, scholarships, special student aid funds, or work-study programs. Some campuses will help you find housing. Find out what is available at your school, and be prepared to use it when you need it.

4. *Attend classes and be active in class.* Attending class and arriving on time are subtle points that indicate that you are serious about your commitment to learning. Take part in classroom discussions and hand in assignments on time. Speaking up in class forces you to think about the points being made and keeps you interested in what is being discussed. However, ask relevant questions, such as for further explanations of points that you need to have clarified or for a definition of an item not fully understood. Ask questions about the implications of the

information learned. This will help you to understand and absorb information more fully.

5. *Have a good attitude about college life.* Know your strong points and your weaknesses, understand your goals and work toward them, and most important, understand what a college can and cannot do for you. Take responsibility for your own education. You should realize that attending college offers you the raw material for success and education—libraries, teachers, textbooks. However, only you can educate yourself. Take advantage of what is around you and use it to your best advantage according to your own needs.

6. *Have the "know-how" to be successful.* Make sure that you know how to study, take notes, take tests, use time wisely. Be sure you can use reference sources such as the library. Develop memory skills. Try to get along with your teachers and your fellow students. You should be at ease in expressing yourself and in understanding words. Learn from experience. Always look for ways to do things better. Notice that this book covers most of these needs—take advantage of it.

7. *Know the rules and be familiar with the various college calendars.* You should know about various social, cultural, and sports events. You should know deadlines for withdrawal from classes without penalty, and deadlines for making up incomplete grades. Be aware of prerequisites and other requirements for the program you are enrolled in. Know which student government activities are available and how they can help you.

PERSONAL PROBLEMS

If you are to be a successful student, you must give special attention to your personal problems. Even if they aren't directly related to school activities, they can certainly affect your behavior in class, and must be dealt with, usually promptly. The key to solving personal problems is to know where help can be obtained. Some frequent personal problems and suggestions for help follow.

1. *Money and job-related problems.* Going to college is expensive, both in tuition and in living expenses. You may need to get a part-time job in order to go to school. Fortunately, college administrators realize this. Check your college's job board. Many businesses prefer to hire college students (often because they feel college students are more responsible and more capable), and they will list their job needs with your school. You may be able to find a job in the field in which you are studying. Also, most schools have work-study programs. A major advantage of a work-study job is that your working hours are usually more flexible. Also, your job is located on campus, so your travel time is reduced. You might even have an opportunity to work for a professor who can later recommend you for a job in your chosen field.

Sometimes you may need money for tuition, books, or rent, and you haven't found a job yet. See if your college has a loan office. Student loans may be available, at little or no interest, on a short-term basis. You might also want to investigate the possibility of a scholarship to help pay your school expenses.

The main point is that you should seek out the college office that can help you with your problem. It may be the job center or the student loan office or the office that has scholarship applications. Know what help is available and seek it out.

2. *Housing.* On a large college campus, if you are not a local resident you will probably need housing. Large colleges usually have dormitories. If they are full, or for some other reason are not available to you, check with the college housing office. They are prepared to tell you about the availability of apartments in the price range you are seeking and which they will recommend. You don't have to spend valuable time looking for these facilities.

3. *Mental health.* Personal and college pressures can be devastating. Don't be afraid to speak to an advisor or counselor or to a teacher who you think will be helpful. Most of these people are trained to be of help to you, and if they can't help you directly, they can refer you to the proper places. If you have marital or parental conflicts, physical health problems, or drug-related or even social problems, people in the community are eager to help you. Your college counselor knows where these people are and can put you in touch with them. If your grades are poor, they can help you cope with that problem. The important thing is to know that help is available. Seek it out and take advantage of these college and community services.

4. *Career goals.* There are many college and community programs that can help you with this problem. If you are not really sure about whether your chosen field is right for you, aptitude or interest tests are available. Take them and use the results to guide your final decision. Speak to the teachers who teach courses in your chosen field. Some colleges provide the opportunity for you to spend a day with a chemist at work, or an accountant at work, or a journalist, or a medical laboratory technician. Take advantage of this opportunity if it is available. The insights you can gain are not attainable in any other way.

Again, try to solve problems by speaking to the people who can help you. Don't try to solve them alone. Know what services are available to you at your college and in the community, and use them when you need them.

EXERCISE 1

1. Following is a list of courses that you want to take during your first two semesters. How can you arrange them so that you have a balanced schedule each semester? List the courses in the spaces provided.

   a. chemistry
      (3-hour lab)   5 credits
   b. accounting   5 credits
   c. mathematics   3 credits
   d. history   3 credits
   e. English
      literature   3 credits
   f. English
      composition   3 credits
   g. ceramics   2 credits
   h. music
      appreciation   2 credits
   i. speed reading   2 credits
   j. physical
      education   2 credits

   First Semester

   a. _____
   b. _____
   c. _____
   d. _____
   e. _____
   f. _____
   g. _____

   Second Semester

   a. _____
   b. _____
   c. _____
   d. _____
   e. _____
   f. _____
   g. _____

2. Use the same list as above. You have a job working 15 hours per week and you have decided that you should take these courses over a period of three semesters. Set up your schedule of the same courses over a three-semester period. List them in the spaces provided.

   First Semester

   a. _____
   b. _____
   c. _____
   d. _____
   e. _____

   Second Semester

   a. _____
   b. _____
   c. _____
   d. _____
   e. _____

   Third Semester

   a. _____
   b. _____

   c. _____
   d. _____
   e. _____

3. Determine where on your campus you would go for each of the following services or information. Tell whom you would see and/or the type of service and its location.

	Person and/or Service	Location
a. academic advisement	_____	_____
b. short-term loan for tuition	_____	_____
c. job	_____	_____
d. parking permit	_____	_____
e. withdrawal from a course	_____	_____
f. replacement of a lost I.D. card	_____	_____
g. lost and found	_____	_____
h. credit by examination	_____	_____
i. student organizations	_____	_____
j. tutoring assistance	_____	_____
k. getting a transcript	_____	_____
l. other college catalogs	_____	_____
m. theft	_____	_____
n. registration information	_____	_____
o. personal problem that is interfering with studying	_____	_____
p. clubs	_____	_____

q. athletic
   schedule   _____   _____

r. college
   calendar   _____   _____

7

Using Time Effectively

"Hey, Jim, are you going to the game tonight?"

"Gosh, I can't, Harry. I can't spare the time. I've got all this studying to do for my biology class."

Has that ever happened to you? Or do you find that because you have both schoolwork and a job, you aren't getting better grades? Or, even if you are able to handle the job and the classwork, you don't have any time at all for fun?

None of this has to be so. If you use your time wisely, you can do well in school, you can hold a job (working a reasonable number of hours), and you can still have time for recreation. You don't have to find more time—you just have to use your time more efficiently. Learning to take charge of your time will help put you in control of your life. Time, in a sense, is like money. Only so much is allotted to you each week. If you spend it wisely, you'll have more left over to have fun with.

How do you take charge of your time, especially when you have schoolwork, a job, family responsibilities, and a social life (and you would even like to get some sleep once in a while)? The first step is to analyze how you are spending your time now. Then replace that with a new, more flexible, more efficient time schedule. Here's how to do it.

ANALYZING YOUR SCHEDULE

First, you must keep a record of how you spend your time for one week. Actually write down everything you do. Carry a small notebook around with you. A typical Monday might be written something like this:

7:00– 7:30	Awoke and got ready for the day.
7:30– 8:00	Breakfast. Also read newspaper.
8:00– 8:15	Walked to school.
8:15– 8:30	Arrived early for my 8:30 class. Chatted with other classmates who arrived early.
8:30– 9:30	English class.
9:30–10:30	Coffee break in cafeteria.
10:30–11:30	Mathematics class.
11:30–12:30	Lunch.
12:30– 1:30	Psychology class.
1:30– 2:00	Took bus to work.
2:00– 5:00	Work.
5:00– 5:30	Took bus home.
5:30– 6:00	Relax.
6:00– 7:00	Dinner.
7:00– 9:30	Study.
9:30–11:00	Watched TV.
11:00	Bed.

After doing this for a week, make a list of all the various activities included on your schedule, and next to it write the amount of time you spent on each activity. You may be surprised to see how much time was not spent wisely. Let's look at Monday's schedule as an example.

7:00–8:00	An hour to dress, have breakfast, and read the newspaper is well spent.
8:00–8:30	Looking over your notes just before and after attending class makes for better understanding and retention and saves time. Although socializing is a desirable activity, reviewing notes between 8:15 and 8:30 would be better use of your time. Also—and here is a study time usually overlooked by students—what do you think about while walking to school? Aren't there some items for class that you need to remember—a formula for your mathematics class, names of people and what they

did for your psychology class, perhaps a subtle point made in your English class? What a great time to study without using extra time—while walking to school.

9:30–10:30   A one-hour coffee break is too long. Half an hour for coffee and interesting conversation would be better. Then, follow with 15 minutes to review what happened in your English class and 15 minutes to review prior mathematics notes.

11:30–12:30   You deserve a leisurely, one-hour lunch. Have lunch with friends, if possible. If you have five to ten minutes to look over notes just before your psychology class, it would be helpful.

1:30–2:00
5:00–5:30   Spend this time wisely. Review your psychology lesson and use any extra time for planning. You might plan a semester paper or a party or other social event. The point is to use that one hour constructively. If you take the bus to work and back home five days a week, you have five hours of time that you can use for school or leisure activities. Read a book for fun, or read a required document—it doesn't matter, but don't squander five hours per week.

5:30–6:00   You deserve time to unwind after the tough day you've had.

7:00–11:00   It's very possible, at least some days, that you don't need as much as two and a half more hours to study if you have made good use of your time earlier in the day. Of course, if there is an exam to prepare for, or a special report or paper due, you may have to extend your study time somewhat. The rest of the time can be used for recreation.

If this schedule was your actual Monday schedule, you probably felt squeezed for time. After all, all that you seemed to be doing all day was studying and running from class to work. If you make the minor revisions suggested above, you should have much more time—and this is only for Monday. You can apply the same time-saving methods all week long. If possible, try to keep most of the weekend for fun and recreation.

PREPARING AND USING A NEW SCHEDULE

To make the best use of your time, you should make a weekly schedule. In order to do so effectively, keep the following guidelines in mind.

1. Set up your schedule to account for all the time from waking until going to bed.
2. Your schedule should be flexible. It should allow for last-minute invitations (or assignments), extra work shifts, unexpected guests, even illness or emergencies.
3. Allocate the times for your fixed activities first. These are your commitments—class hours, work hours, other activities whose hours are set and cannot be changed.
4. Make sure you have provided time for both work and play.
5. Make use of time that might otherwise be wasted. Time spent alone while walking from one place to another, riding in a public conveyance, shopping, or eating can be put to good use. You can mentally review class notes or even have vocabulary words or other material on 3 x 5 cards to review during these times.
6. Before setting up your schedule, try to be aware of your biological clock. Schedule activities around it, if possible. You might, for example, want to do your tough studying when you are at peak efficiency. Time will be used more efficiently this way.
7. If possible, allow for study periods just before and just after class.

Look at the weekly schedule on p. 155. This is a reasonably flexible schedule. It allows for contingencies, and the amount of time allowed for study depends on the need. You should not accept the common error that a certain amount of time should be devoted to study for every hour that you attend class. How much time you devote to studying a particular subject depends upon many things—your prior knowledge of the subject, your interest in it, what grade you wish to receive in the course, your course load, and other priorities. Certainly you wouldn't want to devote as much time to a subject in which you have only a casual interest and which is not related to your major as you would to a course in your major in which you have a vital interest and whose content is important to your expected life's work. Also, some subjects simply require more work and attention than others. Teachers require more, or the subject itself is inherently more demanding. A course in music appreciation (not your major) in which you must do reading and learn about certain musicians and their compositions is not as demanding as a course in sociology (your major) in which, as part of the course requirement, you must knock on doors for a survey and then analyze the results of that survey and report on it for your semester project.

Note, also, the following points about the schedule on p. 155. On Saturday, do chores first and enjoy your recreation last. During the study hours on Saturday, take brief breaks as needed. Also, reserve Saturday for work on long-range projects or extra study (term papers, study for final exams, extra study for tough subjects). Even though the

CHAPTER 7 USING TIME EFFECTIVELY

	Monday	Tuesday	Wednesday	Thursday	Friday	Saturday	Sunday
7–8		arise, dress, breakfast →				dress breakfast	
8–9	Review English	Review english	Review english		Review English	study as needed chores	church recreation
9–10	ENGLISH break	HISTORY	ENGLISH break	HISTORY	ENGLISH break	laundry housecleaning shopping other	social activities sports hobbies other
10–11	review math MATH	review history coffee break review accting	review math MATH	review history coffee break review accting	review math MATH		
11–12	LUNCH	ACCTING	LUNCH	ACCTING	LUNCH	recreation sports	
12–1	review psychology PSYCH	lunch	review psychology PSYCH	lunch	review psychology PSYCH	social activities hobbies fun activities	
1–2		travel to work					
2–3			WORK				
3–4							
4–5							
5–6		return home rest					
6–7			DINNER				
7–8							review tough subjects
8–9		Study first, as needed					prepare for week
9–10		Then, recreation					Then
10–11							relax, TV, recreational reading other

schedule is flexible, you should hold Saturday mornings for schoolwork as needed. Sunday evening should be reserved for reviewing the notes of the past week in preparation for classes during the coming week. On Tuesdays and Thursdays, try to leave five to ten minutes just before your accounting class to review your notes. If you happen to have lunch alone, you can get a lot of work done at that time.

After you have made an analysis of how you are spending your time, prepare your own weekly schedule and a long-range schedule that covers at least one semester. The weekly schedule should look something like the one on p. 155. Leave room at the bottom of the schedule (or, if necessary, attach a blank sheet to it) to record the things you need to do that week. Such things as medical appointments, social events, and items that are due that week should be listed. The long-range schedule should be a listing of things that need to be done in the future, such as reports or projects for school, sports events you wish to attend, or even vacation plans.

The most important thing about preparing a time budget is to stick to it. Be flexible and make appropriate changes as the need arises, but stick to the general schedule.

Become time-wise and enjoy life more.

The following pages include three blank weekly schedule forms to get you started. You don't have to make out a new sheet each week. Make one out and change it only when your circumstances change—when you begin a new semester, or when summer comes along, or if you change your hours or work. You can accommodate a special circumstance during a particular week by making a note of it in the space at the bottom of the schedule. You could also have a separate sheet on which you write the things that need to be done that week. Following the schedule forms are exercises which can help you sharpen your ability to analyze your time needs. Do them carefully and learn to use time wisely.

CHAPTER 7 USING TIME EFFECTIVELY

	Monday	Tuesday	Wednesday	Thursday	Friday	Saturday	Sunday
7-8							
8-9							
9-10							
10-11							
11-12							
12-1							
1-2							
2-3							
3-4							
4-5							
5-6							
6-7							
7-8							
8-9							
9-10							
10-11							

	Monday	Tuesday	Wednesday	Thursday	Friday	Saturday	Sunday
7-8							
8-9							
9-10							
10-11							
11-12							
12-1							
1-2							
2-3							
3-4							
4-5							
5-6							
6-7							
7-8							
8-9							
9-10							
10-11							

	Monday	Tuesday	Wednesday	Thursday	Friday	Saturday	Sunday
7-8							
8-9							
9-10							
10-11							
11-12							
12-1							
1-2							
2-3							
3-4							
4-5							
5-6							
6-7							
7-8							
8-9							
9-10							
10-11							

EXERCISE 1

Tell how you would change the following time schedule to make it more efficient. Write your answer on the lines below the schedule.

7:00–8:00	Dress, eat breakfast, read newspaper.
8:00–9:00	Go to school, have coffee break with friends in cafeteria.
9:00–11:30	Classes.
11:30–12:30	Lunch.
12:30–1:00	Review classwork.
1:00–2:00	Nap.
2:00–4:00	Join friends for social gathering.
4:00–5:00	Relax.
5:00–6:00	Dinner.
6:00–7:30	Telephone friends, write letters.
7:30–8:30	Watch TV.
8:30–11:00	Study.

EXERCISE 2

You can choose your own working hours and your own class hours as well as the time for all other activities. How would you schedule the following activities during a day? Indicate your schedule on the lines below. Classes and labs can begin as early as 7:30 A.M. and go through evening classes, which end at 10:00 P.M.

English class (one hour), history class (one hour), chemistry class (one hour), chemistry lab (three hours), work (three hours), study (three hours), three meals (two and one-half hours), breaks, and travel (one and one-half hours), sleep (eight hours).

8

Working with Professors

You're a pretty good student, you are conscientious, you put in your study time, you attend classes and take good lecture notes, you're interested in what you are studying, you even earn above average grades. Then why is it taking so long to get through college? You have had to drop four courses, and that has cost you almost a semester. You didn't drop because of illness or other personal problems or because it was too much for you to handle. It wasn't really your fault—the professors were just impossible. The first professor was unbelievably boring; he lectured in a monotone and put the class to sleep. The second professor walked into class the first day and told us to look at each other because half of us wouldn't be there by the end of the semester. Then she spent the rest of the hour telling us about all the work we would have to do and how tough her exams were. She was right about the first statement. You didn't stay very long. The third professor seemed to think he was in a vacuum. He came in, lectured for an hour without stopping, never allowed any questions, and walked out when the hour was over. You dropped the fourth class because the professor didn't seem to care what you did. She gave an assignment, then asked if there were any questions. If there weren't any, she would spend most of the time telling us about her personal experiences. When she did answer a question, she would act as though you hadn't read the assignment carefully enough.

Don't you need to have a good feeling about the instructor if you are to learn from a class? Actually, you don't have to like your instructor in order to learn. You may dislike the personal activities or political affiliation of an actor, but that doesn't stop you from enjoying his dramatic performance. You probably won't like every employer you have, but hopefully that won't stop you from being successful on the job. Teachers, like everyone else, have a variety of personality traits. You can learn from almost any teacher. Dropping a class is giving up and is costly to you in time and money. The following pages will offer suggestions for coping with your professors and getting the most out of their courses.

First, remember that college teachers normally have freedom to conduct their classes in any way they see fit. Although this sounds arbitrary and unfair, it actually is a good thing. Most teachers teach best when they can incorporate their own style and personality into their presentations. If you don't like the method of presentation or the rules set down by a teacher, don't let that interfere with your goal of learning, becoming educated, passing the course. This particular teacher is but a passing phase in your life. Get from the teacher what you can by paying attention to the content, to what is said rather than how it is said. This can be tough, but if there is no other teacher for the course, you have no choice except to transfer to another school. If the teacher does lose a lot of the class, you have a more ideal learning situation; a smaller class could mean that more attention is paid to you. Also, a more demanding teacher is often the one that you look back upon and realize you learned more from.

HOW TO CHOOSE PROFESSORS

Sometimes you do have a choice of teachers for a particular class. What are some of the things you should consider in choosing a particular instructor?

1. What is the teacher's reputation among other students? Is the teacher considered tough (not necessarily a bad trait, as discussed above), weak (you may not learn as much), an easy grader (requires motivation on your part), helpful and giving of time, especially if you have difficulty understanding the course content? These points should be considered before you select from among several teachers who are offering the course for which you are planning to register.

2. What is the teacher's reputation in his field of knowledge? If you are fortunate, your school may have a person of national or even international fame on the staff. Taking a course from such a person can be an inspiring learning experience. In addition, if this course is in your major, this professor might be able to help you find a job later on or give you a valuable recommendation to graduate school. On

the other hand, a person with an outstanding reputation can sometimes be a poor teacher. He or she may be very knowledgeable, but poor at imparting that knowledge to students. Both these points must be considered before you make a decision.

WHAT PROFESSORS DO FOR YOU

Here are some further points to consider in working with professors. Most of them are honest and capable or they wouldn't have been hired for the job. What do college professors do for you?

1. They take materials that they have spent many years learning and digesting, and they condense them for you.
2. They think about the best ways to present this material. They then prepare lectures or teaching aids in order to present it that way.
3. They prepare and grade testing material. This is time-consuming. Do you really prefer a teacher who gives no exams (or perhaps just one) and gives everybody an A or a B? How much would you really learn?
4. They sacrifice money, so they probably really like to teach. Most of the time, teaching doesn't pay as much as other jobs for which their special knowledge qualifies them.

WHAT PROFESSORS EXPECT

What do college professors expect of you?

1. They expect you to attend classes and be on time.
2. They would like you to show some interest, if not enthusiasm, in class.
3. They expect you to be prepared when you come to class. This means that you should have done any reading assignments in advance, and if possible, either know something about the subject to be covered or ask questions about ideas that puzzle you.
4. They expect written assignments to be turned in on time.
5. They expect an attitude of willingness to learn when in class rather than an "I challenge you to teach me" attitude.

HOW TO HELP YOUR PROFESSORS AND YOURSELF

What should you do for yourself and your professor when taking a class?

1. You should attend all classes and you should arrive on time. It is not true that you should purposely arrive late in order to let the professor know you. You will be known all right, but in a negative context.
2. You should realize that when you do assignments you are doing them for yourself, not for your professor. From a really selfish viewpoint (which most college teachers don't have, because they are usually genuinely concerned if you don't do your work), it doesn't really matter to your teacher if the work isn't done. He has less material to grade, and whether you learn or not, he still has his job. You, however, are wasting your time if you don't do the assigned work.
3. You should tell your professor if you feel that a lecture was especially good or if you were inspired by it. This gives valuable feedback. Also, one of the important rewards of teaching is to know that you are appreciated. If you feel that a particular professor is really outstanding, don't only tell that professor. Tell other students. Write a letter to the college administration and tell them how you feel.
4. You should have a list of your teachers' names, office hours, and office locations. This is important if you need to consult with them. In the space below, list the name, office hours, and office location of three of your teachers.

NAME	OFFICE HOURS	OFFICE LOCATION
1. _____	_____	_____
2. _____	_____	_____
3. _____	_____	_____

5. You should ask questions if you do not understand something. Before asking questions, however, be sure that you have explored the obvious places for an answer. Don't, for example, ask a question whose answer is clearly stated in your reading assignment. Ask questions about items in the textbook or other reading that you don't understand. Ask for clarification of points made in class that you don't fully understand. Also, when you do ask a question, phrase it clearly so that it can be answered clearly. Don't say, "I don't understand about the causes of the revolution." Say instead, "I don't understand how economic conditions were a cause of the revolution. Which particular economic conditions were they, and how did they lead to war?"

You can help your teacher do a better job of teaching. A very interesting article appeared in the March 1974 edition of *Psychology Today* magazine that concerns itself with how students can change the behavior of teachers in the classroom. Students were taught how to influence teachers to do a better job of teaching and develop a more positive feeling about those particular students.

EXERCISE 1

Below are descriptions of classroom situations that would cause many students to drop the class, although it is not advisable to do so. Briefly describe how you might handle each situation in order to stay in the class and still learn the course content. Space is provided for your comments.

1. Professor X teaches a history class and is really very boring. She really knows her subject matter, but she presents it in such an uninteresting way. First she asks us to read about the subject of her lecture in the textbook. You read about a fascinating period, you can visualize the scene, and you are excited about the events. Then in class Professor X bores you with statistical details and concentrates on names and dates instead of events. Not only that, she speaks in a monotone and gives the impression that she herself is bored. She ignores people who wish to ask questions. How can you make her more responsive to your needs and interests in this class?

2. Professor Y teaches advanced mathematics and is unpredictable. Sometimes he is brilliant in his clear explanation of difficult ideas. At other times he just can't make himself clear and doesn't seem able to answer questions well. He always tries, however, and you are always welcome to seek help during conference hours. Unfortunately, his tests are difficult, and they always seem to center around the points he didn't make clear. He is a rather likeable person, but when students are a bit noisy in class he is embarrassed to discipline them. This sometimes makes for an unpleasant situation. It would be easy to drop the course, as several students have already done, and take it with someone more predictable. How might you handle this situation?

3. Professor Z is a joke. You need to take the class to graduate, and he is the only one teaching it. He never arrives on time, and when he does, he fumbles for several minutes putting his notes in order and getting ready to lecture. He usually starts on one subject, then changes to another, then comes back to the first. When he returns a test, you can tell that either he didn't read it very carefully or an assistant probably graded it. At least half the time he dismisses the one-hour class after about 40 minutes. You are frustrated and disgusted, but you do need the class. What can you do? _____

9

Remembering What You Learn

You have good techniques for studying textbooks, you take notes well, your research skills are expert, you get along with your professors, college life is great as far as you are concerned—except for one thing. You can't remember. Why spend hours reading and studying and researching if you can't remember the information when the test comes around? You get along well with people, but you're embarrassed when you don't remember their names.

Have you ever experienced this problem? Do you forget names of people, or dates that signify such information as important historical events, or the six causes or seven results or ten properties that you need to know for your various courses? Well, it doesn't have to happen.

You can remember what you want to, when you want to, and for as long as you want to if you have the confidence in your ability to remember, and most important the desire to remember. Add to that some good techniques for remembering—the "how" to remember—and your improved memory skills will be a source of satisfaction to you.

Basically, your motivation (desire and confidence) and your purpose (reason to remember) help you to remember facts. If you don't really want to remember certain information, or if you have no real reason to remember it, then you won't. You can't recall the causes of the revolution for that history course you are taking, but you don't have trouble remembering the make, model, color, and other specifications of the car you are planning to buy. Become interested in what you want to remember. The information will then have more meaning to you.

Also, make sure that you understand what you want to remember. It is especially difficult for you to remember things that don't make sense to you.

Look at the following list of ten groups of three letters each for no more than five seconds. See how many of them you can remember in the exact order in which they appear. Remember, time yourself for five seconds. Then try to write down the groups of letters from memory before going on.

JMP
LQN
SPK
GBD
SMF
TRL
CWR
VTD
RQP
MBT

How many groups did you remember in the exact order in which they appeared? Most students can't recall more than three or four groups. Now try these groups. Follow the same directions as above.

BOY
SEE
CAN
BUT
THE
LAP
TEN
GOT
SEA
ART

How many did you recall this time? Most students can recall more than they did in the first group. Now try it one more time with the group below.

THE
BOY
AND

HIS
DAD
SAW
THE
BIG
RED
CAR

Did you remember all or almost all of these? How do you account for this improvement? In the first group, you were not able to relate the letters to each other in any way that made sense. In the second group, the letters made sense as three-letter words, but the words did not relate to one another. In the third group, the letters made sense as individual words, and the words made sense as a unit of thought. Does this mean that when items make sense and when they relate to one another you can remember them better? What is involved in memory improvement?

In order to improve your memory, you should consider the following:

INTENSE ORIGINAL IMPRESSION

Very often, it isn't that you forgot an item as much as that you didn't really observe it in the first place. Have you ever been introduced to someone and a moment later realized that you can't remember that person's name? You probably didn't pay attention to the name in the first place, so you didn't really hear it. Have you ever put something away and later not remembered where you put it? Rather than forgetting where it was, you just didn't pay attention when you put it away in the first place. Forcing yourself to have a strong, visual, intense impression in the first place will help you to remember things. Have you heard the expression, "First impressions are lasting"? Well, that is true if your first impression is a strong, vivid one.

How can you develop an intense original impression? Whenever you read something that you need to remember, look away after every paragraph or two and tell yourself what was said. (Remember the second R of PQ3R in Chapter 3?). This will force concentration. If you want to remember the name of someone to whom you were just introduced, repeat the name when you learn it. Say, "Hi, Sue. I'm glad to meet you," rather than just "Hi."

ASSOCIATION

The key to learning any information is to relate it to something you already know. All learning takes place that way. You don't begin to learn psychology by taking an advanced course—you take the introductory course, where the information is usually cut up into small, easy-to-digest pieces that you can relate or associate with things you already know about. This knowledge becomes part of you, and the advanced course can then build upon the information you learned in the introductory course by helping you associate with it.

Look at the following group of dots. Are there any missing?

. . . .
. . . .
 . . .

Obviously, you don't know. Now look at the same number of dots arranged somewhat differently. Are there any missing?

. . . .
. .   .
. . . .

Can you see that the third dot in the second row is missing? The way in which the dots are arranged or related to one another tells you that. Also, you won't forget this information, because the logical order of arrangement makes it easier to force a strong original impression.

Make your associations as personal as you can. When you study the psychology of emotions, try to relate the information to your own feelings. When you study accounting, pretend that it is for a personal business that you are preparing that balance sheet. In history, pretend that you are there. This will not only help you make strong associations, but will also make for an intense original impression.

When you are studying a chapter in a textbook, the PREPARE technique (see Chapter 3) helps you relate details to important points. When studying spelling, you can remember that the word *stationery* (referring to writing materials) is spelled with *ery* at the end, as opposed to *stationary* (standing still), if you relate it to the word *envelope*, which you know begins with an *e*. There was a national campaign in the early 1970s to use the acronym *WIN* (Whip Inflation Now) to get people to be more conscious of that issue.

VISUALIZATION

It is important for you to visualize what you want to remember, and especially to visualize it with an association. One important point—the wilder, more ridiculous the visualization, the better you will remember it, because in order to dream up a wild image you have to concentrate more and you have to force a strong original impression and association. Let us say that for a history exam next week you have to remember the names of the first several presidents of the United States in the order in which they served. How can you use visualization and association to help you? You know, of course, that Washington was the first president. John Adams was the second. Well, somehow you have to relate the two in some wild, outlandish way. Visualize Adam (from the Bible) standing on a ton of coal with a washcloth in hand, washing the ton of coal one piece at a time. This will relate the first two presidents. (Actually try this. Don't just read about it—really do it. When you finish, you will not only know the names of the first few presidents of the U. S. in order, you will also remember them later.) Now picture Thomas Jefferson (our third president) and his son (it doesn't matter whether he had a son) watching Adam. They are having an argument because Jefferson wants his son to help Adam, and his son thinks that washing a ton of coal, one piece at a time, is ridiculous and he won't do it. As the argument continues, Jefferson's son becomes madder and madder. Picture Jefferson and his mad son (Mad (i) son). Who are the first four presidents? Of course, they are Washington, Adams, Jefferson, Madison. Continue to make up your own outlandish story for the next several presidents, or for any other list of items you need to remember. Really do it! You will learn the items and remember them for as long as you wish.

Pegging

Another highly successful technique for combining visualization and association is to use the peg. This memory technique can give you the power to remember whatever you wish for as long as you wish. Nursing or anatomy students can use it to recall the bones of the body in any order desired. History students can use it to recall and relate causes and events, historical dates, and names. Other students can peg to remember the various properties of chemicals or to recite the major and minor concepts of a theory or philosophy, etc. What is the peg and how does it work?

Visualize, in order, 10 to 20 locations or items in your home. You would ordinarily go from room to room. Let us pretend that you chose the following 10 items: sink, gas stove, refrigerator, TV set, couch, bed, desk, chest of drawers, bedroom door, and bedroom window. Learn these 10 in the above order. (This is very easy to do, because you are familiar with them in their various locations.) These are your pegs upon which you will hang information. Now let us say you are taking a nutrition course and you must remember the seven basic food groups in the following order: (1) green vegetables, (2) citrus foods, (3) potatoes, (4) milk, (5) meat, fish, and eggs, (6) breads and cereals, and (7) butter. The first peg is the sink and the first item is green vegetables. Visualize a sink whose basin is made of string beans pasted together and which is standing on a pedestal made of asparagus. You turn on the faucet and green peas pour out and fill up the basin. Actually visualize this—see it happen in order to get a strong first impression. Next, picture yourself opening your oven and dozens of lemons and oranges fall out, or perhaps you turn on the stove and instead of flame, orange juice squirts out. Remember, the wilder your visualization the more easily you will remember. Now, stop for a moment. What are the first two groups? If you remember green vegetables and citrus fruits, go on to the third group. If not, strengthen the first two. Now open the refrigerator and see it full of potatoes whose eyes are looking at you—some may even be winking at you. Wink back. Close the door. Open it again, slowly. Can you see those potatoes waiting to wink at you again? Now look at your TV set. It is made of milk cartons. Turn it on and a waterfall of milk pours out of the TV screen. It floods the floor; you are up to your ankles in it. Now stop. Go back. What are the first four groups? Strengthen your visualization of any you do not remember immediately. Use the same approach to visualize the other groups, relating each to the proper peg.

Linking

Another technique closely related to pegging is *linking*. When you link items, you associate them to each other in sequence. You can link a shopping list, or a list of chores to be done, or the ten causes of a war, or eight chemical properties of a substance, or the bones of the body, or the steps of a lab experiment, or the concepts involved in a theory of economics. You can learn to remember sophisticated concepts by linking. However, it is important for you to realize that remembering and understanding are different. You must already understand whatever it is that you need to remember. Also, you must link in a way that forces you to remember. ASOE is such a way. ASOE is an acronym that stands for action, substitution, out of proportion, and exaggeration. Let's consider each of these. (Incidentally, you should reserve the linking method for occasions when you have difficulty remembering what you need to remember. If the information is easy to retain, you don't have to apply this extra step.)

Action. When you want to link two items, give them action. Suppose you were having difficulty remembering three characteristics of gaseous particles for a chemistry course, namely that they move rapidly, expand considerably, and completely fill the area into which they are released. Imagine a gaseous particle as a racing car, running a race. It zooms ahead of the other cars, moving very rapidly to the finish line. Really visualize that happening in your mind. Follow the action, then see it at the finish line. It is proud to be the winner, so it puffs itself out with pride until it seems that it will burst. See it expanding. Now notice that next to it is another gaseous particle (racing car) that is also expanding, and another, and another. The entire racetrack is filled with expanding gaseous particles (race cars). Again, be sure that you see the action in your mind. Now look away. What was the first picture that you visualized? (The rapidly moving car.) What is the first characteristic of a gaseous particle? (It moves rapidly.) What is the next picture that you see? That is, what is happening to the gaseous particle (racing car)? (It is expanding considerably.) What is the second characteristic of a gaseous particle? (It expands considerably.) Now look at the expanding particle. Do you see the same thing happening to other gaseous particles (racing cars)? Do you see each one filling up the area? Does it remind you that the third characteristic of a gaseous particle is that it fills the area into which it is released?

Before continuing, one important point must be made. You might feel that it takes more time and energy to link items than it does to just simply say the items over and over again until they are memorized. That is not so. In rote memory, you can easily forget any item, in or out of order. When linking, all you need remember is the first picture that you visualize. This, in turn, reminds you of the second item, which then reminds you of the third item, and so on. You can learn as many as 40 items this way and not forget any of them. Rote memory will not do this for you. Informal studies done by this author have shown that with this method you can learn (more easily and more quickly, without forgetting) the sequence of blood flow for a physiology class, bones of the body for an anatomy class, economic principles of various kinds, various principles of accounting, famous psychologists and their theories, case studies for law students, and so on. It is especially easy to link ten or more items this way.

Substitution. Substitute one thing for another in order to form a strong link. When you do this, the substituted item takes the place of the original item. This often makes for a bizarre picture, but that is all right, because the more bizarre the picture, the more easily it is remembered. In the example above, racing cars were substituted for the gaseous particles.

Out of Proportion. This refers to size. Make things much bigger than they really are. If the gaseous particles were giant racing cars, the information would be more easily remembered. The important thing, again, is that you actually visualize the objects you are linking rather than just think about them.

Exaggeration. This refers to numbers. Don't just see one or two gaseous particles (racing cars). See hundreds, thousands of them. This greatly reinforces your link. Seeing the gaseous particles (racing cars) filling the racetrack strengthens your memory for this information.

How might you link a faucet and a banana? You might see them as a banana on a sink next to a faucet—a still picture. There is no ASOE in this picture, however. It would be better to visualize turning on a faucet and seeing bananas come out. They are very long bananas, and they soon fill up the sink and begin to overflow onto the floor. See hundreds of bananas. This scene has action (the movement of the bananas), substitution (bananas, rather than water, flow from the faucet), out of proportion (they are very long bananas), and exaggeration (hundreds of bananas). If you really visualize this scene, it will not be easily forgotten. It is particularly important to have a strong image at the beginning of your series of links (strong first impression).

Now look at the bananas. They are being sliced by hundreds of knives. You wonder where the knives are coming from, and you look up and see them as fruit hanging from a tree. Look at the tree. See the knives. It really is a strange tree, because its fruit is knives, and instead of leaves there are necklaces in and around the knives.

Think back to the first picture you saw. Do you remember the faucet and the bananas coming from it? What happened to the bananas? (They were being sliced by knives.) Where are the knives coming from? (Do you see the tree?) Do you see the necklaces around the knives? You have now memorized five items in order—faucet, banana, knife, tree, and necklace. You can easily and quickly learn to visualize 20 or more pictures and remember them in correct order, without an error. You can do the same with items you need to remember for your courses. Silly? Maybe. Does it work? Definitely. Linking is an effective technique for remembering what you want to remember.

CONCENTRATION

Concentration is paying attention to one thing only and eliminating thoughts of everything else. In forming a strong original impression and in associating and visualizing, you are concentrating. You are forcing attention to one thing only. This in turn forces stronger, more vivid impressions and better memories. Again, practice reading a paragraph or two, then look away to tell yourself what was said. Just knowing that you are going to do this will force you to concentrate. Also, keep your purpose in mind. Knowing what it is that you want to remember will help you to recognize it when you come to it.

Read the following paragraph for the purpose of finding out four ways in which the president may suppress security threats. Visualize what is being said. Concentrate on discovering this information only. Then, from memory, write the answer on the lines below.

The enforcement of general law and local regulations, the maintenance of public order and safety and the suppression of crime in the Republic are fundamental responsibilities centralized in the president as chief executive. Under the Constitution, he may employ one or more of the armed forces to put down rebellion, insurrection or invasion. If national security is threatened, he may declare martial law throughout the land or in any specific portion of it. When the situation seems to warrant it, he may suspend the right of habeas corpus or deport any alien he believes to be dangerous to the nation.

_____

_____

_____

_____

Did you answer the question correctly? Did visualizing help you to concentrate?

If you need to learn and remember information, do so in a place that is relatively quiet and free of distractions. Keep people away, don't be near a phone, face away from the window, turn off the TV set, don't have a picture of a loved one near. Be sure to have a goal in mind. Don't say (casually) that you are going to remember the information in the chapter. Instead, determine to remember specific information—the six characteristics, or the eight causes, or how the two theories differ. Read a short section to find the answer to a particular question; when you finish, look away, and before going on, tell yourself the answer to that question. (Refer to the PQ3R study method in Chapter 3.) Practice increasing your concentration span. One way to do this is as follows: Have someone place ten objects on a table in front of you. See how quickly you can observe and remember all of them. Time yourself. Then look away and name the objects. When you can do this reasonably quickly, add more objects. Later, things you need to remember for your classes can be substituted for objects on a table. You may have to do pegging in order to develop expertise in this exercise.

REPETITION

Overlearning will help you to remember information that is hard to recall. One way to overlearn is to repeat the information to yourself several times after you think you know it perfectly. Also, strengthen the images or associations that give you the most difficulty. If you can't remember one of the six causes of the revolution or two of the six physical properties of that chemical, just work on those. Then recall the whole thing. Then recall it again.

Use the "some, sum, some" method for verbatim memory. If you must remember a speech or a poem or a play, for example, first memorize a small segment of it (let's call it part A). Then learn the next segment (call it part B). Then repeat A and B. Then learn the third segment (part C). Then repeat A, B, and C. Then learn part D. Then repeat A, B, C, and D. Continue in this way until you have learned the entire item.

INTENTION

This one factor (and it's a psychological one) can make a big difference. Decide before you begin to study that you will remember the information that you need to remember, and then do the things (the suggestions in this chapter) that will guarantee it. However, if you decide that you never could remember well, so you won't be able to do any better now, then you really won't. Don't allow yourself to fall into this trap.

USE OF ACRONYMS

An acronym is a word formed from the first letter of each of a group of words. The acronym NOW stands for the National Organization of Women. You may have remembered the names of the five Great Lakes by thinking of the acronym HOMES (Huron, Ontario, Michigan, Erie, Superior). Acronyms are very useful and effective ways to remember information. To be most effective, you should review what the acronym stands for after about 2 hours, again after 8 hours, and then after 24 hours.

SEQUENCE OF STUDY

When you study several subjects in turn, use a sequence that will allow you to study subjects that are as different as possible after each other. Research has shown that the more alike two courses are, the more one will interfere with your memory of the other. (This is called retroactive and proactive interference.) Therefore, if you are studying, for example, for courses in medical laboratory technology, biology, and history, it would be better if you studied history second, between the other two.

The following exercises will provide practice in learning to remember. Do them carefully, applying the suggestions given in this chapter. Then try the skills on the materials you want to learn— textbooks, research materials, names of people, numbers.

CHAPTER 9 REMEMBERING WHAT YOU LEARN 183

EXERCISE 1

1. Flying from New York to California is compared with driving from New York to California in the following paragraphs. Three advantages of each are given. See if you can list them after just one reading. Concentrate. Visualize the advantages and associate them either with flying or driving.

> There is no doubt that flying from New York to California has many advantages over driving. For one, you will get there faster. Flying takes only a fraction of the time that driving does. Your trip will probably be more comfortable, especially considering the service on airplanes today. And you will arrive feeling less tired than if you drove.
> Driving on the other hand, offers opportunities and advantages that flying cannot provide. You can enjoy scenery not visible from the air and visit places that you have never been to before. If you plan your trip carefully, you can even stay longer in some places you've always wanted to see. Also, it is considerably less expensive if there are three or four people going.

Advantages of flying _____

_____

_____

Advantages of driving _____

_____

_____

2. The following excerpt from President Johnson's address to Congress after the Kennedy assassination refers to some of President Kennedy's aspirations. There are eight of them. Study them carefully. Visualize and associate similar items together. Concentrate. Then, from memory, try to list them in the space provided.

> The dream of conquering the vastness of space—the dream of partnership across the Atlantic and across the Pacific as well—the dream of a Peace Corps in less developed nations—the dream of education for all our children—the dream of jobs for all who seek them and need them—the dream of care for our elderly—the dream of an all-out attack on mental illness—and, above all, the dream of equal rights for all Americans whatever their race or color. . . .

3. Read the following paragraph to discover the various frames of reference from which the study of adolescents may be approached. Then, without looking back, list them in the space provided. To be successful, get strong first impressions by concentrating and visualizing.

> The study of adolescents may be approached from various frames of reference. One of these, the biological approach, involves defining adolescent behaviors and development in terms of biological criteria. The second, or chronological frame of reference, concerns adolescence as influenced by age. Society uses this frame of reference, for example, in determining the age of adult legal liability. A third approach, the psychological, focuses on personality, values, and individual experiences. Another popular method of characterizing the adolescent, the psychoanalytic, stresses the significance of psychosexual development. Adolescence is perceived as a time when the Oedipal feelings of early childhood are reawakened and produce psychological conflict in teenage boys and girls. From another, or sociocultural, point of view adolescence varies according to time, place, circumstance, and culture or subculture involved. In addition to these ways of perceiving youth, the historical frame of reference portrays changes in their status throughout the ages.

4. What are some of the physical and chemical properties of chlorine? Read the following paragraph to discover them. Then, without looking back, list them in the space provided. Visualize and concentrate.

> We can select a few of the physical and chemical properties of chlorine as an example. Chlorine is a yellowish-green gas with a disagreeable odor. It will not burn, but will support combustion of certain other substances. Chlorine is used as a bleaching agent, as a disinfectant for water, and in many chlorinated substances such as refrigerants and insecticides. When chlorine combines with the metal sodium, it forms a salt, sodium chloride. These properties, among others, help to characterize and identify chlorine.

_____

_____

_____

5. Try to remember the ten effects that fear of speaking in public may have on people. Then list them in the space provided. (Hint: There are two effects experienced before the speech, four at the time of the speech, and four during the speech.) Visualize and concentrate in order to have a strong first impression. Associate the items with when they happen. Acronyms can also help.

> What are the effects of this fear? Before the speech people are likely to experience an inabilty to eat or sleep; at the time of the speech people are likely to experience trembling, perspiring, shortness of breath, and increased heartbeat; and during the speech people are likely to experience excessive self-doubt, loss of contact with the audience, a jumping back and forth from point to point, and occasional lapses of memory.

_____

_____

_____

6. Read the following table to discover some of the differences between a mixture and a compound. Then write the information in the

space provided. It is important that you understand these differences in order to remember them. Associate, concentrate, and visualize.

	Mixture	*Compound*
Composition	May be composed of elements, compounds, or both in variable composition.	Composed of two or more elements in a definite fixed proportion by weight.
Separation of components	Separation may be made by simple physical or mechanical means.	Elements can be separated by chemical changes only.
Identification of components	Components do not lose their identity.	A compound does not resemble the elements from which it is formed.

Composition

    Mixture _____

    _____

    Compound _____

    _____

Separation of components

    Mixture _____

    _____

    Compound _____

    _____

Identification of components

    Mixture _____

    _____

    Compound _____

    _____

7. Below are six guidelines for getting the most out of visual aids. Study them and then, from memory, list them in the space provided. Visualizing, associating, and linking can be very helpful in doing this exercise.

> Since visual aids are very powerful types of speech amplification, you should take care to use them to your advantage. The following are some of the guidelines that will enable you to get the most out of your visual aids:
>
> 1. *Show visual aids only when you are talking about them.* It takes a very strong-willed person to avoid looking at a visual aid while it is being shown. And while people are looking at a visual aid, they will find it difficult to pay attention to the speaker's words if they are not related to that visual aid. So, when you show a visual aid, talk about it; when you have finished talking about it, put it out of sight.
>
> 2. *Conversely, you should talk about the visual aid while you are showing it.* Although a picture may be worth a thousand words, it still needs to be explained. You should tell your audience what to look for; you should explain the various parts; and you should interpret figures, symbols, and percentages.
>
> 3. *Show visual aids so that everyone in the audience can see them.* If you hold the visual aid, hold it away from your body and let everyone see it. Even when the visual aid is large enough, you may find yourself obscuring someone's view inadvertently if you are not careful in your handling of your aid. If you place your visual aid on the chalkboard or mount it on some other device, stand to one side and point with the arm nearest the visual aid. If it is necessary to roll or fold your visual aid, you will probably need to bring transparent tape to hold the aid firmly against the chalkboard so that it does not roll or wrinkle.
>
> 4. *Talk to your audience and not to your visual aid.* Even though most of the members of the audience will be looking at your visual aid while you are speaking, you should maintain eye contact with them. The eye contact will improve your delivery, and you will be able to see how your audience is reacting to your visual material.
>
> 5. *Don't overdo the use of visual aids; you can reach a point of diminishing returns with them.* If one is good, two may be better; if two are good, three may be better. Somewhere along the line, there is a point at which one more visual aid is too many. Visual aids are a form of emphasis;

but when everything is emphasized, nothing receives emphasis. If you have many places where visual aids would be appropriate, decide at which points the visual aids would be most valuable. Remember, a visual aid is not a substitute for good speechmaking.

6. *Think of all the possible hazards before you decide to pass objects around the class.* Since we are used to professors passing out materials, we sometimes become insensitive to the great hazards of such a practice. Audiences cannot resist looking at, reading, handling, and thinking about something they hold in their hands; and while they are so occupied, they are not listening to the speaker. More often than not, when you pass out materials you lose control of your audience—lessening your chances of achieving your purpose. Even when only two or three objects are passed around, the result may be disastrous. Most members of the class become absorbed in looking at the objects, looking for the objects, wondering why people are taking so long, and fearing that perhaps they will be forgotten. Anytime you pass something around, you are taking a gamble—a gamble that usually is not worth the risk.

---

8. Six items of legislation passed by the Eighty-Ninth Congress are mentioned and commented upon below. Study them, and list them from memory. Use all of the clues for remembering that are appropriate in order to do this successfully.

The following were the chief items of legislation in the first session of the Eighty-Ninth Congress.

1. *Civil rights act of 1965.* In states and counties where fewer than 50 percent of the voting-age population were registered or had voted in 1964, the law suspended all literacy, knowledge, and character tests for voters. The Attorney General was authorized to send Federal registrars into such counties to register voters in keeping with the Fifteenth Amendment's guarantee of the right to vote.

CHAPTER 9   REMEMBERING WHAT YOU LEARN   189

   2. *War on poverty*. The antipoverty program initiated in 1964 was continued by (a) greatly expanding the provisions of the Economic Opportunity Act; (b) expanding aid and construction in depressed areas, especially Appalachia; (c) authorizing grants and loans to stimulate business and employment in such areas.

   3. *Education*. For the first time, large-scale aid was given to elementary and secondary education. Parochial schools were aided, but under the supervision of public-school administrators. A feature of the system was the granting of aid to schools according to the number of needy children in a school district rather than according to the wealth of the state. Aid to higher education was continued, and undergraduates were made eligible for scholarships.

   4. *Medicare and health*. A medical care program for those 65 and over was set up under the Social Security system and was financed partly by payroll taxes and optional monthly payments by the enrollees. There was a limit to the amount and duration of aid provided, so that medicare fell far short of meeting the needs of those afflicted by long-term illness. Title 19 of the Medicare Bill gave grants to states which would provide medical benefits to indigents and handicapped of all ages; this was not under Social Security. Other legislation gave aid to medical education and research, combated water and air pollution, and contributed funds to sewage treatment.

   5. *Immigration*. The national origins quota system was repealed; however, quotas were set for each hemisphere. Relatives of Americans, refugees, and immigrants with needed skills were to be admitted freely.

   6. *Housing and urban renewal*. A Department of Housing and Urban Development was established and given Cabinet rank. The first Secretary was Robert C. Weaver; he was also the first Negro to serve in any Cabinet. Housing and urban renewal programs were extended: a rent subsidy plan to aid low-income families was passed, but no money was provided at that time.

---

9. Read the following paragraph to discover ways in which the automobile influenced the American scene. Then list them from

memory in the space provided. Use the appropriate memory clues for doing this successfully.

> By far the most significant and pervasive gift of the new technology had been the automobile; in 1929 some 5.6 million automobiles were built and 26.5 million registered. The automobile had been a powerful influence in lifting the nation out of the primary postwar depression, and within a few years it was no longer a luxury but an ordinary necessity. The car brought the farm to the town by shortening the farmer's trips. It made it possible for the worker to live many miles from his job, and at the same time it decentralized industry. Counties had been laid out so that a farmer could drive his horse to the county seat and back in a day; now the county seat was rarely more than an hour away, and local government became obsolescent and burdensomely expensive—and still is. School buses made it possible to consolidate country schools into better schools. Churches, medical services, and hospitals became more available. Trucks brought farm and garden products hundreds of miles in a single night to city markets, and express trucks accelerated interurban deliveries of freight.

_____

_____

_____

_____

_____

_____

10. Below are ten suggestions for developing physical fitness. Read them carefully and then, from memory, list them in the space provided. Visualizing and associating by linking or pegging are very helpful ways to do this.

> 1. Exercise regularly several times a week. If tennis is not played, another vigorous game should be played in addition to regular conditioning exercises.
> 2. Eat a well-balanced diet with emphasis on green vegetables and proteins. Eat at regular hours each day and do not eat between meals. Eating snacks tends to reduce the appetite with the result that the snacks may replace more vital items in the diet.

3. Do not eat immediately after strenuous exercise. Allow the body time to cool off and body functions time to return to normal.

4. Drink at least six glasses of water a day. Drinking cool liquids during and after strenuous exercise will help reduce body temperature.

5. Do not drink alcoholic beverages of any kind.

6. Shower immediately after practice or workout. Do not sit or lie around in damp clothes. Use soap and hot water to clean all parts of the body thoroughly.

7. Wear clean clothes not only for appearance, but also to help prevent skin irritations and infections.

8. Wear a sweater or jacket after playing to prevent colds or sore muscles.

9. Obtain at least 8 hours of sleep every night. Regular hours are more beneficial to the body than just a set number of hours.

10. Keep a balance in life by not overdoing any one phase of it. Take time to develop the physical, mental, social, and spiritual sides of life.

___

Before doing the exercises that follow, review the information about linking and pegging.

11. Carefully link or peg the items on the shopping list that follows. Then, from memory, write the items in the space provided, in the exact order in which they appear.

   1. milk
   2. eggs
   3. cigarettes
   4. celery
   5. canned beans
   6. ice cream
   7. bread
   8. toothpicks
   9. olives
   10. candles
   11. bacon
   12. hot dogs
   13. canned peas
   14. tomatoes
   15. canned salmon

Now don't look back. (Cover up the items if you need to.) List the 15 items in the space provided.

1. _____   6. _____   11. _____

2. _____   7. _____   12. _____

3. _____   8. _____   13. _____

4. _____   9. _____   14. _____

5. _____   10. _____   15. _____

12. Use the same directions as for exercise 11 above. The items in this exercise, however, are a list of 12 cities in the United States. Remember, they must be listed in the exact order in which they appear. (Hint: Visualize something that represents each city to you, e.g., a blackjack table for Las Vegas, and link them.)

1. Philadelphia   5. Los Angeles   9. Houston
2. New York City   6. Washington, D.C.   10. New Orleans
3. Las Vegas   7. Chicago   11. Phoenix
4. San Francisco   8. Miami   12. Salt Lake City

Now, without looking back, list them in the same order.

1. _____   5. _____   9. _____

2. _____   6. _____   10. _____

3. _____   7. _____   11. _____

4. _____   8. _____   12. _____

10

Taking Tests

This author knows some students who feel that if they really understand the content of a course they are taking, they can't help but get excellent grades in that course. Well, it really isn't so. Ordinarily, in order to receive good grades in a course you have to know the material, and equally important, you have to convince your teacher that you know the information. You do this mostly by scoring well on exams. Knowing the material is not really enough to receive a good exam grade; you also have to be test-wise. You need to acquire good techniques for taking tests. A difference of as many as two grades can be seen between two people who are equally knowledgeable about the subject matter if one is a poor test-taker and the other is a skilled test-taker.

PREPARATION FOR TESTS

How do you become a skilled test-taker? The following thoughts and suggestions may be of help to you.

Don't panic. Tests, because they result in grades which can affect a person's future, become very important and sometimes cause panic. This does not have to happen to you. View a test as a way of finding out how much you know about the subject. In order to avoid panic, you need knowledge and a feeling of confidence in your ability to answer the test questions. The best way to do this is to be prepared. Ideally, you should be studying and preparing for the test on a regular, ongoing basis from the beginning of the semester. You don't always do this, of course, but if you study effectively, and use the procedures suggested in Chapter 3 ("Studying Textbook Chapters"), you should feel confident enough not to panic. Before studying for an exam, there are several things you should keep in mind.

Try to find out what the form of the exam will be. Will it be a short-answer test or an essay test? If it is a short-answer test, will it be true–false, multiple choice, fill-in, or matching? Will you be penalized for guessing? If an essay-type test, will you have to answer all questions or will there be an option? How many questions will there be? Will questions come mostly from the textbooks, from class discussions and lectures, or from outside assigned readings? Most teachers will answer some if not all of these questions, and this information gives you clues to studying. You can also find clues to the type of questions in other places. There are classroom clues, for example. Think about what the teacher has stressed in class. Was there more concentration on going over the textbook, or was the textbook used as background and elaborated on in discussions and lectures? Does your teacher concentrate on ideas and concepts, or on people, places, or other details? There are also clues from prior exams. Where did the questions come from? Again, were questions mostly from the textbook, from lectures or class discussions, or from outside reading assignments? What kinds of questions were asked? Were they about ideas and concepts or about details?

Another important step in studying for an exam is to try to predict test questions. Think about the course, the teacher, and the content. Then write out seven to ten questions that you think might be asked. (Make sure that you know the answers to these questions, of course.)

Other than being prepared, there are other things that can help prevent panic. You should be fully rested. Going out the night before an important exam will not help you be at your best. Also, an all-night cramming session can lead to panic. Make sure that you arrive for the test on time. Arriving at the test room after the exam has begun and feeling rushed may result in your forgetting important information. Set out everything that you may need the night before—writing materials, paper, rulers.

Above all, learn how to relax. The emotional reactions of tensions and anxiety that often come with preparing for an important exam can lead to panic. Studies have shown that one way to achieve a deep feeling of relaxation is to first tense and then relax different muscle groups. A procedure for doing the tension-release sequence follows. You should do it in a quiet atmosphere, if possible.

1. Take a deep breath, tense the muscle group, and count slowly to five.
2. When you reach the count of five, exhale and relax. Feel the relaxation flow through that muscle group.

3. Practice no more than twice each day and at least one hour apart.
4. Make sure that no part of your body is touching any other and that you are not using muscles for support.

Practice the tension-release cycle in the following muscle group order:

1. Both hands and arms. Tighten fist, forearm, and biceps.
2. Forehead and top of head. Frown hard by raising eyebrows hard.
3. Jaws and cheeks. Clench your teeth and purse your lips.
4. Chin and throat. Draw corners of your mouth down hard.
5. Chest and back. Take a deep breath, tighten chest and back muscles.
6. Abdominal muscles. Take a deep breath, make abdominal muscles hard.
7. Legs and feet. Push down hard with toes, tense leg muscles. (Watch out for cramps.)
8. Concentrate on relaxing your entire body, feeling warm, relaxed, and very heavy. Allow yourself to sink deeply into chair or cushion. Notice the soothing feeling of deep relaxation.

The above procedure is a somewhat sophisticated method for reducing anxiety. A simpler, but very useful alternative might be to do the following just before a tension-producing activity, such as an important test, or a prepared talk in a speech class. Breathe deeply and imagine a very relaxing scene. You might think of a quiet, calm ocean view, or you might see a country scene with a lot of greenery and perhaps a waterfall whose peaceful sound of falling water is the only thing that breaks the stillness in the air. At any time that you become tense during the exam or speech, stop for a moment and breathe deeply and visualize that scene again. This can bring an immediate feeling of serenity and peace. Feel the tension flow out of your body. Try it now, before reading on.

Sometimes, when studying for a test, you will force yourself to remember information that you think will be asked. You don't have a good, solid grip on that information, however. You should write these ideas down as soon as you receive your test paper (perhaps on the back of the paper). You don't have to write the entire idea down, just a few key words that will act as a reminder to you.

SHORT-ANSWER (OBJECTIVE) TESTS

You should use a somewhat different approach to short-answer (objective) tests than you would to essay tests. The following suggestions apply to the short-answer test.

1. Make sure that you read and understand and carefully follow all directions. More students lose points on tests because of not following

directions than for almost any reason other than actually not knowing the answer. What kinds of directions can be confusing on a short-answer test? Read the directions below and then answer each of the questions that follow them.

A. In the space provided, mark the following statement F if false and T if true. Then, if false, cross out the word which makes it false and write the correction above it.

_____ California is on the east coast of the United States.

B. Which of the following words is opposite in meaning to the first word? Circle the letter before the correct answer.

happy: a. joyous b. incompetent c. sad d. brave

C. Which one of the following people was not a U. S. president? Circle the letter before the correct answer.

a. Franklin b. Washington c. Hoover d. Kennedy

D. Which of the following are cities named after U. S. presidents? Circle the letter before the correct answers.

a. Cleveland, Ohio
b. The state of Washington
c. Lincoln Park, Chicago
d. Madison, Wisconsin
e. Dallas, Texas

The first question, correctly answered, should look like this:

__F__ California is on the ~~east~~ *west* coast of the United States.

This type of question is sometimes called the modified T–F question. If you don't correct the false answer, you will lose credit on this question even if you know that it is false.

For the second type of direction, your teacher will include both a word having the same meaning and one having the opposite meaning. If you didn't read the directions to mark the word which is opposite in meaning, you might have marked the word which has the same meaning, thus losing points unnecessarily.

You can lose credit on the third type of direction if you don't notice that it asks for an exception, something that doesn't belong. Be aware of this type of question.

The fourth type of direction has several things for you to watch out for. Notice that it asks for more than one answer (it asks for cities, not for just one city). You must also be careful that you look for a city named after a president, not just the name of a president. Choices *a* (Cleveland, Ohio) and *d* (Madison, Wisconsin) are the correct answers here. Choice *b* is a state named after a U. S. president, not a city. Choice c is a park. Choice e, of course, doesn't even mention the name of a U. S. president.

When answering a matching-type question, read the directions to discover if a choice can be used more than once. If the directions give no clue, ask the exam proctor.

There is one direction which you should not necessarily always follow. Sometimes the directions will tell you that you will be penalized for guessing and that you should not guess. What should you do about this direction? How does the test-maker know when you are guessing? Actually, the grading of these questions is based on statistical probability. For true–false questions, you have an even chance to guess correctly. For multiple choice questions with four choices, your chances are one out of four, and with five choices, one out of five. This means that if you guess at all the questions on a true–false test, you would probably get half of them right (50%), even if you didn't know the answer to any of them. If you could do that with the questions on an exam whose answers you didn't know, and added that to the questions whose answers you did know, you would receive a score much higher than you really deserved. That's the reason for the penalty for guessing. On a true–false test, the scoring is minus two points for each wrong answer, one point for each correct answer, and no points for questions left unanswered. A simple way to calculate the score is to total the right and subtract the wrong. The reason is that you have a 50–50 chance of guessing the answer to any question correctly. This means that if you guessed at 20 questions, chances are that you would guess 10 answers correctly and 10 answers incorrectly. If you subtract the number of wrong answers (10) from the number of correct answers (10), your guesses would be canceled out. You would receive credit only for the answers you knew. The same reasoning is used for multiple choice questions—the scoring is adjusted for the number of choices given.

There is a flaw in this reasoning, however, which you can use to your advantage. The above reasoning assumes that you know absolutely nothing about the questions that you guess at—that the test might as well be written in a foreign language. In reality, however, you often have some inkling as to the correct answer. In multiple choice questions you can often eliminate at least one of the choices as being incorrect. This puts the odds in your favor. How should you, as a test-wise student, deal with this kind of test scoring? If you have any idea, even a remote idea as to the correct answer on a true–false question, or if you can eliminate at least one choice of a multiple choice question, then you should guess. The odds are in favor of your guessing. If you have absolutely no idea as to the correct answer, then do not guess. Incidentally, if there are no directions about being penalized for guessing, you should assume that there will be no penalty. In that case, of course, you should guess at answers to questions you are not sure of.

2. Read the entire exam first, answering easy questions that take no extra time as you go along. There are several advantages to doing this. First, in case you run out of time, you are sure to receive credit for the questions that you know the answers to. You should not assume that the easier questions are those that you see first. You may know the answers to the last 10 questions of a 100-question true–false test. However, you may spend so much time thinking about some of the earlier questions that time will run out before you get to the last 10 questions. You lose 10 points (a full grade) unnecessarily. Second, later questions may provide a clue to remembering prior questions. Often, seeing a question sets off a chain of associations that reminds you of the answer to an earlier question. If you tried to answer each question in turn, without reading all questions first, you would be spending time unnecessarily and may not have time to finish the exam. Third, reading all questions first allows time for "blocked" information to appear. Your mind is really quite remarkable in this respect. As soon as your mind sees a question, it starts working on it. It continues to work on it while you are working on other questions. You save time this way. If you have ever tried to remember something but you just can't—it's on the tip of your tongue—even though you stop trying, you still think. Four hours later, when you are occupied with something totally different, you remember what you had been trying to think of. If you have experienced this phenomenon, you can see the advantage of reading all the questions first.

3. When you finish the exam, reread it if you have time. Don't change any answers, however, unless you are absolutely sure that you have made a mistake. Most of the time, if you are not sure, your first answer will be the correct one. However, do look over the paper for silly errors. Sometimes you may have skipped a line when answering a question. This could put all answers below that on the wrong line. Catching this error when you review the test allows you to correct it.

4. On true–false tests watch out for key words that allow or don't allow for exceptions. Words such as *all*, *always*, and *never* do not allow for any exceptions. Statements using these words are suspect, and the answers are likely to be (but not always) false. Words that allow for exceptions such as *some*, *sometimes*, and *often* represent a more common life situation and are more likely to be true. There aren't too many things for which there are no exceptions.

5. In true–false statements, if any part of a statement is false, it is all false. Read the following three statements. Then mark T or F in the space provided to indicate whether each is true or false.

_____ Monday always follows Sunday except during the last Monday in February during a leap year.

_____ Kangaroos hop, birds fly, mice have tails, and snakes have feathers.

_____ Some good places to study are in the library, in a quiet room at home, and in the stands during a football game.

Notice how most of each of the above statements is true, but one part of it is enough to make the statement false.

6. For multiple choice questions try to predict the correct answer before looking at the choices, then look for that answer. This forces you to concentrate on the question and to find the correct answer more quickly. Also, when looking at the choices, eliminate those which are obviously incorrect. It is very difficult to make up an exam with every choice for every question being reasonable and appropriate. Your knowledge of the subject should make it clear that perhaps one of the four or five choices is incorrect.

7. In multiple choice, you should choose the best choice from among those given. The most correct answer may not be among the choices. An example of that can be seen in the following question.

A well-known animal native to Australia is the

    a. zebra

    b. platypus

    c. polar bear

    d. elephant

You would probably agree that the most well-known animal common to Australia is the kangaroo. However, kangaroo is not a choice. Choice b, platypus, is an animal native to Australia. It is the only possible correct answer, even if it is not the most desirable one.

8. In multiple choice, make sure that the answer is related to the question. A true statement by itself isn't necessarily the correct answer to the question being asked. Circle the letter before the correct answer to the following question.

Which of the following statements gives a purpose for fighting the Civil War?

    a. The Battle of Gettysburg was a turning point in the war.

    b. The southern states had seceded.

    c. Lincoln wanted to be a great general.

    d. General Grant was later to become president of the United States.

Even though choices a, b, and d are true statements (choice c could be true, but there is no evidence of that), only choice b (The southern states had seceded) is listed by historians as a purpose for fighting the war. These kinds of choices often appear in multiple choice questions. Be careful not to be trapped by them.

9. In multiple choice, be aware of grammatical or other language clues among the choices. Answer the following questions by putting a circle around the letter before the correct answer.

One of the heaviest members of the animal world is an

    a. hippopotamus
    b. elephant
    c. rhinoceros
    d. black bear

Each of the animals is heavy, but the use of the word *an* tells you that the author is looking for a word whose first sound is a vowel sound. Only choice *b*, elephant, can be the correct answer. Now try to answer this question.

Which bodies of water provide an ideal means of transporting freight in the United States? Circle the letter before the correct answer.

    a. the Mississippi River
    b. the Gulf of Mexico
    c. the Great Lakes
    d. the Ohio River

Did you notice that the question asks for more than one body of water? Did you notice also that among the choices only choice *c*, the Great Lakes, represents more than one body of water? Choice *c*, then, has to be the correct answer. Teachers often provide these clues when they construct tests. They may not mean to, but when writing many questions, a clue of this sort can slip by without being noticed.

10. In matching questions, don't assume that an answer can be used only once unless the directions say so. If you are not sure, you should ask about it.

11. Write the answer that you think your teacher expects, even if you don't fully agree and even if you think you can convince your teacher that your answer is better. The test is no place to challenge your teacher.

12. Sometimes you can recognize certain ways of writing questions that your teacher uses (and probably doesn't even realize). For example, a correct answer might almost always be longer or more detailed or more specific. In multiple choice questions, choice *a* might almost never be the correct response. In matching questions, the correct match may always be as far away as possible. Whenever you recognize these test-making strategies, keep them in mind when you answer the questions.

ESSAY (SUBJECTIVE) TESTS

Following are suggestions for taking essay-type tests. Although some of these suggestions are the same as for short-answer tests, their particular applications are to essay questions.

1. Try to create a balance between the time you take on a particular question, your ability to answer the question, and the relative weight that the question has. If a question counts 20 or 25 points, you should spend more time on it than you would on a 10-point question. Of course, how well you can answer the question is also a factor. If you can write a superb answer in less time than it takes to answer a 10-point question which you know little about, do so. Don't spend excessive time just because the answer is heavily weighted; however, consider its relative weight and give it appropriate time. A good procedure is to answer the questions that are easy for you regardless of weight, because doing so will probably take you less time than its point allowance might suggest. Then answer those questions which pay more in points. The main idea is that you should not spend so much time on the "cheap" questions that you don't have enough time for the more important "expensive" ones.

2. Follow directions carefully. For example, in an essay exam, you may have five questions given, but you only have to answer four of the five. If you didn't know that because you didn't read the directions, and you answered all five questions, you are at a disadvantage. First, you divided the time that you spent into five answers instead of four, and so you didn't have as much time for each question as you could have. Second, you might have been able to answer four questions well, but not five. When the directions are to answer four questions out of five and you answer all five (one inadequately), what does an instructor do? Does he take the best four answers and ignore the fifth? Unfortunately, no. Most instructors grade the first four questions and ignore the fifth answer. But your last answer may have been the best one, so you will lose points unnecessarily.

What are some of the kinds of directions that may be asked on essay exams? Following are examples of some of the most common, with explanations of their meaning and (in some cases) strategies for answering them.

a. *Compare.* The direction "compare" asks you to show how things are alike. If you were asked to compare two chemical elements, for example, you should show how they are similar. You would probably stress similar physical and chemical properties.

b. *Contrast.* When you contrast things, you show how they are different. If you were asked to contrast two chemical elements, you would probably show differences in physical and chemical properties.

c. *Name or enumerate.* This direction asks you to list items that are asked for, but not to go into detail. Going into detail in this instance would not improve your grade, and could hurt it.

d. *Explain.* When you are asked to explain, you should give reasons for something or make it clear in some other way. You should answer the questions "why" and "how" whenever it is appropriate to do so. If you were asked to explain the theory behind the combustion engine, you should tell how the engine works and why it responds as it does.

e. *Define.* In order to get the most credit for a definition you should do two things. You should name the general class to which the item that you are defining belongs, and you should show how it is different from other members of that class. If you had to define an *allen wrench* for a class that was studying these items, you would say that an allen wrench is a tool, or even a type of wrench (general class), and then show how it is different from other tools, or wrenches. In another class you might define *love* as an emotion (general class), and then show how it is different from other emotions (hate, anger, jealousy).

f. *Discuss.* This is a most difficult direction to follow unless you know your subject well. You must explain different aspects of the question. You should comment on the pros and cons, on kinds of causes or effects or qualities. Try to include examples when you discuss an item.

g. *Defend.* When you defend a position, you give specific evidence showing why that position is correct. You show the advantages or the strengths of that position and ignore or attach less importance to the disadvantages or weaknesses.

3. Always read all questions. Organize your answer in your mind first in order to avoid overlapping. (It's even a good idea to outline it briefly on scrap paper, if possible.)

4. Answer easier questions first (that is, questions that you can answer easily). There are at least two reasons for doing this. First, it allows time for blocked information to appear. Having read all the questions, your mind works on the answers to the tougher questions while you are answering the easier questions. Second, if time runs out, you will have completed your best answers, for which you will probably earn the most credit. You will probably answer more questions, because you don't need to spend as much time on them as you do if you aren't as sure of the answers.

5. If you have time, when you finish the exam, look over the paper carefully. Don't change answers unless you are sure that you have made an error. However, check for the following items.

a. Did you follow directions? Sometimes in reading the paper after you have finished the test, you may discover that you misread a direction.
b. Did you omit a question or part of a question? Sometimes a question has several parts, and you are so concerned about answering parts A and B that you completely forget about C. (Maybe that's why you finished so early.)
c. Did you say something that you didn't mean to say or that isn't clear? Sometimes you will discover in reading your paper that in the enthusiasm of writing your answer, it didn't really come out on paper the way you meant it to, or it isn't quite as clear as you thought it was.
d. Did you make any gross English errors? Poor English or faulty punctuation prevents an exam paper from being clearly understood.

Also, when looking over your paper, pretend that you are the teacher. Looking at it from that point of view, can you do anything differently in order to earn more points?

6. Always leave space after each answer in case you need to make changes or in case you want to add information. Be sure to answer only what is asked for. Do not volunteer additional information. If it is correct, it won't earn you more points, and if it's incorrect, you could lose points. In either case you have used up time which you may need for other answers.

7. If it is at all possible, write something for each question. Even partial credit is better than none. When you write an answer, begin with the key, basic information. Then fill in the supporting details. This permits your instructor to see your best answer first—a psychological advantage for you. Also, in case time runs out, you have already written what will earn more points for that question than you could if you answered it any other way.

8. Be sure that you write clearly and neatly. Try not to cross out too much. Be legible. Try not to spell words incorrectly. All this makes for a good effect, which is greatly to your advantage.

9. Sometimes, no matter how well you plan, you don't have enough time to answer a question or two. A note to your instructor saying this, with a brief statement of what you would have written, can earn you some points. You might say something like, "I didn't have time to answer this question. If I did, I would have discussed how the laws taking away freedom and the soaring inflation rate were factors in the revolution. I also would have discussed. . . ." Even if this earns very few points, it can help.

Following the suggestions in this chapter should help make you test-wise, and this should result in better grades. So that you can practice doing this before the real test comes around, do the exercises on the following pages. Be careful though. Some of them are purposely tricky.

EXERCISE 1

Answer the following questions by marking F if the statement is true and T if the statement is false. Mark your answer on the line following each statement.

_____ 1. The American flag has fifty stripes. _____
_____ 2. The following vehicles are used in land transportation: automobile, bus, train, airplane, taxicab. _____
_____ 3. Florida is a state in the southeast portion of the United States. _____
_____ 4. All doctors are wealthier than all grocery clerks. _____
_____ 5. A concert pianist will never make an error during a concert. _____
_____ 6. Summers are usually warmer than winters. _____
_____ 7. A violin is a musical instrument. _____
_____ 8. A sick person must call a physician if he is to get well. _____
_____ 9. A wealthy person is always happier than a poor person. _____
_____ 10. Health insurance always saves money for the person who has it. _____
_____ 11. In order to vote in most states, you must register in advance, you must study the issues carefully, and you must either cast your ballot at the voting booth on election day or file an absentee ballot. _____
_____ 12. All auto mechanics are experts in the repair of all kinds of automobiles. _____
_____ 13. In Florida or California, during the summer, the temperature usually goes above 60F. _____
_____ 14. Most people enjoy singing at one time or another. _____
_____ 15. Happiness, anger, jealousy, sleep, and love are examples of emotions. _____
_____ 16. In the same year, February follows January, March follows April, August follows July, and December is the last month. _____
_____ 17. The victim of a fatal heart attack will never recover sufficiently enough to return to his job. _____
_____ 18. It is never unwise to study for an exam. _____
_____ 19. It is usually not a good idea for a pedestrian to avoid crossing the street when cars are approaching at full speed. _____
_____ 20. A woman cannot have a happy marriage if she isn't good-looking unless her husband is wealthy. _____

EXERCISE 2

Do the following number problems. Mark 3 if the answer is 5; 5 if the answer is 7; 6 if the answer is 9; 8 if the answer 6; and 4 if the answer is not 5, 7, 9, or 6.

1. 4 plus 2 equals _____ .
2. 5 plus 6 minus 4 equals _____ .
3. 2 plus 8 plus 4 minus 2 equals _____ .
4. How much does 3 plus 2 equal? _____ .
5. 14 plus 6 divided by 4 equals _____ .
6. How old are you? _____ .
7. Today is what day of the month? It is the _____ of the month.
8. New Year's Day is on January _____ .
9. Christmas Day is December _____ .
10. In _____ years, we will reach the year 2000.

EXERCISE 3

1. In the space below, name the last four presidents of the United States, in alphabetical order. Then, after each name, tell the years in which he served.

   _____

   _____

   _____

   _____

2. In the space below, list each of the following occupations in the order of how much money you think is earned by an average person in that job, with the person earning the most money listed first. Then make another list according to how dangerous to life you think that occupation is, with the most dangerous listed first. Then, in the first list, place a 6 in front of the job you would most like to have and a 1 in front of the job you would least like to have. Place the numbers 1–6 after the occupations in the second column, then list them again in alphabetical order.

   Doctor, waiter, janitor, actress, engineer, dishwasher.

   _____   _____   _____

   _____   _____   _____

   _____   _____   _____

   _____   _____   _____

   _____   _____   _____

   _____   _____   _____

3. Define the following three terms according to the suggestions given on p. 202.

   orange _____

   _____

   _____

   chemistry _____

   _____

   _____

cow _____
_____
_____

4. For each of the following statements, circle the letter before the correct answer.

Which of the following is the author's favorite west coast city?
   a. Portland, Oregon
   b. Las Vegas, Nevada
   c. San Francisco, California
   d. Phoenix, Arizona

A fruit that contains a lot of iron is an
   a. cherry
   b. apple
   c. banana
   d. grapefruit

Which of the following statements is true?
   a. Some of the courses that you might find in a college home economics department are Sewing, Food preparation, How to shop wisely, and Animal husbandry.
   b. Some outdoor recreational activities are swimming, boating, football, and going on picnics.
   c. Some measurements of volume are ounces, bushels, feet, pints, and quarts.
   d. Some famous American people are Ben Franklin, Helen Keller, Henry Ford, Sigmund Freud, Elizabeth Taylor, and George Washington.

Answer Key

The answers given herein are suggested answers only. They are not meant to be exclusive or final. Although they represent the best judgement of the author, it is recommended that teachers accept any answer that is adequately supported by the student.

CHAPTER 1 IMPROVING VOCABULARY

Exercise 1 (p. 13)

1. lured, tempted
2. bitter
3. exausted
4. high blood pressure
5. symptoms that may precede the development of disease
6. hydrates—solids that contain water as part of their crystalline structure. anhydrous—without water
7. pimples
8. white fatty coating
9. giant
10. famous, well known
11. daily
12. lie, tell a falsehood
13. diminished, soothed
14. soft, flabby, limp
15. pretty, attractive, beautiful
16. surname, last name
17. avoided, shunned
18. lessening, decreasing
19. contorted—twisted, bent
20. exculpated—exonerated, cleared of blame

Exercise 2 (p. 17)

1. *bindum*—name
2. *gulded*—dived, jumped
3. *subtuk*—vote
4. *insul*—dress
5. *remdock*—instructor, test giver
   simburn—answers
   tookle—grade
6. *pernioffing*—reducing
   crawlit—deflation
7. *gondek*—determination
   borcron—hard work
8. *lister*—carbon
   beldum—use, asset
9. *korded*—stored
   rejnill—memory
10. *boralis*—lemonwood
    sapsog—hickory
    colit—bow

Exercise 3 (p. 19)

1. c	3. a	5. d	7. a	9. b
2. a	4. b	6. c	8. a	10. d

Exercise 4 (p. 21)

1. b
2. c
3. c
4. a
5. d, b, a
6. a, d
7. b
8. c
9. 4, 3, 9, 7
10. 10, 4, 8, 3

CHAPTER 2 LEARNING TO OUTLINE

Exercise 1 (p. 35)

1. refer to text
2. colors
3. games
4. types of fabric
5. cosmetics
6. animals used as pets
7. wild animals
8. cities
9. U.S. cities
10. parts of the face
11. parts of the body (visible)
12. parts of the body (not visible)
13. (athletic) games
14. (athletic) games using a ball
15. male relatives
16. branches of science
17. performers (on a stage)
18. allied health occupations
19. professions
20. office supplies

Exercise 2 (p. 37)

1. refer to text
2. United States presidents
    Washington
    Lincoln
    Roosevelt
   United States rivers
    Mississippi
    Colorado
   United States mountains
    Rockies
    Alleghenies
3. European countries
    Germany
    Sweden
    France
      Type of government
      Important cities
        Paris
        Marseilles
   Asian countries
4. Federal government
    Congress
      House of Representatives
      Senate
     Supreme Court
   State government
   City government
     Police department
     Fire department
5. Counseling services
     Curriculum advisement
     Scholarships and grants
     Occupational
       Job information
       Job interviews
   Library services
     Reference guides
     Interlibrary loans
     Exhibits
   Checkout materials
     Fiction
     Nonfiction
     Recordings

Exercise 3 (p. 39)

1. refer to text
2. *Heart Disease*
   I. Preventing heart disease
      A. Cigarettes
      B. Diet
         1. Cholesterol
         2. Weight Control
      C. Exercise
   II. Treating heart disease
      A. Drugs
      B. Surgery
3. *Communicating Effectively*
   I. Effective speaking
      A. Eye contact
      B. Enthusiasm
      C. Voice
         1. Pitch
         2. Volume
         3. Tone
   II. Effective writing
      A. Mechanics
         1. Spelling
         2. Punctuation
      B. Grammar
         1. Nouns
         2. Verb form
            a. Irregular form
            b. Subjunctive form
4. I. Types of R. N.s
      A. Baccalaureate nurse
      B. Diploma nurse
      C. Associate degree nurse
   II. Career opportunities
5. Types of Mechanical Aids
   I. Slides
      A. Definition
      B. Use
   II. Opaque projections
      A. Definition
      B. Use
   III. Overhead projections
      A. Definition
      B. Use

Exercise 4 (p. 43)

1. refer to text
2. I. Types of insurance
      A. Automobile insurance
         1. Collision
         2. Fire and theft
         3. Bodily injury
      B. Health insurance
      C. Homeowner's insurance
      D. Life insurance
         1. Term life
         2. Limited payment life
         3. Endowment life
   II. Costs of insurance
      A. Individual costs
      B. Group plans
3. Frames of Reference for Studying Adolescents
   I. Biological frame of reference
   II. Chronological frame of reference
   III. Psychological frame of reference
   IV. Psychoanalytic frame of reference
   V. Sociocultural frame of reference
4. Specialties Within Psychology
   I. Clinical psychology
      A. Psychotherapy
      B. Testing
      C. Research
   II. Social psychology
      A. Social behaviors
      B. Communication
   III. Physiological psychology
   IV. Developmental psychology
   V. Industrial psychology
      A. Machine design
      B. Worker morale
      C. Training programs
      D. Marketing and advertising

ANSWER KEY

Exercise 4 (p. 43) (cont.)
5. Legislation of the Eighty-Ninth Congress
   I. Civil Rights Act of 1965
      A. Special rules in low voting states
      B. Federal registrars to register voters
   II. War on poverty
      A. Expanded Economic Opportunity Act
      B. Expanded aid in depressed areas
      C. Authorized grants and loans
   III. Education
      A. Aid to elementary, secondary, and parochial schools
      B. Aid to needy children
      C. Aid to higher education
   IV. Medicare and health
      A. Program for those on social security
         1. Financing
         2. Limits
      B. Program for those not on social security
      C. Other aid
   V. Immigration
      A. Quotas changed
      B. Skilled people admitted freely
   VI. Housing and urban renewal
      A. Cabinet rank established
      B. Programs extended
6. Junior College Programs
   I. The transfer program
      A. Costs
         1. Tuition
         2. Living expenses
      B. Size
   II. The technical-vocational program
      A. Type of training
      B. People serviced
   III. The adult–continuing education program
      A. Types of programs
      B. People serviced

Exercise 5 (p. 49)
1. Teacher judgment
2. Teacher judgment
3. Teacher judgment

CHAPTER 3 STUDYING TEXTBOOK CHAPTERS

1–6 Teacher judgment

CHAPTER 4 LEARNING TO TAKE NOTES

Exercise 1 (p. 81)

1. refer to text
2. Keeping Financial Records
   1. The journal
      — Def: record of daily activity
      — Show
      A. Date of transaction
      B. Description of transaction
      C. Amount of money involved
      D. What is affected by transaction *re D: such things as assets, liabilities capital, type of income or expense*

ANSWER KEY 215

2. The ledger
   — All journal info. goes into it
   — SomeX's* income/expense go to profit/loss statement and only the profit or loss is posted in ledger
   — Bznses use as many accts as needed for operation
3. Vitamin A
   A. Made in body from carotenes
   B. Deficiencies result in stunted growth
      night blindness
      diseased skin and membrane
      Xerophtalmia (causes blindness)
   C. Needed for *rhodopsin* which is needed for night vision
      — needed to maintain *adrenal cortex* which controls use of protein for energy
   D. Stored in liver—too much can be toxic (hypervitaminosis syndrome)
      — adult rec. allowance—5000 I.U.
   E. *Sources*
      liver, butterfat, egg yolk, green/yellow vegs
   F. Affected by how foods are prepared. Mineral oil interferes with vit A absorption
4. *Jobs Cards and Resumes*
   A. Job card
      — use when filling out applic. on spot
      — should contain
      1. Soc. Sec #
      2. School info.
      3. prior job info. *beg. and ending dates, salaries*
      4. name/address of former supervisors
      5. armed service info.
      6. info. re references
      7. other pertinent info.
   B. References
      — Don't use relatives, friends
      — Inform references—get OK
      — If open letter of refer. is available carry it with you
   C. Resume
      — really expanded job card
      — give original copy (typed, is preferred)
      — enclose when sending letter also take copy to interview
      — shows how well you org. info.
5. *Different kinds of language*
   A. To bring about human contact
      — purpose—to show real self
        to make closer human contact
      — not the same as speaking fluently and/or elegantly

---

*abbreviation for *sometimes*

- B. Commercial speech
  - — the language of wheeling & dealing
  - — it deals with people as objects rather than humans
  - — it is cold, practical language
- C. Cliché talk
  - — superficial, talk to fill time
    doesn't really make for human interaction, just words
- D. Speech as a weapon
  - — hurts human contact
    i.e. married people having argument
- E. Nonverbal communication
  when people talk there is verbal-nonverbal commun.
- F. nonverbal *Sometimes a "no" is really a "yes."*
  - — tone, inflection, other voice charact.
  - — body language via eyes, stance, facial expression

6. Appeal to Authority
   A. Improper appeals to authority
      - — An expert in one field is not necessarily an expert in another field i.e. athletes who endorse razor blades
      - — Accepting an opinion of an expert when the experts disagree
      - — When experts disagree, ask for reasons and arguments for their opinions
      - — If all else fails, check the record of the expert.

7. Checking a Bank Statement
   A. Steps to be taken
      - — Put cancelled checks in numerical order
      - — Compare bank statement/checkbook deposits (list deposits not in BS* in 1st sect. of recon)
      - — check off cancel. cks. from prior month list cks. still outstanding in 1st sect. of recon
      - — Ck off cancelled cks listed on BS, list any outstanding cks.
      - — if errors are found, note them in 2d sect. of recon.
      - — list service chges or adjustments in 2d sect. of recon.
      - — do addit. & subt. from recon.—checkbook & BS should match
   B. Bank errors
      - — Someone else's ck. or deposit posted to your acct.
      - — Your dep. or ck. posted to someone else's acct.
      - — Dep. or ck. posted in wrong am't
      - — balance incorrectly brought forward
      - — bank math errors
   C. Report bank errors immediately see that error is corrected in next BS

8. History Textbooks
   A. They indoctrinate
      - — which "facts" are selected
      - — books appear objective, but history is basically controversial
      - — books play down bad things & highlight good things
      - — minority contrib. are mostly ignored

*abbrev. for bank statement

B. This creates bias in us as adults . . we aren't prepared to face today's problems & challenges
   C. Hist. books leave out the contrib. of many important people.
9. Status and Roles
   A. Def: status—a position in society or in a group   *i.e., teachers, policemen, father, football player*
      — we can have several positions at the same time
   B. Def: Role—the behavior of one who occupies a particular status—what person does in the status
   C. Norms surround each status and each role (called role requirements)   *i.e., student expects to behave in certain ways—same for teacher, father, or policeman.*
   D. Within role requirements there can be variation in behavior i.e. teacher can be tough or easy
   E. Def: achieved status —an earned status—i.e. policeman, teacher
   F. Def: Ascribed status—automatic status—we have no choice—i.e. your sex, race, or nationality.

Exercise 2 (p. 101)

1. refer to text

2. How archery was discovered can only be conjectured. Possibly a man idly experimenting with a tree branch that had a piece of vine, gut, or rawhide attached to it discovered that it could cast a light stick of wood farther than he could throw a heavier spear. As the idea developed, better pieces of wood were found for bows, and feathers or leaves were added to the sticks to guide them better in flight. The idea of adding sharp stones to the ends of the arrows was probably the next stage of development. Once the bow was perfected, it became man's most important weapon. We can imagine his feeling of relief when he no longer had to flee the beasts or to fight in close combat with clubs or spears or when he could take game at greater distances than previously.

Dev. of bow and arrow
1. accidental discovery
2. better materials were found
3. sharp stones were added to end of arrow

   The bow is thought to have been known to all Eastern Hemisphere tribes except the aboriginal Australians. The Israelites, Babylonians, Mongolians, Assyrians, Chinese, and Japanese all favored the bow and arrow. The Egyptians used bows and arrows in overthrowing the Persians and then successfully waged war on many other countries. The success of the bow and arrow as a weapon of war spread rapidly, and many nations gave up their chief weapons— slings and javelins—for this more efficient device.

"C" bow was efficient

   The Greeks and Turks are credited with originating composite bows made of wood, horn, and sinew and shaped like a "C" when unstrung. These composite bows were extremely efficient. Interestingly, many of our modern bows tend to resemble them. An ancient Turkish bow is said to have shot an arrow more than 800 yards. This record flight was unsurpassed until Danny LaMore won the National Flight Championship at Lancaster, Pennsylvania, on August 17, 1959, with a free-style flight (bow held by the feet and pulled with both hands) of 937.17 yards and a regular flight (hand-held) of 850.67 yards. At the same meet Norma Beaver set a women's national record of 578.7 yards.

bow used in wars until 1860

The bow was the chief weapon of warfare for centuries—until the battle of the Spanish Armada in 1588. For that battle, the English had experimentally equipped ten thousand troops with firearms, with outstanding success. The bow soon became a secondary weapon, and after the last big battle was fought with bows and arrows by the Chinese at Taku in 1860, it became obsolete as a weapon of war. However, some tribes in Africa and South America still use bows and arrows in warfare (as is evidenced by small, slow-flying planes that become "pincushions" over certain jungle areas) and also depend on them as their chief means of taking game and fish.

used as sport in England

After the decline of the bow as a weapon, archery was forgotten until countries such as England saw its merit as a sport. King Henry VIII was an enthusiastic archer and an ardent bettor who staged large matches and invited wide participation. With the help of this kingly interest, archery became very popular in England, and proficiency in the use of the longbow was common.

Archery known to American Indians then replaced by firearms

Archery was known to the Indians of America when the Pilgrims arrived. The Indians soon gave up their bows and arrows for the more efficient firearms, and so history repeated itself. Archery began as an American sport in 1828 when a group of archers formed the United Bowmen of Philadelphia—which still exists. In 1879, the National Archery Association was founded and yearly national tournaments were begun, the first being held in Chicago.

Archery as a popular sport

For more than 100 years, target-archery competition prevailed in America. In 1934, when the NAA held its tournament in Los Angeles, a group of archers interested mainly in bow hunting began agitating for a new kind of game that was suited for off-hand shooting, which was more usable for hunting. Six years later, in 1940, the National Field Archery Association was organized. For ten years competition was restricted to bare-bow shooting, or the use of a single-pin sight. Today, the values of the two main styles of shooting are recognized and tournaments are conducted in two divisions, free style and instinctive.

ANSWER KEY 219

The future of the sport looks bright. Archery tackle sales are among the highest of all sporting goods and still rising. People of all ages are taking up the sport. There were 1.7 million bow twangers in 1946, according to the National Recreation Association; in 1960 they numbered more than 4.7 million—up 176 percent and the trend is still upward. The greatest increase can be seen in the large numbers of newly licensed bow hunters each year. From 1950 to 1966, the number of licensed archery deer hunters in Michigan alone jumped from a few thousand to over forty thousand. Practically every state has special bow seasons which commonly precede the regular deer seasons and usually last much longer. In Michigan, for example, the bow season is five weeks long, while the regular deer season is only fifteen days. Because archery has many merits, it is probable that people of all ages will continue to enjoy it in the years ahead.

Since its inception, the Outdoor Education Project of the American Association for Health, Physical Education, and Recreation has done much to promote archery, primarily in schools and colleges. The numerous workshops conducted throughout the country have enabled thousands to receive training under expert instructors. This effort is expected to continue.

[margin note: Sales up — continuous interest in archery as a sport]

3. Aptitude Tests

Entrance examinations taken for acceptance into college are a kind of intelligence test, usually divided into several areas. In order to be accepted in many universities you must achieve stated minimum scores on individual tests or an accepted combination of scores. Girls generally make higher scores on verbal tests and lower scores on mathematical or quantitative tests.

[margin note: used as college entrance exams]

A standard entrance test for many colleges and universities is the *Scholastic Aptitude Test* (SAT), which is a three-hour objective test designed to measure your verbal and mathematical skills. It is offered by the College Entrance Examination Board, a nonprofit membership organization that provides tests and other educational services for schools and colleges. The College Board also offers achievement tests in various subjects which you may take the same day as the SAT if the college you plan to attend requires it.

[margin note: SAT — 3 hr. test — measures verbal/math skills]

Another test that many colleges use for their entrance examination is the *American College Test* (ACT) which gives scores in four areas (English, mathematics, social science, and natural science) followed by a composite

[margin note: ACT measures Engl., math, Soc. Sci., Natural Science]

score. Some colleges, particularly public junior colleges, do not require a minimum score in order to be accepted, but use the scores to supplement high school grades for placement in various courses.

Another entrance test, the *School and College Aptitude Test* (SCAT), is divided into two areas (verbal and quantitative) with a total which is not an average of the two.

The purpose of all these aptitude tests is to determine the ability of a person to succeed in academic work, and in this sense, the tests reveal the intellectual ability of the person taking the test. However, since the questions are related to particular bodies of knowledge, the tests also measure achievement. An individual who has had little or no familiarity with the information being tested will not do well and still may be intelligent.

Intelligence Tests

An intelligence test refers to the intelligence quotient (IQ) or "ability" of the person taking the test. When comparing aptitude tests and IQ tests, it is important to realize that the aptitude test gives scores in different kinds of mental ability, that is, English and mathematics; an IQ test reports mental perception with only one score. That score can then be compared with the average scores made by thousands of others.

The *Otis Quick Scoring Mental Ability Test* and the *Henmon-Nelson Tests of Mental Ability* give the test taker a rough estimate of his IQ. A more nearly valid test of an individual's IQ can be obtained when a test is administered individually by a skilled tester.

One problem with all aptitude and intelligence tests is that the individuals taking them must have come from homes with similar cultural and linguistic backgrounds. If they have not, the scores are not valid. Schools and test centers have gradually become aware that there are other ways to measure intelligence than through a measure of verbal skills, because intelligence may be defined as the capacity to profit by experience or as the ability to solve problems.

4. Everyone likes a good listener, but not everyone likes to listen. Often we have our own ideas, and we would prefer that others listen to us. However, approximately one-third of career communication is now oral, and new devices such as televised telephones and conference telephone systems will make listening even more important.

Employers often complain that their employees, especially their new employees, make mistakes because they do not listen carefully enough. There is some truth in their complaint, but listening is not the employees' responsibility alone. It is just as important for employers and managers to be good listeners. In fact, listening may be used to define power: the president of an organization is the most powerful person in it because he has more sources for listening than anyone else. *(Importance of listening)*

Anyone who wants to learn to listen more effectively should first realize that he can never completely understand what another person says. Understanding is always imperfect because the backgrounds of the speaker and listener are never identical, and therefore no word means exactly the same thing to both. As a result, the listener always over- or under-reacts to the message. However, if he learns about the factors that influence listening, a person can understand the message more completely and recall its details more exactly.

Factors that influence listening include the clarity of the message, the importance of the message to both speaker and listener, the listener's preparation for receiving the message, and the physical conditions under which listening takes place. Many things, then, can go wrong in the listening experience. A good listener must eliminate as many of the possibilities for error as he can—before, during, and after listening. *(factors that influence listening)*

Blocking

Inaccurate listening usually occurs because the listener has composed a message of his own that competes in his brain with the speaker's message. The result of this competition may be total blocking: the listener simply does not hear the speaker. Or it may be partial blocking: the listener hears only a portion of the speaker's message. In this case he may confuse the details of this portion with the details of his own message. *(total blocking / partial blocking)*

The basic reasons for blocking are to be found in the very nature of listening. Listening requires that the listener accept the speaker's goals, at least temporarily, in order to comprehend them. Listening also usually requires the listener to accept the speaker's techniques for reaching these goals. Therefore, even if the listener disagrees with the goals and with the speaker's techniques for reaching them, he must overcome his opinions enough to be able to recall the information he has been given. *(2 reasons for blocking)*

Creative listening goes beyond simple good listening. The creative listener uses material he hears to form new thoughts and ideas of his own, during or after the listening experience. There is always some danger in listening creatively because one's own thoughts may interfere with the *(creative listening)* speaker's message. However, creative listening should be the goal of the career person who wishes to train himself not only to understand oral information, but also to use it to stimulate and expand his own thought.

Boredom

One of the greatest threats to effective listening is boredom. Boredom usually occurs because the listener already knows the material, or because he believes it irrelevant to his own goals.

Even the most boring listening experience can be made interesting if the listener tries to listen critically. Critical listening involves determining if the speaker is presenting the details in a logical order, if other listeners are properly involved in what he is saying, and if they appear to understand the message. Critical listening should always be undertaken for positive goals, not for the negative goal of enhancing the critical listener's prestige. A good critical listener can be very helpful to a speaker. He can ask questions that will help other listeners to learn, and he can tell the speaker where his message needs clarifying or expanding.

Information outside his own field need not bore the career listener. He should realize that careers are highly interrelated, and it is precisely where career fields meet that executive management is needed. Therefore, listening to information outside one's field is a form of management training. The career person who wishes to advance to the management level should listen eagerly to information both inside and outside his immediate area of responsibility.

Anxiety

Everyone is slightly afraid of even the kindest superiors. Everyone wants to be considered intelligent and promotable. But everyone sometimes fears that he is not outstanding, and this fear can make it hard for the listener to understand what his superior is saying.

A certain amount of anxiety about one's career abilities and listening skills is normal, and some tension is believed necessary for learning to occur. However, excessive anxiety prevents one from receiving the message. The anxious listener must therefore decrease his nervousness. He can do this by concerning himself with the physical and organizational techniques of listening.

Getting oneself in a proper physical position to listen greatly increases one's ability to take in facts. People who sit near the door at the rear of a large auditorium soon become tired from straining to hear; they expend effort needlessly. A good listener tries to get away from distractions such as swinging doors, windows open on street sounds, and even certain people who he knows may become restless and fidgety during the listening period. — *distractions*

The listener himself is often his own greatest distractor. He may tap his foot, drum a pencil, twist his hair, bite his fingernails, and thereby create small, distracting pains that prevent him from paying full attention to the speaker. — *more distractions*

By maintaining eye contact with the speaker, a listener not only prevents himself from becoming distracted, but he increases the number of cues that he receives from the speaker. If he is listening to a mechanical source such as a tape recorder, he should look at the recorder rather than at another person. If printed material is being used with the mechanical source, the listener should look at the printed material when the source instructs him to look at it. If the source does not tell the listener where to look, and the listener grows bored looking at the source, he should look at a neutral area such as a wall or desk surface; he should not look at pictures on a wall or out a window at passing cars because these stimuli may distract him. — *importance of eye contact*

5. Somatotyping

<u>People are built differently.</u> Some are slight with long levers and small muscles; others have short levers and large muscles. Some are streamlined; others are truncated. The basic build of most people is between these extremes. Biological heredity is responsible for basic body structure. The size of bony segments, bone length, number of muscle fibers, and even intestinal length are relatively fixed from conception.

<u>A number of attempts have been made to classify the human body.</u> Sheldon offers a reasonable scheme. His system is called somatotyping and recognizes three main categories: endomorphy, mesomorphy, and ectomorphy. — *3 types*

The endomorph is characterized by a large soft bulging body—the so-called "pear-shaped" build. Identifying traits include short neck, large round head, wide feminoid hips, short arms, broad stubby hands, hammy legs, and small feet. Body mass is concentrated toward the center of the body in fatty breasts, protruding abdomen, and heavy buttocks. Generally, endomorphs have fragile tendons and ligaments and intestines of great length—some 12 to 15 feet longer than the average. They usually reach sexual maturity late. Their response to fitness training is slow, but they are capable of vast improvement. Running is hard for endomorphs because they are troubled by foot problems. — *endomorph – characteristics*

Endurance work is also difficult because they have great body bulk, but strength work is more promising because of their lever advantages.

The ectomorph is characterized by linearness and slight build. Identifying traits include poked neck (thin with slight musculature); short torso; shallow chest depth; long arms, legs, and feet; thin wrists; and knees and elbows that appear to be knotted. Ectomorphs have light musculature; and, generally, their ligaments and tendons are flimsy. They carry little body fat and their intestines are about 12 to 15 feet shorter than the average. Their response to training is slow, and they are easily injured. Strength development poses a problem because they have slight muscling and long levers, but endurance development offers greater promise. *[margin: ectomorph characteristics]*

The mesomorph is characterized by a body mass that is away from body center: he has extremely well-developed and well-defined muscles. Identifying traits include long torso, short heavy neck, short powerful levers, narrow waist and hips, wide shoulders, deep chest, and flat abdomen. Their ligaments and tendons are strong, and their skeletal muscles are capable of great strength and endurance. Intestinal length is average—about 32 feet. They respond quickly to training and are capable of incredible physical feats. *[margin: mesomorph characteristics]*

Every individual has some characteristics of each of these three components; extreme cases are rare. Each component is rated on a scale from one to seven, seven being the largest amount and one being the least. The endomorphy rating is given first, followed by mesomorphy and ectomorphy, in that order. Three numbers in sequence give the rating. For example, a 4 5 2 is an endomorphic mesomorph—mesomorphy is most prominent and endomorphy is next in prominence. A 3 5 3 is a mesomorph and a 2 5 6 is a mesomorphic ectomorph. The average male falls in the "average" category for each component, while most women are higher than "average" in endomorphy because of biological sex differences. Females tend to have wider hips and more subcutaneous fat stored in the hip and thigh areas. *[margin: how to somatype]*

Somatotyping permits an understanding of individual differences. It focuses on the individual and on the characteristics of his physique, illustrating that basic structural differences may be the result of biological inheritance. Most people would probably choose to be mesomorphs, but an individual's will cannot determine his body structure. *[margin: uses of somatyping]*

The health needs of each category are unique. For example, the endomorph should know that his group is prone to degenerative and hypokinetic disease. He should be aware that he may always have a serious problem with weight control and that his motor potential is less than average. However, he should also realize that, within the limitations of this inheritance, he can contribute maximally to his health, although his life may be prematurely terminated if he does not pay close attention to his health needs. Health problems in the endomorph are common and often severe. — *health factors*

The body-type classifications described here are subjectively determined and are variable. By constant exercise and extreme dieting, the mesomorphic endomorph may appear more mesomorphic and less endomorphic than an endomorphic mesomorph who eats too much and does not exercise. The concern is to recognize *gross* individual differences and to personalize fitness goals accordingly rather than to assume that every person has the same physical potential and that his present physique is solely the result of his choosing. The somatotype is only one of many factors to consider in forming a realistic self-image. It is not very useful alone, but when combined with other measurements, it increases understanding of individual fitness. — *variability of body types* — *Is somatyping really necessary or important?*

6. Learning to Listen

How to become a good listener (4 ways)

1 Part of learning in college comes through listening to a lecturer. Sitting and listening is rather passive and not always conducive to learning. To give yourself the best opportunity to learn in the classroom, you must become as actively involved as possible. The first step in becoming a good listener is very simple. Sit up straight in your chair! This first step sets the stage for your *active* listening.

2 A second step for making classroom listening an active process is to develop the habit of using questions to analyze what the speaker is saying. Ask yourself questions that will help capture the essential meaning in the lecturer's flow of words: "Why is he saying that?" "What does he mean by that?" "What is the main point of what he is saying?"

3 A third step that will help you develop into an active listener is to take notes on what the lecturer is saying. The act of writing will make you physically as well as mentally active as you try to determine the important ideas and facts that should be captured in your notes.

4 A fourth step involved in becoming an active listener is to familiarize yourself with the lecturer's topic before the lecture through assigned reading. If you have prior knowledge of the lecturer's subject, you can develop a

keener interest in what he is saying and the time you spend in class will be more valuable for you. By contrast, if the subject is "foreign," then what the lecturer is saying will mean little and the hour will be lost.

Remember the four steps of active listening: (1) be physically alert; (2) ask yourself questions; (3) take notes; (4) develop familiarity with the topic to be discussed.

7. It is unfortunate that a significant number of physicians have found it lucrative to abandon general practice in order to "treat" the obese. In some areas of the United States this abandonment has helped to create a "doctor shortage." It is perhaps tragic that most obesity "treatments" dispensed by these men are unsuccessful, although they are dispensed at great cost to the patient. One of the areas notoriously neglected in the education of physicians is the area of nutrition, and most fad diets or ill-considered nutritional regimes published in popular magazines carry the endorsement of a physician. Fortunately, some physicians are very knowledgeable in the area of nutrition in spite of their limited initial preparation.

<u>Following is a discussion of some of the chief misapprehensions about weight reduction which have made huge profits for the unscrupulous or the ill-informed.</u>

Perspiration

Steam cabinets, plastic steam-bath suits, and portable sauna baths are just a few of the many devices used to cause the body to perspire. When the body perspires, moisture and its corresponding weight is lost. But as soon as one drinks water, all the lost weight is restored and the body's fatty deposits remain untouched.

Salt

One well-known beauty expert has urged women to omit some of the salt they use in meals, because this salt is used by the body for fluid retention. A number of self-proclaimed obesity experts have therefore recommended dietary salt restriction for weight reduction. The salt and water balance of the body is a basic and critical matter of health and is controlled by the cortex of the adrenal glands. Except in cases of severe edema, salt restriction is not a wise practice from the standpoint of health. As in forced perspiration, the dehydrating of the body can cause weight losses of short duration but it does not reduce the fatty deposits which cause obesity.

Appetite Killers

One method of reducing the fat stored by the body is

the decrease of the amount of food consumed. Many people soon find that the limiting of food intake is often difficult; they become receptive to any "crutch" which will help support their will-power in their attempts to eat less. One of the earliest "crutches" did not rely on drugs, but did fit very well with the concept of body dehydration for weight reduction. The consumption of water or of any beverage with meals was strictly forbidden. It is still rather common today for students to enter college with the deeply ingrained misconception that "Water with meals makes fat."

In recent years an entire family of anorexigenic drugs has been developed. Anorexigenics have proven to be temporary and useful "crutches" in the early treatment of the individuals for whom weight loss is difficult. Too great a reliance on the anorexigenic, however, causes the treatment of obesity to fail. The use of anorexigenics in a patient who has a deeply rooted neurosis, the outward manifestation of which is compulsive or emotional overeating, is dangerous. Such patients need treatment aimed primarily at the correction or alleviation of their real illness, the neurosis. Neurotics need crutches. They are the least likely to be properly motivated to reduce and are the most likely to depend excessively on medication; there is a great chance that they will become habitual users of the drug. Excellent appetite suppression is obtainable with drugs, but anorexigenics, although useful in the treatment of obesity, are never the *only* treatment.

The drugs preferred and most commonly used because of their anorexigenic potency and lack of side effects are phenmetrazine, dextroamphetamine, phendimetrozine, methamphetamine, diethylpropion, chlorphentermine, benzphetamine, and phentermine. Of these, phenmetrazine and dextroamphetamine are the most popular. They are stimulants of the benzadrine and dexedrine category and in some patients they can cause coronary attacks or cerebral hemorrhages. These drugs can only be obtained legally through a physician's prescription and are of greatest therapeutic value in patients whose obesity stems from compulsive overeating due to a depressed mental state.

Other appetite killers are called "bulkers" and are supposed to function by expanding in the stomach and causing the stomach to feel full. Research by Jolliffe showed that these "bulkers" were no more effective than a placebo, which also helped patients to lose weight. The primary value of these "bulkers" seems to be as a psychological aid for those who have insufficient will power to reduce the amount of their food consumption. "Bulkers" are dangerous for people with ulcers, colitis, or ileitis.

One of the more popular commercial preparations for appetite suppression is a milk-sugar candy which supposedly contains a few vitamins and minerals and which is supposed to reduce the appetite if it is taken shortly before a meal. The theory behind this preparation is similar to the theory of parents who exhort children not to eat sweets before meals. The vitamins and minerals have no therapeutic value; one could expect the same effect from any candy which was eaten in the same way. A half-slice of bread taken shortly before a meal would be just as effective. The effect of such before-meal snacks toward the reduction of appetite is minor.

[margin: use of candy as appetite killer]

The Machines

In general, "reducing" machines specialize in arm and leg exercises or in surface agitation to increase blood flow to certain areas of the body. Although a half hour of special arm and leg exercises may be very tiring, one could lose far more weight by spending that half hour in a leisurely walk. Most studies agree that physical activity involving the large muscle system of the legs expends the most energy. Stair climbing requires the expenditure of more calories than is required by almost any other activity. Accordingly, an increasing number of physicians recommend running and walking as an aid to weight control. Regular running also helps to strengthen and maintain the health of the cardiovascular and respiratory systems. Atherosclerosis is more apt to occur in vascular systems where blood flow is slow and is seldom accelerated by vigorous exercise. A daily walk of about an hour's duration interspersed with weekly running to the point of exhaustion has been recommended by Mayer as a practical aid to the maintenance of better weight and health.

[margin: machines — compared to exercise — advantages of running]

8. Crowd

An outline of the major collective behavior concepts would start with the crowd. A *crowd* is a temporary collection of people in close physical contact reacting together to a common stimulus. For example, the passengers on the flight from New York to San Francisco whose pilot suddenly decides he would like to go to the North Pole might be transformed from an aggregation into a crowd (or even a mob). Crowds have certain characteristics in common. *Milling* usually occurs as a crowd is being formed. In one sense *milling* refers to the excited, restless, physical movement of the individuals involved. In a more important sense *milling* refers to a process of com-

[margin: DEF: characteristics; 1. milling]

munication that leads to a definition of the situation and possible collective action. Not long ago, a Berkeley classroom suddenly started shaking with the first tremors of an earthquake. Almost at once the people began turning, shifting, looking at each other, at the ceiling, and at the instructor. They were seeking some explanation for the highly unusual experience and, whether spoken aloud or not, the questions on their faces were clear: "What is it?" "Did you feel it?" "What should we do?" Buzzing became louder talking, and some shouted, "Earthquake!!!" The students began to get up and move toward the doors. Many continued to watch the ceiling. . . . Milling may involve the long buildup of a lynch mob, or the sudden reaction in a dark and crowded theater when someone shouts, "Fire!!!" Milling helps ensure the development of a common mood for crowd members.

2. suggestibility
3. anonymity

A person when he is part of a crowd tends to be *suggestible*. He is less critical, and he will readily do things that he would not ordinarily do alone. This is in part because, as a member of a crowd, he is *anonymous*. There is a prevailing feeling that it is the crowd that is responsible, not the individual. Once one becomes a member of an acting crowd, it is extremely difficult to step back, get perspective, and objectively evaluate what one is doing. Crowd members have a narrowed focus, a kind of tunnel vision. The physical presence of a crowd is a powerful force—a person almost has to separate himself from the crowd physically before he can critically examine his own behavior. There is also a *sense of urgency* about crowds. Crowds are oriented toward a specific focus or task: "We've got to do *this*, and we've got to do it *now!*" Some form of leadership usually appears in the crowd but, as the mood of the crowd changes, the leadership may shift quickly from one individual or group to another.

4. sense of urgency

Types of crowds
—passive
—active
—goal oriented

There are many different types of crowds. Some are passive—those watching a building burn or those at the scene of an accident. Some are active—a race riot or a lynch mob. Some crowds have a number of loosely defined goals. Other crowds are focused on a specific goal. Turner and Killian distinguish between crowds that direct their action toward some external object—harassing a speaker until he leaves the platform or lynching a criminal—and expressive crowds, that direct their focus on the crowd itself—cheering at a football game or speaking in tongues at a church service.

Audience, Mob, Riot

audience
—characteristics

Audiences and mobs are specific types of crowds. An audience at a concert, football game, lecture, religious service, or burning building may usually be likened to a passive crowd. Emotional contagion is possible in such situations, and individuals are responsive in a group in ways that they would not be as individuals. Audiences at performances of rock and roll stars and in Pentecostal church services may become very expressive in a variety of possibly unpredictable ways. Comedians expect audiences to laugh at their jokes. But most comedians have "bits" that they do when audiences are unpredictable and don't laugh (Johnny Carson gets audience sympathy by jokingly mentioning his "war injuries"). Much of audience behavior is predictable, or at least predictably unpredictable. The football fan knows he is going to cheer at the game, the comedian's "rejection bits" are well prepared, and rock concerts are adequately staffed with police to protect the musicians and nurses to minister to the fans that pass out. At the same time, audiences demonstrate collective behavior characteristics in that their behavior is frequently spontaneous, and members are suggestible and anonymous.

[margin: mob characteristics] A *mob* is a focused, acting crowd. It is emotionally aroused, intent on taking aggressive action. A lynch mob would be an example of such a crowd. A water-fight between several fraternities in Berkeley on a warm spring day in 1956 spontaneously turned into a panty raid. Thousands of eager young males marched with determination through the campus community methodically stealing panties from numerous sorority houses. Afterwards, many of the participants expressed amazement that they had been involved in such behavior.

[margin: riot characteristics] A *riot* describes the situation in which mob behavior has become increasingly widespread and destructive. Riots may involve a number of mobs acting independently. Throughout our history, the United States has had riots over the issue of race: New York, 1863; Chicago, 1919; Detroit, 1943. In the 1960s, urban riots occurred with increasing frequency. The issues were social class and poverty as well as race. The Watts riot in Los Angeles in the summer of 1965 lasted six days. Nearly 4,000 people were arrested, and property damage was estimated at over $40 million. Thirty-four people were killed and over 1,000 people injured. Most of the killed and injured were Negroes. More than forty people died, and property damage was estimated at $50 million in the Detroit riot in the summer of 1967. The relatively minor incident which set off the week-long confrontation was the police closing of a "blind pig," an after-hours tavern. A crowd collected as the police carted off the tavern's patrons, a stone was thrown, a shoe store was set on fire, and the riot was on. Campus

disturbances occurred in the late 1960s at San Francisco State, Berkeley, Harvard, Columbia, Cornell, and at a number of other schools. It is likely, however, that to call these occasions riots, as the press often did, is an exaggeration of what actually happened. Riots have taken place at prisons and sporting events. A highly unusual situation occurred in 1969 when a disagreement at a soccer match led to a riot which in turn led to a short war between the two countries Honduras and El Salvador.

Summary

In this chapter we examined a form of activity that is outside the organized, ordinary, and predictable—collective behavior. Collective behavior refers to spontaneous, unstructured, and somewhat unpredictable actions by groups of people. A number of concepts and terms central to the study of collective behavior were discussed. We examined types of collectivities: crowds, audiences, and mobs.

9. A number of other professions are specially prepared to work with physicians or independently to assist in adjunct areas:

Optometry

1 The optometrist is an individual who has received special preparation to measure visual acuity and to prescribe corrective lenses for visual defects. The optometrist examines eyes without the use of drugs, and he does not treat diseases of the eye. Most optometrists have been prepared to recognize pathological conditions of the eye and to refer these conditions to an ophthalmologist. Optometry is a well-recognized profession and preparation leads to a bachelor's degree or, for advanced study, the degree O. D., Doctor of Optometry.

Opticianry

2 An optician is a skilled technician specially prepared in compounding, filling and adapting prescriptions written by an ophthalmologist or optometrist.

Nursing

3 Nurses are prepared to staff a variety of positions. The primary preparation leading to the title R.N. (registered nurse) is instruction in caring for the sick. Minimum preparation beyond high school is not specified in a number of states, but individual curriculum requirements dictate the length of the programs in these states, with a two-year minimum required for licensing in 31 states.

allied health occupations

232 ANSWER KEY

[margin note: 3 types of RN's / Baccalaureate nurse / Diploma nurse / Associate degree nurse]

There are three categories of professional preparation presently recognized that lead to the title R.N. The Baccalaureate Nurse has a bachelor's degree in nursing following four years of preparation in a degree-granting institution. The Diploma Nurse has received three years of training, usually associated with an accredited hospital school of nursing. The Associate Degree Nurse receives two years of professional preparation beyond the high school diploma. Graduates from each of these three categories must take State Board examinations before receiving the R.N. classification. *[margin note: career opportunities]* The career possibilities available for individuals prepared in nursing include serving in hospitals, clinics, nursing homes, doctors' offices, public health departments, schools, and industrial plants. The demand for Registered Nurses far exceeds the supply.

Hospital demands have necessitated creation of the practical nurse. The licensed practical nurse (L.P.N.) must meet certain requirements in 48 states and in the District of Columbia. *[margin note: LPN]* Texas and California license a vocational nurse (L.V.N.). Usual preparation of the L.P.N. or L.V.N. is one year of study beyond the high school diploma.

Medical Technology

[margin note: 4 / medical technologists / lab technologists / lab technician]

Medical technologists provide services under the supervision of physicians. Laboratory technologists are primarily prepared to work under the direction of a pathologist in making tests on blood, urine, and tissues. The findings from these tests are used by the physician in making a diagnosis. Because of the scientific demands of their work, laboratory technologists must have at least three years of college work in the basic sciences plus a year of supervised laboratory experience.

Laboratory technicians are prepared to carry out types of work similar to those undertaken by technologists but not requiring as high a degree of specialized preparation. X-ray technicians are prepared to operate X-ray machines by taking pictures and developing the plates for reading by a radiologist.

CHAPTER 5   USING THE LIBRARY

Exercise 1 (p. 125)

1. teacher judgment
2. teacher judgment
   teacher judgment
3. teacher judgment
4. teacher judgment
   teacher judgment
5. teacher judgment
6. teacher judgment
   teacher judgment
7.–10. teacher judgment

Exercise 2 (p. 127)
1. Ja, F, Mr, Ap, My, Je, Jl, Ag, S, O, N, D,
2. jt auth
3. il, por
4. bi-m, bi-w, m, q, semi-m, w
5. September 1978
6. after January 8, 1979
7. teacher judgement (there are 10)
8. Retirement Living, 50 plus
9. Current Health 2, Family Health, World Health
10. Christian Century, Christianity Today, U.S. Catholic

Exercise 3 (p. 137)
1. National Geographic
2. Cookery—Shellfish, Shellfish fisheries
3. Science 201: August 18, 1978
4. Joseph Conrad: Problem Child
5. Shifting Gears in Urban Transportation
6. Art—United States
7. Volume 78
8. C-Rations—New Look, New Taste
9. J. Barron
10. Ebony, Vol. 33; S.D. Lewis
11. Research Questions from the Cabinet
12. Popular Science, Vol. 213
13. North Bonneville, Wash.
14. U.S. News, Vol. 84
15. Newsweek
16. T. Alexander
17. J.N. Baker and D. Shapiro
18. Around the world tours, Around the world voyages
19. Chaplains, Military
20. Aviation World

CHAPTER 6 BECOMING A SUCCESSFUL STUDENT

Exercise 1 (p. 147) teacher judgment

CHAPTER 7 USING TIME EFFECTIVELY

Exercise 1 (p. 161) teacher judgment

Exercise 2 (p. 163) teacher judgment

CHAPTER 8 WORKING WITH PROFESSORS

Exercise 1 (p. 171) teacher judgment

CHAPTER 9 REMEMBERING WHAT YOU LEARN

Exercise 1 (p. 183)

1. You will get there faster. The trip will be more comfortable. You will arrive less tired. You will enjoy scenery. You can stay longer in places. It's less expensive.
2. Conquering space, Atlantic-Pacific partnerships, Peace Corps, education for all, jobs for all, care for elderly, attack mental illness, equal rights for all.

3. biological, chronological, psychological, psychoanalytic, sociocultural, historical
4. yellowish-green, disagreeable odor, will not burn, support some combustion, bleaching agent, disinfectant, forms sodium chloride when combined with sodium.
5. can't eat, can't sleep, trembling, perspiring, shortness of breath, increased heartbeat, excessive self doubt, loss of contact with audience, jumping back and forth from point to point, memory lapses
6. mixture—can be element, compounds, or both in any proportion
compound—two or more elements in fixed proportions
mixture—made by physical or mechanical means
compound—done by chemical changes only
mixture—do not lose their identity
compound—compound does not really resemble elements from which formed
7. Show only when talking about them
Talk about them when showing it
Make sure everyone can see them
Talk to audience, not visual aid
Don't overdo their use
Consider hazards before deciding to pass them around class
8. Civil rights act of 1965
War on poverty
Education
Medicare and health
Immigration
Housing and urban renewal
9. Took us out of postwar depression
Shortened trips—brought people closer together
Made local government obsolescent
School buses made for consolidated, better schools
Churches, medical services, hospitals more available
Delivery of food and freight was accelerated
10. Exercise regularly
Eat well balanced diet
Don't eat after strenuous exercise
Drink at least six glasses of water per day
Don't drink alcoholic beverages
Shower after practice or workout
Wear clean clothes
Wear sweater or jacket after playing
Get enough sleep
Live a well balanced life
11. refer to text
12. refer to text

CHAPTER 10 TAKING TESTS

Exercise 1 (p. 205)

All answers must be placed on the line *following* each statement.

1. T	6. F	11. T	16. T
2. T	7. F	12. T	17. T
3. F	8. T	13. F	18. F
4. T	9. T	14. F	19. T
5. T	10. T	15. T	20. T

Exercise 2 (207)

1. 8
2. 5
3. 4
4. 3
5. 3
6. 4
7. teacher judgment
8. 4
9. 4
10. 4

Exercise 3 (p. 209)

1. teacher judgment
2. teacher judgment
3. teacher judgment
4. c, b, b

Index

A

Acronyms, 182
Action, and remembering, 178–179
ASOE, 178–180
Association, 175–176

C

Call number, 119
Card catalog, 117–120
Career goals, 146
"Compare," on tests, 201
Concentration, 180–181
Context clues, 4–8
"Contrast," on tests, 201

D

"Defend," on tests, 202
"Define," on tests, 202
Definition, 6
Derivation, of words, 12
Dewey Decimal System, 119
"Discuss," on tests, 202

E

Encyclopedias, 123–124
Enjoyment, courses for, 142–143
Etymology, 12

Exaggeration, and remembering, 180
Examples, and word meaning, 5–6
"Explain," on tests, 202
Explanation, of words, 6–7

H

Housing, 146

I

Ideas
   key, 27
   relating, for outlining, 26–30
Intense original impression, 175
Intention, and remembering, 182

J

Job-related problems, 145. *See also*
   Time, effective use of

L

Librarians, 124
Library
   and card catalog, 117–120
   exercises for use of, 125–126
   reference aids in, 120–124
   services in, 124
Library of Congress System, 119

Linking, 178-180

M

Mental health, 146
Money and job-related problems, 145

N

Notation, outline, 30-34
Notetaking
   from books not owned by you, 80
   from books owned by you, 75-80
   exercises for, 81-116
   from lectures and class discussions, 68-75
   and POWER courses, 143
   reasons for, 67-68

O

Outlining
   exercises for, 35-51
   notation for, 30-34
   reasons for, 25
   suggestions for, 26-30

P

Pegging, 177-178
PEP, 142-143
PLUG AWAY courses, 142, 143
POWER courses, 143
PQ3R method of study, 55-62
   exercise for, 62-66
Prefixes, 9
   list of, 10-11
   of numbers, 11-12
Proactive interference, 182
Problems, personal, 145-146
Professors, 165-172
   choosing, 166-167
   exercises for working with, 171-172
   expectations of, 167
   helping, 167-169
   value of, 167
Proportion, and remembering, 179

R

Readers' Guide to Periodical Literature, 120-122
   abbreviations used in, 129-132
   exercises for use of, 127, 133-134
   sample pages from, 135-138
Reference aids, 120-124
Relaxation, tension-release procedure for, 194-195
Remembering, 173-192
   aids to, 175-182
   exercises for, 183-192
Repetition, 181-182
Restatement, 4-5
Retroactive interference, 54-55, 182
Roots, word, 9-10
   list of, 10-11

S

Schedule
   analyzing daily, 152-153
   blank forms for weekly, 157-159
   preparing and using a weekly, 153-156
Scheduling, of courses, 141-144
Situation, and word meaning, 7
Structural clues
   types of, 9-10
   examples of, 10-12
Students, successful
   characteristics of, 144-145
   and course schedules, 141-144
   exercises for becoming, 147-149
   and personal problems, 145-146
Study, sequence of
   and remembering, 182
Studying. See Remembering, aids to; Tests, preparation for; Textbook chapters, studying; and Time, effective use of, for studying
Substitution, and remembering, 179
Suffixes, 9
   list of, 12

T

Tests
   essay (subjective), 201-204
   exercises for taking, 205-210
   preparation for, 193-195
   short-answer (objective), 195-200
Textbook chapters, studying
   general techniques for, 53-55
   PQ3R method for, 55-66

Time, effective use of, 151–163
    exercises for, 161–163
    for studying, 154–156
Topic, development of, 27–29

V

Visualization, 177–180
Vocabulary, improving
    aids to, 4–12
    exercises for, 13–23
    reasons for, 3

DISCHARGED

RESERVED   APR 1 8 1996
                 DISCHARGED
   DISCHARGED   APR 1 8 1999

   OCT 0 4 1991

   DISCHARGED

   APR 2 1 1993
   DISCHARGED
   DEC 0 2

   NOV 1 9

   DISCHARGED
   MAY 1 7 1999